# Heroes, Heavies and Sagebrush

Dr. McClure is the author of *The Truman Administration and the Problems of Postwar Labor* and *The Versatiles,* with Alfred E. Twomey; Dr. McClure is the editor of the anthology *The Movies: An American Idiom.*

Mr. Jones and Dr. McClure, together with Mr. Twomey, are the authors of *The Films of James Stewart.*

# Heroes, Heavies and Sagebrush

## A Pictorial History of the "B" Western Players

Arthur F. McClure

and

Ken D. Jones

South Brunswick and New York: A. S. Barnes and Company
London: Thomas Yoseloff Ltd

A. S. Barnes and Co., Inc.
Cranbury, New Jersey 08512

Thomas Yoseloff Ltd
108 New Bond Street
London W1Y OQX, England

Library of Congress Cataloging in Publication Data

McClure, Arthur F
    Heroes, heavies and sagebrush.

    1. Moving-picture actors and actresses, American
—Portraits. 2. Western films—Pictorial works.
I. Jones, Ken D., joint author. II. Title.
PN1998.A2M25        791.43'52              73-126945
ISBN 0-498-07787-X

Printed in the United States of America

*Roy Barcroft died on November 28, 1969, after appearing in westerns for more than thirty years. This book is dedicated to his memory.*

# Contents

# Preface

This work is an effort to synthesize the historical evidence which has been discovered about a small part of American popular culture. We feel strongly that while popular history is often the last to be written and taken seriously, it is by no means less important than other significant portions of American history.

It would be impossible to thank everyone who has helped us prepare this volume. Thanks is due to those many actors and their families who answered our correspondence. We wish to acknowledge special assistance generously extended by Mrs. D. Victorek, collector extraordinary; William T. Stewart, expert necrologist; Miss Lucy Smith, memorabiliac supreme; and Mr. Nick Williams and Mr. John Cocchi. Miss Peggy Hendrix, faithful typist, was indispensable in the completion of this manuscript.

Most of the photographic material was provided by the Ken Jones Collection, Columbia, Missouri. Although the errors of omission ought to be more numerous than those of commission, we accept joint responsibility for the entire book.

Our gratitude for the contributions of our wives, Judy McClure and Nancy Jones, is far from the conventional and must be avowed. And finally, a word for our children, who were not old enough to give help, and yet not too old to be beyond offering it.

A. F. M.
K. D. J.

# Introduction

For many years the "B" western film was something special not only to Americans, but to moviegoers the world over. The "B" western was a source of vicarious experience for a substantive life that young and old alike yearned for in the 1930s and 1940s. Society simply could not provide the same excitement, and audiences for "a few thrilling hours . . . could roughly toss conventions aside and share the fellowship of ranch life and adore the kind of hero who was never bored and never afraid."

The 1930s and 1940s, as with any historical era, presents problems to historians who are all too prone to compartmentalize the American past. Certainly they were disruptive and grim decades for the average American. The "B" westerns made during the period are fascinating historical examples of the romantic flavor of a haunting nostalgia for a more individualistic and flamboyant past. Life in these decades was full of paradoxes and incongruities. But the "reel" life portrayed by these films reveals something about popular culture in America. The "B" western was very much a part of the "evasion of reality" in a mundane world. Many distorted myths about the American West were perpetuated in these films. Some of them were serious distortions, such as the hardening of racial stereotypes. Others included the less serious but just as erroneous impressions of things such as ranch life itself. But their special charm and value as an escape from banality more than outweighed their inadequacies in most instances.

In those bleak years, the "B" western movie was a kind of morality play. Evil would threaten good, but in the end it was good that conquered evil. There were many variations that developed from this theme, but the basic structure of the "B" western remained the same. In many ways the "B" western represented the conflicts between the public and private attitudes of the audiences. In their desire for escapism the audiences identified with the stereotyped hopes, fears, and desires of the characters.

The popularity of the "B" western was an extension of the cowboy myth in American life. Historian Carl Becker noted that Americans are prone to cling to what he called "useful myths." The western film hero received an adoration and continuing loyalty of amazing proportions. Villains were hissed with equal fervor. Westerns moved audiences emotionally as no other type of film. The emotional conditioning provided by these films, and the *durability* of that conditioning should never be underestimated by historians of American life. Some historians have dismissed the "B" western as simply a novelty or tasteless fad with no real substance or significance. However, it is entirely possible that in the midst of the confusion and uncertainty created by the Depression and World War II audiences sustained many of their "faiths" by identifying with such admirable and powerful symbols of straightforward righteousness as seen in the "B" westerns.

The impression should not be left that the actionpacked "B" westerns saved the American national character from collapse. They were, however, an important part of many lives. Many of these westerns when viewed today seem incredibly devoid of almost *any* substance, but they most certainly belong to what has been termed the "only-yesterday" school of history. The films provided a medium through which Americans could relive a life that was largely illusory, but the many players who appeared in them became highly recognizable symbols to moviegoers.

In the "B" western many of the character's physical movements revealed whether it was the hero or the villain. Dialogue was something held to a minimum. Much of these films' excitement come from the action, many times through stock situations.

The plots were straightforward in their pursuit of action fare. Psychology was usually uncomplicated to a point of being nonexistent.

Thomas Mann once wrote that audiences would accept almost any film story, no matter how improbable, if it was "set in a frame of scenic and mimic detail which is true to reality." This is especially true of the "B" western, which portrayed scenes of what Americans felt and visualized to be the individualistic and heroic frontier life (from which they were only a generation or two removed). The outdoor situations and the open spaces of the vast ranges provided the frame of reference for the action. The "mimic detail" of false front buildings and white hats needed only to be added by the studio prop departments.

The scenes were stock situations that were about the same for each western. It did not really matter to audiences because the things that held their attention were the *personalities* of the players themselves. All of these westerns had no hint of the modern cinematic sadism or sex. The men were men, while the women were invariably school teachers, the rancher's daughters, or "saloon hostesses." The "good over evil" theme was a formula for success which producers sometimes felt constituted a justification that not only the most prolific, but also the most consistent output would be accepted by audiences. Consequently, in the 1930s and 1940s, literally hundreds of these films were made. More western stars were working simultaneously in the 1930s and 1940s than in any other period. The stars themselves were grinding out pictures at a prodigious rate, but bit players and character actors were involved in dozens of films each year. This study represents the results of much time spent in tracing the lives of some of these players not only from the standpoint of historical curiosity, but in order to provide an affectionate nostalgic glimpse of a significant portion of western movie fare.

The lives of the various players represent a study in contrasts. Some embody the rags-to-riches-to-lost-fame spectrum so often observed in the lives of Hollywood residents. Some were semi-literate, while others earned academic degrees including the Ph.D. Some retained their wealth and popularity, while still others retained neither. A representative group of actors who played heroes, heavies, sidekicks, Indians, and assorted character types is included in the investigation. Many players have been excluded because they have died or simply disappeared without recognition. Actors who specialized in portraying everything from ranchers, bankers, sheriffs, undertakers, ministers, newspaper editors, and gamblers to the idolized heroes appear in the following pages. For some, the brief biography or still photograph is all that remains as a remembrance of their often lengthy careers.

Novelist and movie buff Wallace Markfield has noted that "the Western was once all leisure and repose, the Westerner a man who shot a gun, rode a horse, fought with his fists, and did, finally, 'what he had to do'—and what he had to do was shoot a gun, ride a horse, fight with his fists." The life story of many former "B" western players is quite indicative of the acceptance of that dictum. They enjoyed their work tremendously, did not take themselves too seriously, and nearly always felt that they were a part of a unique and entertaining contribution to the history of the American film.

# Heroes, Heavies and Sagebrush

The stars of the "B" western were the embodiment of the following "Cowboy Commandments," attributed to Gene Autry.

1. HE MUST NOT TAKE UNFAIR ADVANTAGE OF AN ENEMY.
2. HE MUST NEVER GO BACK ON HIS WORD.
3. HE MUST ALWAYS TELL THE TRUTH.
4. HE MUST BE GENTLE WITH CHILDREN, ELDERLY PEOPLE AND ANIMALS.
5. HE MUST NOT POSSESS RACIALLY OR RELIGIOUSLY INTOLERANT IDEAS.
6. HE MUST HELP PEOPLE IN DISTRESS.
7. HE MUST BE A GOOD WORKER.
8. HE MUST RESPECT WOMEN, PARENTS AND HIS NATION'S LAWS.
9. HE MUST NEITHER DRINK OR SMOKE.
10. HE MUST BE A PATRIOT.

With such a code, certainly no more could be asked of them, or of their loyal audiences.

# 1. Heroes

### Bob (Tex) Allen (1906–      )

Bob (Tex) Allen was born I. E. Theodore Baehr, the youngest of four sons of Eugene B. and Katherine Baehr, on March 28, 1906, in Mount Vernon, New York. After attending public schools in Mount Vernon, he was sent to New York Military Academy for "disciplinary reasons." He graduated from the academy with the highest scholastic average in the class of 1924. He enrolled in Dartmouth College, "flunked out twice," but he returned and graduated with the class of 1929. In his freshman year, he joined the Dartmouth Players and upon graduation went to work for the Curtis Flying Service selling "aeroplanes." After the Curtis Company went bankrupt in the stockmarket crash, Allen became a photographer's model, becoming one of the most successful in America. From modeling with the famous John Robert Power's Agency, he got his start in films which ultimately led to a contract with the Warner Brothers First National Studios. His contract was dropped and he was stranded in Hollywood without a job. He acquired a beautiful bride, Evelyn Peirce, a former MGM Baby Wampus star, and together with about $200, they returned to New York to invade Broadway. After considerable theatrical experience, he returned to Hollywood under contract with Columbia pictures. For several years, he played juveniles, heavies, and some leads for Columbia and finally "talked my way into westerns." Allen was co-starred with Tim McCoy, and after they had appeared together in several westerns, it was decided that Allen should star in his own pictures. These were known as the "Ranger" Series (1936–1937). By this time Columbia had three cowboy series: Buck Jones, Charles Starrett, and Bob Allen. Allen's western series was dropped, "being low-man on the totem pole." His western career came to an end when a possible contract with Republic "came in acropper when they found out I could not play the guitar, and they signed Roy Rogers." Allen had a year's contract with 20th Century-Fox in 1938–1939. He left Hollywood in 1940 for permanent residence on the East Coast. He has appeared on Broadway, some feature films made in the East, plus innumerable television commercials, hundreds of industrial films, and scores of television shows on all the major networks. In private life, between engagements, Allen now operates a highly successful real-estate business on Long Island. He lives in a beautiful Georgian mansion overlooking Oyster Bay. He became a widower in 1960 by the sudden death of his wife. He remarried in 1964 to a widow, the former Frances Cookman of Philadelphia. He now states that "life has been very good to me in many, many ways. . . . It's been fun, and I've enjoyed it. . . ."

*Bob Allen with Indians (?) in* Ranger Courage *by Columbia in 1936.*

*Bob Allen with Lafe McKee in Columbia's* Law of the
Ranger *in 1937.*

### Rex Allen (1922–    )

Rex Allen was born in Willcox, Arizona, on December 31, 1922. His parents owned a typical western ranch and by the time he reached the age of thirteen, he had become widely known throughout the state for his singing ability. Upon graduation from Willcox High School in 1939, Allen was offered a scholarship from the University of Arizona. He turned it down and instead rode on the rodeo circuit for the next two years. He was determined, however, to make singing his lifetime career and he left the rodeo and landed his first professional singing job on a Trenton, New Jersey, radio station. In March 1945 he was hired as a regular on Chicago's internationally famous National Barn Dance Show on radio station WLS. He was extremely successful and became one of the biggest stars on the show. In the same year, however, he was stricken by a serious eye problem which almost put an end to his budding career. After delicate eye surgery in Chicago, he resumed his singing career that was to lead to recording, motion pictures, and television fame. In 1949, he signed a contract with Republic pictures and his first movie was *The Arizona Cowboy*. Allen and his famous horse, Koko, made a series of successful western films including *The Hills of Oklahoma, Under Mexicali Stars, The Rodeo King and the Senorita, Old Overland Trail,* and *Down Laredo Way.* He appeared in 31 feature films and 78 episodes of his television series, *Frontier Doctor.* Allen has also been an extremely successful song writer and has over 300 published songs. He still frequently appears at the big western rodeos. He and his wife, Bonnie, have four children, three boys and one girl. For the past ten years he has been associated with Walt Disney Studio, which "has always featured a product of which we can be proud." He owns the Diamond X Ranch thirty miles north of Hollywood.

*Rex Allen.*

*Rex Allen in* Under Mexicali Stars *(Republic, 1950).*

*Rex Allen, center, with Harry Lauter and Harry Cheshire in* Thunder in God's Country *(Republic, 1951).*

### Richard Arlen (1900–     )

Richard Arlen was born on September 1, 1900, in St. Paul, Minnesota. His father was one of the first graduates of the University of Minnesota and served as a judge. He helped to write many of the early state laws. Arlen was educated at St. Thomas College and served in the British R. A. F. during World War I. He made his motion picture debut in 1920 although he had no desire to be an actor; "it just happened." He has acted on Broadway, silent films, talking films, and television for nearly fifty years. He starred in many action films in the 1930s and 1940s. Since World War II, he has appeared in westerns more than any other type of film. Among them: *Grand Canyon*, *Kansas Raiders*, *Devil's Canyon*, *Flaming Feather*, and *Silver City*. Arlen now lives in Sherman Oaks, California, and is still active as an actor and lecturer. For the past few years he has lectured frequently on uni-

*Richard Arlen, center, with Mary Brian and Fred Kohler Sr. in* Light of the Western Stars *(Paramount, 1930).*

versity and college campuses throughout the United States.

*Gene Autry with Martin Garralaga in* Twilight on the Rio Grande *(Republic, 1947).*

LOBBY CARD: *Gene Autry and the Mounties (Columbia, 1950).*

### Gene Autry (1907–    )

Gene Autry was the screen's first singing cowboy and one of its most successful as well. He was born in Tioga, Texas, on September 29, 1907. In 1925 he was a railroad telegrapher in Sapulpa, Oklahoma, but by 1928 he was a radio singer and Columbia Records recording star. He made his screen debut in 1934 at Mascot Pictures (which later became Republic) as a singing cowboy. Autry was voted the top money making western star from 1937 to 1942, and was among the top western stars in 1936, and 1946 to 1954. He was the first west-

Gene Autry with Nan Leslie in Rim of the Canyon *(Columbia, 1949).*

*Gene Autry with his wonder horse, Champion, in* Cow Town *(Columbia, 1950).*

ern star to be in the top ten movie money makers from 1938 to 1942. He served in the Air Force as a flight officer from 1942 to 1945. Immediately after the war he resumed his radio career with his former sponsor, the William Wrigley Co. He formed Gene Autry Productions, Inc. and later the Flying A Production Co., which made many films for TV. Autry in recent years has become the owner of a number of radio and TV stations, hotels, and the California Angels in the American League.

*Bob Baker with Dorothy Fay in* Prairie Justice *(Universal, 1938).*

### Bob Baker (1914–     )

Bob Baker, one of the singing cowboys spawned in the late 1930s, was born Leland "Tumble" Weed in Forest City, Iowa, on November 8, 1914. He spent most of his boyhood, however, in Arizona and Colorado. He was featured as a singer on the "National Barn Dance" radio show until his mother contacted Universal in 1937. The success of the western musical, pioneered by Republic Pictures, had prompted most of the independent producers and some major studios to look for stars of their own. He was given a screen test at Universal City after being coached by his old friend, Max Terhune, the popular western comic. Renamed Bob Baker, his first film was *Courage of the West*, which was released in December 1937, and had Fuzzy Knight as his comic sidekick. This was followed by three more films with Knight, *The Singing Outlaw, Border Wolves,* and *The Last Stand,* with Constance Moore as the singing leading lady in the last two. The last film in this series was *Phantom Stage,* but Baker and his horse Apache proved to be so popular that Johnny Mack

*Bob Baker with Glenn Strange in* Honor of the West *(Universal, 1938).*

Brown and Fuzzy Knight made six more films with him in 1939–1940. Baker made his last major appearance in *Wild Horse Stampede* for Monogram in 1943 with Ken Maynard and Hoot Gibson. He retired from films in the mid-1940s.

### Smith Ballew (1911–     )

Smith Ballew was born in Palestine, Texas, and began his show business career as a singer in radio. In the early 1930s he became one of the first singing cowboys. His voice was dubbed in for John Wayne's in the "Singing Sandy" series by Lonestar Productions. In 1936 he began to star in a series of musical westerns for Paramount. He later made a series of westerns for 20th Century-Fox and by the late 1930s, he was one of the more popular singing cowboys. In later years he was featured in supporting roles and was still active as late as the 1950s. His films include: *Roll Along Cowboy, Western Gold, Hawaiian Buckaroo, Cowcho's Serenado, I Killed Geronimo.*

*Smith Ballew with Evalyn Knapp in* Hawaiian Buckaroo *(20th Century-Fox, 1937).*

*Smith Ballew, right, with Stanley Fields in* Roll Along Cowboy *(20th Century-Fox, 1937).*

### Jim Bannon (  -  )

Jim Bannon was born in Kansas City, Missouri, and attended Rockhurst College where he was a star athlete. After college he became a sportscaster in Kansas City, St. Louis, and after 1938 in California where he also began working as a radio actor and in small parts in movies. In the early 1940s he appeared as a stuntman in films and starred for Columbia in a series of detective movies based on the radio show *I Love A Mystery*. In 1949 he was given the role of "Red Ryder" in the series of the same name for Eagle-Lion productions. Since the 1950s he has appeared in character parts in many westerns and on television. His brother, Rev. John Francis Bannon S.J., is a noted historian and for many years served as Chairman of the Department

*Jim Bannon as "Red Ryder" with Peggy Stewart in* Ride, Ryder, Ride *(Eagle Lion, 1949).*

*Jim Bannon with Gaylord Pendleton, Steve Clark, Emmett Lynn and Don Kay Reynolds in* Ride, Ryder, Ride.

of History at St. Louis University. Some of Bannon's western films include: *Riders of the Deadline, The Gay Senorita, Jack Slade, Redheaded Cowboy, The Cowboy and the Redhead,* and *The Great Missouri Raid.*

### Donald (Red) Barry (1912–    )

Donald (Red) Barry was born Donald Barry de Acosta on January 11, 1912, in Houston, Texas. He was educated at the Texas School of Mines and in 1936 made his screen debut in *Night Waitress* for RKO Radio. Thereafter in 1939 he appeared in numerous feature pictures including *The Woman I Love, Sinners in Paradise,* and *The Crowd Roars.* Starting in 1939 he began to appear in westerns and attained wide popularity as a Republic western star. During World War II he entertained troops overseas and was voted one of the Top Ten Money-Making Western Stars in the *Motion Picture Herald* Fame Polls in 1942, 1943 and 1944. Barry is still seen in numerous films and television shows in character parts.

*Don Barry with Dick Botiller and Edmund Cobb in* Wyoming Wildcat *(Republic, 1941).*

*Don Barry with Al St. John and Douglas Walton in* Jesse James Jr. *(Republic, 1942).*

*Don (Red) Barry.*

### Warner Baxter (1893–1951)

Warner Baxter was born in Columbus, Ohio, on March 29, 1893. After a stage career he entered films in bit parts beginning in 1916. After starring on Broadway, he was signed by Paramount Studios in 1924. He later starred for Fox and in 1929 won the Academy Award for his role in *In Old Arizona* as the first "Cisco Kid." He retired from films in 1940 to concentrate on his real-estate business. He returned to movies during World War II as the star of the "Crime Doctor" series for Columbia. He was active in films until his death on May 7, 1951.

*Warner Baxter, center, with Cesar Romero and Chris-Pin Martin in* The Return of the "Cisco Kid" *(20th Century-Fox, 1939).*

Warner Baxter.

*Rex Bell.*

### Rex Bell (1905–1962)

Rex Bell was born George Belden on October 16, 1905, in Chicago, and entered films in the late 1920s in juvenile roles. He later was cast in western roles and found his greatest fame there in such films as *The Man From Arizona, Too Much Beef, Idaho Kid, Law and Lead, Gunfire, Fighting Pioneers* and *West of Nevada*. He purchased a large cattle ranch near Searchlight, Nevada, in 1930 and gradually retired from the screen. He was very interested in politics and in 1954 was elected Lieutenant Governor of Nevada. While campaigning for the governorship he was stricken by a heart attack on July 4, 1962, and died at the age of 57. He was survived by his wife, Clara Bow, a silent screen star, and two sons.

*Rex Bell, left, with Al St. John, Steve Clark and Joan Barclay in* West of Nevada *(Colony, 1936).*

### William (Hopalong Cassidy) Boyd (1895–    )

William Boyd was born in Cambridge, Ohio, on June 5, 1895, and came to Hollywood in 1919 where his striking appearance (his hair had become white while he was still in his teens) got him work as an extra in Cecil B. DeMille's *Why Change Your Wife.* The great producer-director was impressed with Boyd and soon began starring him in such films as *The Road to Yesterday* (1925), *The Volga Boatman* (1926), and *King of Kings* (1927). Boyd had an excellent voice and when sound came in he continued making many features including *High Voltage* (1929), *The Painted Desert* (1931), *Lucky Devils* (1933), *Racing Luck* (1935), and *Burning Gold* (1936). In 1935 producer Harry (Pop) Sherman bought the screen rights to Clarence E. Mulford's "Hopalong Cassidy" stories and began readying his first feature. When offered the chance to star in the film, Boyd eagerly accepted. He did not accept the role handed him by Sherman, however. Instead of the clean-cut part of Buck Peters, the "Bar 20" ranch foreman, Boyd insisted on playing the more colorful part of "Hopalong." (As written, Cassidy was a near-illiterate, tobacco-chewing, hard-drinking, and coarse-talking character who got his nickname because of a limp.) The completed film was released as *Hop-a-long Cassidy* by Paramount in the summer of 1935 and showed just how much Boyd had retained of the original literary character—only the limp, caused by a bullet wound. This was dropped in the second film with an explanation that the wound had healed. This initial feature was later reissued under another title as *Hopalong Cassidy Enters.* Boyd's original screen partner was young Jimmy Ellison who created the character of "Johnny Nelson" and played him in eight films before relinquishing the role to Russell Hayden in 1937. Hayden did not continue in the same role, though, but appeared as "Lucky Jenkins." In 1941 he, too, bowed out and the juvenile role was successively played by Brad King, Jay Kirby, George Reeves, Jimmy Rogers and Rand Brooks. The comedy relief was handled by several different actors. First was George (Gabby) Hayes who created the role of "Windy Halliday" in 1936. Other comic sidekicks were Harvey Clark, Frank Darien, Britt Wood and Andy Clyde, who had the part of "California Carlson" from 1940 to 1948. There were 66 Hopalong Cassidy features in all. Sherman produced 54 of them. The first 41 were released by Paramount and the balance through United Artists. The last of these was *Forty Thieves* in 1944. Two years later, Boyd himself began producing the films, and starred himself in an additional 12 features that were released through United Artists. By 1948 the films had just about played

*William Boyd as Hopalong Cassidy.*

*William Boyd with Barbara Britton in* Secret of the Waste-lands *(Paramount, 1941).*

themselves out theatrically when television suddenly revived their popularity. Through a far-sighted clause in Sherman's original 1935 contract whereby Mulford's publishers retained the TV rights, Boyd managed to gain control of all the films. Placing the first on TV in 1948, the popularity of Hopalong Cassidy began to rise and continued to rise until it reached its crest in the early 1950s, leaving Boyd an extremely wealthy man.

*LOBBY CARD:* In Old Mexico *(Paramount, 1938).*

*William Boyd is surrounded by Montie Montana, Herbert Rawlinson, Art Felix, Roy Bucko and Cliff Parkinson in* Riders of the Deadline *(United Artists, 1943).*

### Johnny Mack Brown (1904–    )

Johnny Mack Brown was born on September 1, 1904, in Dothan, Alabama, and became a top football star while attending the University of Alabama. He entered films in non-western roles at MGM including roles in *The Fair Coed* and *Our Dancing Daughters* in the late 1920s (the latter with Joan Crawford). Brown was given the leading role in King Vidor's *Billy the Kid* in 1930 and his career in westerns was launched. In 1931 Universal teamed him with Leo Carillo in *Lasca of the Rio Grande*. This led to roles at Paramount, Fox, Warners and in the classic serial *Fighting with Kit Carson* for Mascot in 1933. In 1935–1936 Brown did a series of westerns for Supreme Pictures, and several serials for Universal throughout

*Johnny Mack Brown with Iron Eyes Cody and Lynn Gilbert in the serial* Wild West Days *(Universal, 1937).*

*Johnny Mack Brown and Nell O'Day in* Boss of Bullion City *(Universal, 1941).*

the 1930s. From 1939 to 1943 he made a number of popular westerns for Universal, after which he teamed with Raymond Hatton in a variety of films for Monogram, the last of which were released in the 1950s. In recent years Brown has worked in TV and as a host-manager of a Beverly Hills restaurant.

*Johnny Mack Brown in* Over the Border *(Monogram, 1950).*

*Rod Cameron in* Stage to Tucson *(Columbia, 1950).*

### Rod Cameron (1912– )

Rod Cameron was born Rod Cox on December 7, 1912, in Calgary, Canada. After going to Hollywood in 1939 he appeared in supporting roles in *Christmas in July, Northwest Mounted Police,* and *Wake Island* in addition to serving as a double for some stars. In 1943, he starred in two serials for Republic—*Secret Service in Darkest Africa* and *G-Men vs. the Black Dragon*—each being 15 episodes. Universal then signed him as their new western star, and he appeared in a number of films in 1944 and 1945 including *Boss of Boomtown, Trigger Trail, Riders of Santa Fe, The Old Texas Trail, Beyond the Pecos, Renegades of the Rio Grande,* and *Frontier Gal.* Fuzzy Knight appeared with him in most of these films. After the war Cameron appeared in westerns for Monogram, 20th Century-Fox, Allied Artists, United Artists and others. He also starred in several non-western TV series including *City Detective* (1953–1955),

*Rod Cameron with Vivian Austin in* Boss of Boomtown *(Universal, 1944).*

*State Trooper* (1957–1959) and *Coronado 9,* all for Revue Studios.

### "Sunset" Carson (1925– )

"Sunset" Carson was born in Plainview, Texas, November 12, 1925. As a boy, he was an accomplished radio performer and later was invited to join the Tom Mix Circus. He journeyed to South America and won a number of rodeo championships there in 1941 and 1942. He was spotted by Lou Grey of Republic Pictures and was signed to a long term contract to star in westerns in 1944 because of his expert horsemanship. Some of his Republic westerns included *Border Town Trail, Bandits of the Badlands, Santa Fe Saddlemates, Oregon Trail, Red River Renegades,* and *Alias Billy the Kid.* Carson also made westerns for RKO, Warner Bros., and Astor and has starred and produced his own live TV shows in recent years. He has made a personal appearance tour of the Orient and gave a command performance for the Royal family in Bangkok, Thailand. Carson and his wife, Margaret, who is from Sydney, Australia, have two children and are active as a family giving personal appearance tours. Carson, who stands six feet six inches, costarred with the late "Smiley" Burnette in several of his films.

*Sunset Carson.*

*Sunset Carson, left, with Rex Lease and Smiley Burnette in* Bordertown Trail *(Republic, 1944).*

### Bill Cody (1891–1948)

Bill Cody, who had been a star in silent films, had a rather brief career in talking films. He was born on January 5, 1891, in Winnipeg, Canada. Cody made two outstanding groups of westerns in the 1930s. The first was a series of eight films for Monogram Pictures in 1932, including *Mason of the Mounted,* and *Ghost City.* Spectrum Pictures Corporation, a newly formed company, released eight Cody westerns in 1935. These included *Vanishing Riders, Lawless Border* and *Western Racketeers.* Cody's son, Bill Jr., was groomed as a future western star and appeared with him in several films as well as in a Universal serial, *The Oregon Trail,* with Johnny Mack Brown. Bill Sr. died January 24, 1948.

*Bill Cody, Gertrude Messinger and a group of cowboys in* Blazing Justice *(Spectrum, 1936).*

*Bill Cody struggles with Gibson Gowland in* Land of Wanted Men *(Monogram, 1932).*

### Ray (Crash) Corrigan (1907–    )

Ray (Crash) Corrigan was born Ray Benard in Milwaukee on February 14, 1907. His strong physical prowess led him into movie stunt work. In 1935, Republic Pictures gave him an acting role in *The Leathernecks Have Landed.* In 1936 he starred in Republic's serial *The Undersea Kingdom.* He then played the part of Briggs in *Country Gentlemen* with Olsen & Johnson and the role of Lt. Hodge in *Join The Marines.* In 1936, he also appeared in *The Painted Stallion,* a high budget serial in which he co-starred with Hoot Gibson and Jack Perrin. He also began the classic *Three Mesquiteers* series in 1936 with Bob Livingston and Max Terhune.

*Ray Corrigan with Max Terhune and John Wayne in* Pals of the Saddle *(Republic, 1938).*

*Ray (Crash) Corrigan.*

*Ray Corrigan with Phyllis Isley (later known as Jennifer Jones) and John Wayne in* New Frontier *(Republic, 1939).*

In 1940, Corrigan starred in the *Range Busters* series for Monogram. Max Terhune played "Alibi" in all 24 of these films. The *Range Buster's* trio was rounded out in various films by John "Dusty" King and Dennis Moore. Corrigan served as co-producer on all of these films. Over the years, Corrigan has appeared in many westerns and is the owner and developer of Corriganville, a leading movie studio ranch which is located in Chatsworth, California, near Hollywood.

### Buster Crabbe (1909–    )

"Buster" Crabbe was born Clarence Linden Crabbe in Oakland, California, on February 7, 1909. As an infant, his family moved to Hawaii where he spent his boyhood years and became an expert swimmer and an outstanding all-around high school athlete. When he was a young man, he returned to the mainland and studied at the University of Southern California. In 1932, he competed as a swimmer in the Olympic games held in Los Angeles. By 1933, he had set more than a dozen world swimming records. While competing in the Olympics, movie scouts from Paramount studios were impressed by his athletic abilities and good looks. His first screen role was in the film version of H. G. Wells's *Island of Lost Souls* with Charles Laughton and Bela Lugosi. He then starred in Paramount's *King of the Jungle*. Thereafter, he appeared in many adventure pictures, serials, and finally westerns. His first western was *To the Last Man* in 1933, which also starred Randolph Scott. Crabbe starred in many western and non-western films in the 1930s. In one film, *Tarzan the Fearless,* he appeared as the King of the Jungle. His popularity increased tremendously with audiences. In 1936, he starred as "Flash Gordon" for Universal, which proved to be highly successful. He then played a detective in the "Red Barry" serial. In 1939, he played in another serial as "Buck Rogers," and in 1940 he made still another "Flash Gordon" series. In the early 1940s, he appeared in various westerns for Republic and in 1941 he starred in a new series as "Billy the Kid" for PRC pictures. His comic sidekick in this series was Al "Fuzzy" St. John. They made 42 pictures for PRC. Throughout the 1940s, he also appeared in many non-western adventure films. In the 1950s, he appeared in various film and television roles including his own television series, *Foreign Legionaire.* He co-starred in this series with an old western movie sidekick, "Fuzzy" Knight, and his son, Cullen "Cuffy" Crabbe. In the late 1950s he appeared in a number of westerns for United Artists, Republic, and Warner Brothers. His last movie was *Gunfighter of Abilene.* In recent years, he has been a representative for a stock brokerage firm.

*LOBBY CARD:* Rustler's Hideout (PRC, 1944).

*Buster Crabbe with June Martel in* Arizona Mahoney *(Paramount, 1937).*

*Buster Crabbe with Al (Fuzzy) St. John in* Lightning Raiders *(PRC, 1945).*

### Ken Curtis (1916–    )

Ken Curtis was born Curtis Gates in Lamar, Colorado, on July 12, 1916. He studied music at Colorado College and later worked for NBC before joining Tommy Dorsey as the male vocalist with his band. He also sang for a time with the Shep Fields orchestra. In the early 1940s he became one of the "Sons of the Pioneers" who were featured in Roy Rogers westerns for Republic. In 1945 he became a singing cowboy in a series of films for Columbia. In the 1960s he became the bewhiskered "Festus" on the *Gunsmoke* television series. Some of his films include: *Apache Rose, Rhythm Roundup, Cowboy Blues, Throw a Saddle on a Star, The Searchers, Two Rode Together, How the West Was Won,* and *The Horse Soldiers.*

*Ken Curtis, with Joan Barton in* Lone Star Moonlight *(Columbia, 1946).*

### Bob Custer (1898–    )

Bob Custer was born on October 18, 1898, in Frankfort, Kentucky. After a career as a cowboy and rodeo performer, he made his first screen appearance in 1924 in a series of westerns for FBO. He was a successful star in silent western films and made the transition to sound easily. In the early 1930s he starred in a number of features for independent producers. In 1934 he made several serials for Mascot, *The Adventures of Rin Tin Tin* and *Law of the Wild.* In 1936 he was featured in the new western series for Reliable Pictures. Custer retired from the screen in 1938. His films include: *Flashing Spurs, Texas Bearcat, Dude Cowboy, Castus Trails, The Oklahoma Kid, Santa Fe Riders, Blood Trail, Polka Dot Bandit.*

*Bob Custer.*

*Bob Custer grapples with Dick Alexander in the serial*
Law of the Wild *(Mascot, 1934).*

*Eddie Dean with "Black" Jack O'Shea.*

### Eddie Dean (   –   )

Eddie Dean was born Edgar D. Glosup in Posey, Texas. From 1930 through 1933 he appeared as a radio singer throughout the middlewest. In 1934 he contracted to sing on the famous National Barn Dance on station WLS in Chicago. He came to Hollywood in 1936 and appeared in small parts in many westerns. In 1944 he was a featured vocalist on the Judy Canova radio show from Hollywood. Dean was a featured performer in a western series for PRC Studios in 1945, and in 1946 and 1947 he was voted one of the Ten Best Money Making Stars in the *Motion Picture Herald* Fame Poll. In 1948 he starred in another western series for Eagle-Lion Productions. He has also been active over the years as a recording artist and has made numerous personal appearances at rodeos and fairs. He is also the composer of a number of western ballads.

*James Ellison, 2nd from right, with Rand Brooks, Lane Bradford, Stanford Jolley and Johnny Mack Brown in* Man From Black Hills *(Monogram, 1952).*

### James (Jimmy) Ellison (1910–      )

James (Jimmy) Ellison was born James Smith in Guthrie Center, Iowa. He worked with the Beverly Hills Little Theatre and following his discovery by a talent scout he made his screen debut in *The Play Girl*. In 1935 he became William Boyd's original screen partner creating the role of "Johnny Nelson" in "Hopalong Cassidy." He played the part for eight films before relinquishing the role to Russell Hayden in 1937. Other films in which he appeared include *The Plainsman, Last of the Wild Horses, Crooked River, Lone Star Lawman,* and *Dead Man's Trail*.

*James Ellison with Evelyn Ankers in* The Texan Meets Calamity Jane *(Columbia, 1950).*

### Gordon (Wild Bill) Elliott (1904–1965)

Gordon (Wild Bill) Elliott was one of the screen's top western moneymakers during the 1940s and 1950s. He was voted one of the Ten Best Money Making Stars in the *Motion Picture Herald* Poll from 1942 to 1952. Elliott reversed the general pattern by abandoning "straight" acting for the western field. His nickname was acquired in 1938 when he played in the Columbia serial *The Great Adventures of Wild Bill Hickok*. He was born Gordon Nance on a farm near Pattonsburg, Missouri, where he learned the cowboy arts of riding, roping and shooting. He moved to Kansas City with his parents, Mr. and Mrs. Roy Nance, when he was ten years old. As a boy he used to tame horses in his father's stockyard. Exposed briefly to the rodeo circuit, he studied acting at the Pasadena Playhouse and most of his early films were non-westerns, his debut being in *Wonder Bar* in 1934. After his appearance in the Columbia serial in 1938, he made a series of eight westerns; another 15-episode serial, *Overland with Kit Carson;* and then another series of eight westerns in which he re-created his role of "Wild Bill" Hickok in several. This was followed by another eight westerns, where he was teamed with Tex Ritter, and his third and last serial, *Valley of Vanishing Men* in 1942 with Slim Summerville. Elliott then signed for eight "Wild Bill Elliott" films for Republic Pictures followed by the Red Ryder series of six-

*Bill Elliott as "Wild Bill Saunders" protects Linda Winters from cattle rustler Matt Brawley played by Dick Curtis in* Pioneers of the Frontier *(Columbia, 1940).*

teen films beginning in 1943. Little Beaver was played by Robert Blake, the same young actor who appeared as one of the doomed killers in *In Cold Blood* many years later. After the Red Ryder series Republic began starring Elliott in their "major" westerns, the first being *In Old Sacramento,* followed by nine more of the higher budgeted films running into the 1950s. After that he appeared in several westerns for Allied Artists and was a TV spokesman for a national cigarette manufacturer. On November 26, 1965, he died of cancer at his Las Vegas home at the age of 61.

*Bill Elliott with Tex Ritter and Shirley Patterson in* North of the Rockies *(Columbia, 1942).*

*Bill Elliott as "Red Ryder" in* Cheyenne Wildcat *(Republic, 1944). "Little Beaver" is played by Bobby Blake.*

LOBBY CARD: Roaring Frontiers (*Columbia, 1941*).

### Dick Foran (1910–    )

Dick Foran was born in Flemington, New Jersey, on June 18, 1910, the son of Senator Arthur F. Foran. He was educated at Princeton University and made his screen debut in *Stand Up and Cheer* in 1934 for Fox. His pictures include *Cowboy From Brooklyn, Fort Apache, El Paso* and *Deputy Marshall, Song of the Saddle, Treachery Rides the Range, Guns of the Pecos, Moonlight on the Prairie, Trailin' West.*

Dick Foran with Joseph Crehan and Anne Nagel in Guns of the Pecos (*First National, 1937*).

*Dick Foran, 1942.*

### Ed (Hoot) Gibson (1895–1962)

Ed (Hoot) Gibson won the title of "Cowboy Champion of the World" at the Pendleton, Oregon, Round-Up in 1912 before launching his screen career as a stuntman and later as one of the western greats of silent and talking films. He was born in Tekamah, Nebraska, on August 6, 1895, and acquired his nickname from hunting owls as a boy. Gibson was a working cowboy in the real West and as a member of Col. Stanley's Congress of Rough Riders before he won his Pendleton title, he gained stature as a skilled bronc rider. For years he was Universal's top western star and was reputed to have earned $14,500 per week. Although he amassed a fortune of more than $2 million, he later lost it. Despite the trend toward singing cowboys in the 1930s Gibson did make numerous westerns. In 1931 and 1932 he made a series of westerns for M. H. Hoffman's Allied Pictures. He also made films for First Division, RKO Radio, and Diversion Pictures before going to Republic in 1937 where he co-starred with Ray Corrigan in one of the greatest western serials in the history of films, *The Painted Stallion,* in twelve episodes. In 1943 and 1944 he starred in Monogram's "Trail Blazers" series with Ken Maynard and Bob Steele. In recent years Gibson played in character roles including *The Horse Soldiers* in 1959 for his old director, John Ford, and his last film, *Ocean's 11* in 1960. He resided in Las Vegas for the last ten years of his life and after undergoing four operations for cancer he suffered a relapse and died on August 23, 1962, in Woodland Hills, California.

Hoot Gibson, right, with Rocky Camron and Bob Steele in "The Trail Blazers" series, Outlaw Trail *(Monogram, 1944)*.

Hoot Gibson with Laurie Anders *in* The Marshal's Daughter *(United Artists, 1953)*.

*Hoot Gibson in an early pose.*

## Monte Hale (1921–    )

Monte Hale was born in San Angelo, Texas, on June 8, 1921. He made his screen debut in *Steppin' in Society* and he sang in *Big Bonanza* in 1944. Through 1945 he was in various westerns, and in 1946 he began starring in a series of Trucolor westerns including *Out California Way*, *Man From Rainbow Valley*, *Home on the Range*, *Under Colorado Skies*, *California Firebrand*, and *Timber Trail*. In recent years he has made TV appearances. He had a small part as a villain in *Yukon Vengeance* in 1954. He also appeared in *Giant* in 1956 with Elizabeth Taylor, Rock Hudson, and James Dean.

*Monte Hale and Roy Barcroft battle over possession of a gun in* Outcasts of the Trail *(Republic, 1949).*

*Monte Hale disarms Richard Anderson as crotchety Paul Hurst looks on in* The Vanishing Westerner *(Republic, 1950).*

**Russell Hayden (1912–    )**

Russell Hayden was born Pate Lucid in Chico, California, on June 12, 1912. He began his Hollywood career by working in the Paramount sound recording and cutting department. He became an actor in 1937 with William Boyd in *The Hills of Old Wyoming* and played in numerous westerns thereafter for Paramount-Sherman and Columbia. Hayden played the role of "Johnny Nelson" and later "Lucky Jenkins" in the Hopalong Cassidy films until 1941. Hayden was voted one of the ten best Money-Making Western Stars in the *Motion Picture Herald* Fame Poll in 1943 and 1944. He is now producer-director for M. H. Productions, which makes films for TV.

*Russell Hayden battles Victor Jory in* Knights of the Range *(Paramount, 1940).*

*Russell Hayden in* Range War *(Paramount, 1939).*

### Tim Holt (1919–    )

Tim Holt was born in Hollywood in 1919 to Margaret and Jack Holt. His christened name is Charles John Holt Jr., but has been called Tim since he was six weeks old. Tim's Dad, Jack Holt, was one of the ranking film stars of all time. It was on his father's picture sets that he learned to ride, and as he now says, "I think I could ride before I could walk." At the age of eleven he went to work on his Dad's ranch as a cowhand in Fresno, California. It was from this early ranching association that his longing for a ranch stemmed. Holt went to private grammar school in the West, then one year of public high school, then back east to Culver Military Academy for his final schooling. During his schooling Tim played football, polo, squash, tennis, and boxed. He graduated Cum Laude from Culver and won the "Gold Spurs," the highest award in horsemanship. After graduation he went back to the Coast and secured one of the leads in the Pennsylvania Dutch Comedy, *Papa Is All*. From there he was signed by United Artists Studio, and he started his upward

*Tim Holt.*

*Tim Holt with Richard (Chito) Martin in Rio Grande Patrol (RKO Radio, 1950).*

*Tim Holt with Richard Martin and Tom Kennedy in*
*Road Agent (RKO Radio, 1952).*

climb to stardom. A few of the pictures he made were: *History Is Made at Night, Gold Is Where You Find It, Stella Dallas, Stagecoach, The Rookie Cop, The Law West of Tombstone, The Spirit of Culver, Laddie, Back Street, Fifth Avenue Girl, Hitler's Children,* and *The Magnificent Ambersons.* Holt enlisted as an aviation cadet and was sent to preflight at Victorville, California, where he graduated. As a Second Lieutenant he taught both on the flight line and in ground school for about three months. He went overseas in B-29s to fight against Japan. He wears the Distinguished Flying Cross, Air Medal with 3 clusters, Asiatic Pacific with 3 clusters, Pacific Defense Medal, Presidential Citation with 2 clusters and the Victory Medal. After the war he returned to Hollywood and made

the following pictures: *My Darling Clementine, His Kind of Woman* and *The Monster Who Challenged the World.* He also made his regular six western pictures a year for RKO. At Warner Brothers he did his favorite picture, *The Treasure of the Sierra Madre,* with Humphrey Bogart and Walter Huston. This picture garnered seven Academy Awards. Holt now lives in Oklahoma and is associated with radio station KLPR in Oklahoma City. He still tries to find time for rodeos, parades and other guest appearances. It gives him a chance to make new friends and to greet the many friends he already has over the state. On occasions he is accompanied by his wife, Berdee, and three children, Jack, Jay and Bryanna.

### Jack Hoxie (1890–1965)

Jack Hoxie was born in Oklahoma on January 24, 1890. As a young man he appeared in rodeos and wound up in California where he made his film debut in 1917 as a stuntman. He became one of the most successful western stars of the silent screen. In the early 1930s, he left films and toured the U. S. with a circus. In 1932 he returned to western films for Universal. He last appeared in films in 1934. In 1937 he organized the Jack Hoxie Circus. He had a brother who also acted in films under the name of Al Hoxie. After his personal appearance tours he finally retired from show business and settled in his native Oklahoma. He died of leukemia on March 27, 1965.

*Jack Hoxie.*

*Jack Hoxie with Dorothy Gulliver in* Outlaw Justice *(Majestic, 1933).*

*George Houston as Wild Bill Hickok with Kenne Duncan in* Frontier Scout *(Grand National, 1938).*

### George Houston (1898–1944)

George Houston was born in Hampton, New Jersey. His blind father was an evangelist. Houston attended Rutgers University, served in World War I, and after several occupational attempts he became a member of the America Opera Company. He sang in many operas and performed in *Faust* for President Calvin Coolidge. He was on the stage in *Shooting Star, New Moon, Casanova, Thumbs Up* and others. Houston made his screen debut in *The Melody Lingers On* for United Artists in 1935 and starred in several musical films including *Let's Sing Again, Captain Calamity* and *Wallaby Jim of the Islands*. He made his first western, *Frontier Scout,* for Grand National in 1938 with Dave O'Brien, Dorothy Fay and Beth Marion. He went on to star in eleven "Lone Rider" films with Al St. John for PRC from 1940 to 1942. He died of a heart attack on November 12, 1944.

### Buck Jones (1889–1942)

Buck Jones was born Charles Gebhart on December 4, 1889, in Vincennes, Indiana. When he was twelve years old, his family moved to the Oklahoma Territory to homestead and located on land near the town of Red Rock. As a young man he worked on the famous Miller Brothers "101" Ranch near Bliss, Oklahoma, as a hired hand. He also spent a year in Indianapolis working as a mechanic because of his fascination for auto racing. He then enlisted in the United States Army and as a member of the U. S. Sixth Cavalry he served in the Philippine Islands. After his Army discharge, he signed on for exhibitions of bronc riding and trick ropings and traveled with the Miller Brothers "101" Ranch Wild West Show to

New York. In the spring of 1914, while playing Madison Square Garden, he first met Odelle Osborne, a circus rider from Philadelphia whom he married in Lima, Ohio, a year later. He was married in a circus ring amidst a great deal of publicity. He and his wife formed their own family riding expedition circus and toured many towns in the West. For a short period they appeared with Ringling Brothers Circus in 1917 then settled in Los Angeles where he worked as an extra in westerns at Universal Studios. A daughter, Maxine, was born in Los Angeles. She later married Noah Beery Jr. and was the Jones's only child. Jones began as a high salaried stunt man for Canyon Pictures and Fox Studios. His first starring film

*LOBBY CARD (Universal, 1935).*

*Buck Jones with Stanley Fields in* Rocky Rhodes (*Universal, 1934*).

for Fox was *The Last Straw,* made in 1920. Jones became an immediate hit and one of the most popular western stars of the silent films. Under the banner of his own Buck Jones Productions he made the film *The Big Hop,* and also invested in his Buck Jones Wild West Show. Both of these ventures proved to be financial disasters and so he returned to Hollywood and contracted for a series of eight westerns for Beverly Pictures at a much lower salary than he had received in the silent days. The first of this series was the *Lone Rider,* his first talking film role in 1930. He followed with several other good westerns in the 1930–1931 period. From 1931 until 1934, he made a number of westerns for Columbia including *Branded, South of the Rio Grande, Forbidden Trail,* and *The Fighting Ranger.* He also appeared in two western films, *High Speed* in 1932 and *Child of Manhattan* in 1933. He then independently pro-

duced a series of 22 pictures which were released by Universal between 1934 and 1937. After a dispute with Universal, he returned to Columbia and made six more films in 1937 and 1938. In 1941, after several films for Paramount and Republic, he made two serials, *White Eagle* for Columbia and *Riders for Death Valley* for Universal. He had previously appeared in four other serials during the 1930s. His career was on the wane when he signed a contract with Monogram in 1941 for the famous "Rough Riders" series. He co-starred with Tim McCoy and Raymond Hatton and appeared in eight of these westerns. His last film was *Dawn on the Great Divide* which was released and shown after his death. Jones died as a result of the tragic Cocoanut Grove night club fire in Boston on the evening of November 28, 1942. As the result of the blaze, 481 people eventually died. Jones was the guest of honor at a party when the fire broke

*Buck Jones with Nan Grey is honored with the official sombrero of the Texas Centennial in 1936.*

out. He was in Boston to end a personal appearance tour of ten principal cities on behalf of the War Bond and Navy recruiting drives. He died two days later on November 30, 1942. Jones was a popular western hero for a period of more than 20 years, and was one of the few western stars to continue in popularity so long.

### Tom Keene (1904–1963)

Tom Keene started in Hollywood the best way— at the top. His first screen role was as the star of Cecil B. DeMille's *The Godless Girl* in 1928. Then he starred with Renee Adoree in *Tide of Empire* for MGM. Born George Duryea, on either October 31 or December 20, 1904, in Rochester, New York, Keene, who took dramatics at Columbia University and Carnegie Tech, had been a success on the Broadway stage before DeMille brought him to Hollywood. He was in *Tol'able David* and *Our Dailey Bread*, and then producer Wallace Reid cast him as a western hero in *Dude Wrangler.* He was mainly in westerns for the rest of his screen career. Changing his name to Tom Keene he starred in twelve westerns for RKO-Pathe between 1931 and 1933. He appeared in some Paramount westerns in the mid-1930s and starred in a series for Crescent Pictures in 1936– 1937. Keene's co-star in two of these films was Rita Casino, who later became Rita Hayworth. He did a series of four westerns for Monogram in 1937–

*Tom Keene in* God's Country and the Man *(Monogram, 1937).*

1938 and a second series of eight for them in 1941– 1942. In many of these pictures Frank Haconelli appeared as his comic sidekick. After a fling at Broadway in the mid-1940s as Richard Powers,

*Tom Keene with Effie Ellsler in* Drift Fence *(Paramount, 1936).*

Keene returned to Hollywood and played character parts for Republic, PRC, and as a contract player for RKO from 1946–1949. In 1950, he starred in his first serial, Republic's 12-chapter *Desperadoes of the West*. He starred in some TV westerns in the 1950s. In later years he devoted more of his time to the real estate and insurance business. On August 4, 1963, he died of cancer at the Motion Picture County hospital in Woodland Hills, California.

### John (Dusty) King (1909–    )

John (Dusty) King was born Miller McLeod Everson in Cincinnati on July 11, 1909. He was educated at Cincinnati University and became a checker and stoker at a Cincinnati grain elevator. He then became associated with radio and furniture firms and the Crocker Cadillac Agency and worked in New Mexico and Arizona lumber camps.

King was also a singer and announcer over radio stations WCKY, and WKRC in Cincinnati before he joined Ben Bernie's band in 1934. He made his screen debut in *Love Before Breakfast* in 1936. He also appeared in *Show Boat* and from 1940 onward in many westerns for Monogram.

*John "Dusty" King, center, with Frank Ellis and Dave Sharpe in* Texas to Bataan *(Monogram, 1942).*

## Allan (Rocky) Lane (1904–    )

Allan Lane was born Harry Albershart in Mishawaka, Indiana, on September 22, 1904, and attended Notre Dame University. After a career that included being a professional football player, a photographic illustrator, and a stage actor he went into the movies and made many westerns in the 1940s and 1950s. He portrayed Red Ryder in a number of them. Among his credits are *Daredevils of the West,* (serial) in 1945, *Sheriff of Sundown, Stagecoach to Denver, Vigilantes of Boomtown, Bold Frontiersman, Bandit King of Texas, Code of the Silver Sage, Desert of Lost Men, Desperadoes Outpost,* and *El Paso Stampede.* Lane was voted one of the Top Ten Money-Making Western Stars in the *Motion Picture Herald* Poll in 1951 and 1953.

*Allan Lane in* Covered Wagon Raid *(Republic, 1950).*

*LOBBY CARD:* Santa Fe Uprising *(Republic, 1946).*

*Allan (Rocky) Lane with Eddy Waller in* Renegades of
Sonora *(Republic, 1948).*

## Al (Lash) LaRue (1917–    )

Al LaRue was born on June 15, 1917, in Michigan but he was raised in Gretna, Louisiana. His father was a traveling hotel representative and real-estate operator so he rarely remained in the same school very long. When it came time for him to enter high school, he enrolled in St. John's Military Academy in Los Angeles, from which he graduated. After his schooling, he traveled around the country working at various jobs. Upon returning to Hollywood, he obtained a bit part in an Eddie Dean film at PRC Studios. He learned to wield a 15-foot bullwhip skillfully and this became his trademark in his western films. His films include *Song of Old Wyoming, Caravan Trail, Wild West, Law of the Lash, Son of Billy the Kid, Mark of the Lash, The Black Lash, The Return of the Lash,* and *The Frontier Phantom.* Al (Fuzzy) St. John appeared as LaRue's bewhiskered sidekick in several of these films. In recent years LaRue has appeared in motion pictures, television, and rodeos. He still resides in Hollywood.

*Lash LaRue, right, with Frank Lackteen, Al (Fuzzy) St. John and Noel Neill in* Son of a Bad Man *(Screen Guild Productions, 1949).*

*Al (Lash) LaRue.*

### Bob Livingston (1908–    )

Bob Livingston was born Robert E. Randall on December 9, 1908, in Quincy, Illinois. His father, Edgar Randall, was an Associated Press editor and wrote the famous "Say Bill" columns during World War I. His mother, Clarena Meyers, was also a well-known writer. The family moved to Glendale, California, when Livingston was twelve years old. As a young man, he worked on a ranch, as a seaman, as a lumberjack, and finally as a reporter for a Los Angeles newspaper. He appeared in a number of theatrical productions in Pasadena. In 1929 he was signed by Universal for their "Collegian Series" and played in several additional pictures until 1933 when he was signed by MGM. He worked as a drama coach and actor at MGM until the mid-1930s. In 1936 he starred as "The Eagle" in Republic's *The Vigilantes Are Coming*, which was a remake of Rudolph Valentino's 1925 silent picture. He then starred in Republic's first color

picture, *The Bold Caballero*. In 1936 he began starring as Stoney Brooke in the classic *Three Mesquiteers* with Max Terhune as Lullaby Joslin and Ray (Crash) Corrigan as Tucson Smith. This series is considered to be one of the best western series ever produced. Livingston's popularity was so great that Republic also used him in a wide variety of non-western films. In 1939 Republic starred him as a first movie Lone Ranger in *The Lone Ranger Rides Again*. He continued to star in the "Three Mesquiteers" westerns and made a total of 29. In 1942 he contracted to star in a series of westerns for PRC as the "Lone Rider." His sidekick in this series was Al (Fuzzy) St. John. His career prospered through the 1940s as did that of his brother, Jack Randall, who died in 1945 while filming Universal's *The Royal Mounted Rides Again*. In recent years, Livingston has been active in the business field.

*Bob Livingston, center, as "Stoney Brooke" with Max Terhune and Ray (Crash) Corrigan in* Range Defenders *(Republic, 1937).*

*Bob Livingston, right, with Ray (Crash) Corrigan and Julia Thayer in* Gunsmoke Ranch *(Republic, 1937).*

### Jack Luden (1902– )

Jack Luden was born John Luden in Reading, Pennsylvania, on February 6, 1902. His father, Jacob C. Luden, was the famous manufacturer of cough drops. After spending two years at Johns Hopkins University, in 1925 Luden enrolled in Paramount Pictures acting school at Long Island, New York. He made his film debut in 1926 and was loaned to FBO where he starred in his first western, *Shootin' Irons*. He was quite active during the transitional years from silents to talking films. In 1931 he starred for Columbia in a western series. After 1935 and through the late 1940s he appeared in many character roles for Republic, PRC, and Monogram in support of Gene Autry, Don (Red) Barry, and others. His pictures included *The Last Outlaw, Pioneer Trail, Stagecoach Days, Boss of Raw Hide, The Texas Rangers,* and *Bordertown Trail*.

*Jack Luden with Marin Sais and Joan Barclay in* Pioneer Trail *(Columbia, 1938).*

### Ken Maynard (1895– )

Ken Maynard was born on July 21, 1895, in Mission, Texas. He was educated at the Virginia Military Institute and at fourteen joined a wagon show. After service with the Army he became a trick rider with Ringling Brothers Circus in 1923. He was signed by Independent producer J. Charles Davis for a series of eight westerns and his first starring role was in *$50,000 Reward* in 1924. Maynard became a tremendous success in these westerns, and he was signed by First National to star in a series of higher-budgeted westerns from 1926 to 1929. In 1929 Maynard went to Universal where he made films that were part talking and part sound. From 1930 through 1932 he made his first series of all-talking westerns for Tiffany-Stahl Studios. He made eight westerns for World Wide Productions in 1932–33 and then returned to Universal for another series in 1933–34. He made his only serial for Mascot films, "Mystery Mountain," in late 1934. In 1935–1936 he made a series of eight westerns for Columbia Pictures and in 1937–38 four more for Grand National. He ended his work in the 1930s by appearing in Four Colony "State-Righters," *Flaming Lead, Death Rides the Range, Phantom Rancher,* and *Lightning Strikes West*. In 1943–1944 he teamed up with Hoot Gibson for

*Ken Maynard, with Lina Basquette, Hooper Stehley, Edmund Cobb and Tom London in* Texas Terrors *(Tiffany, 1931).*

Monogram's famous "Trail Blazers" series. The first three—*Wild Horse Stampede, The Law Rides Again,* and *Blazing Guns*—were made by Gibson and Maynard. In the last three, Bob Steele co-starred—*Death Valley Rangers, Westward Bound,* and *Arizona Whirlwind*. Maynard's last film, *White Stallion,* was made in 1945. Maynard was married for 28 years to a former Ringling Brothers aerialist who died in 1968. He keeps active per-

*Ken Maynard with Bob Steele and Hoot Gibson in* Arizona Whirlwind *(Monogram, 1944).*

forming at rodeos and state fairs. (Maynard's horse, Tarzan, lived for over 25 years and appeared in most of his films.) He now lives quietly in San Fernando, California.

*LOBBY CARD:* Wheels of Destiny *(Universal, 1934).*

Ken Maynard.

### Kermit Maynard (1902–1971)

Kermit Maynard, the younger brother of western star Ken Maynard, was born on September 20, 1902, in Mission, Texas. He graduated from Indiana University, Bloomington, Indiana, and after his college days, he went to work for the George H. Hormel Packing Company in Austin, Minnesota, where he worked as a claim agent. He first appeared in western films in 1927 as a double for various stars in dangerous action scenes. He was also a rodeo performer and won the World's Championship in trick and fancy riding in 1933. In 1934, he signed a contract with Ambassador Pictures and starred in a series of films about the Royal Canadian Mounted Police. The first film in this series was *Fighting Trooper* followed by *Northern Frontier* and *Wilderness Male* in 1935. He had roles in many westerns in the 1930s and 1940s and was actively doing stunt work in the late 1950s. He died on January 16, 1971, at his North Hollywood home.

*Kermit Maynard.*

*Kermit Maynard with Cliff Parkinson and Olin Francis in* Rough Ridin' Rhythm *(Ambassador-Conn, 1937).*

### Tim McCoy (1891–    )

Tim McCoy was born on April 10, 1891, in Saginaw, Michigan, and he was educated at St. Ignatius College, Chicago. He is one of the most authentic cowboys ever to appear in American westerns. His white Stetson has gone virtually unsullied through hundreds of fist fights, dust storms, and Indian raids in films. McCoy is one of the world's leading authorities on American Indian history. As a boy, he worked on cattle ranches in Wyoming and learned Indian sign-talk. After serving in World War I, he became an aid to General Scott, Indian fighter of the late 19th century and later army chief of staff. He was ranked by General Scott as one of the three best Indian sign talkers in the U. S. Army. In the early 1920s McCoy went into pictures as a result of Jesse Lasky's need for a technical advisor in the classic westerns *Covered Wagon* and *The Vanishing American*. Irving Thal-

berg, production chief for MGM, started McCoy on his acting career. He made a series of films for MGM between 1926 and 1929, the first of which was *War Paint*. Several of these were filmed on location in Wyoming on Indian reservations. McCoy made the only serials of his career for Universal, *The Indians Are Coming* in 1930 and *Heroes of the Flames* in 1931. In late 1931 he began a series of sixteen westerns for Columbia Pictures, which were released between 1931 and 1933. Columbia also used McCoy in a group of non-western films in 1933 and 1934 involving subjects ranging from auto racing to fire fighting. He made eight more westerns for Columbia in 1934–1935 including *The Westerner, Fighting Shadows,* and *The Prescott Kid*. McCoy made westerns for several companies including Puritan Pictures, Monogram Studios, and Victory Pictures through 1938.

*Tim McCoy with Nora Lane in* Outlaw Deputy *(Puritan, 1935).*

*Tim McCoy has the best of John Merton in* Lightnin' Bill Carson *(Puritan, 1936)*.

In 1938–1939 he starred in some westerns in which he played G-man "Lightning Bill" Carson. In these films he used Mexican, Chinese, and Gypsy disguises for "undercover" work. In 1940–1941 he made six westerns for PRC in which he battled not only outlaws but Axis agents as well. In 1941–1942 he appeared in Monogram's "Rough Riders" series with Buck Jones and Raymond Hatton. This famous series was McCoy's last before entering the service in World War II. He became a Lt. Colonel in the U. S. Army as a member of the Adjutant General's staff. Since World War II, he has been active in television, and has made some guest appearances in films including *Around the World in 80 Days*, Alex Gordon's *Requiem For A Gunfighter,* and *Run Of The Arrow*. In the 1950s, he was a contestant on the TV quiz show *$64,000 Challenge* and was the subject of a *This Is Your Life* show. He has also appeared with several circuses and still is active with an 18-act motorized touring production throughout the United States. The eleven-month season is climaxed every year with a banquet in Greenville, South Carolina. The

*Tim McCoy battles Dick Curtis as James Burtis looks on in* Ghost Patrol *(Puritan, 1936)*.

Scott-McCoy Caravan travels more than 10,000 miles a year. McCoy now resides in Nogales, Arizona, one of the two survivors along with Ken Maynard of the onetime "Big Five" of American western movies.

Joel McCrea with Henry Hull and Virginia Mayo in Colorado Territory (Warner Bros., 1949).

Joel McCrea with Barbara Stanwyck in Trooper Hook (United Artists, 1957).

## Joel McCrea (1905–    )

Joel McCrea was born in Los Angeles on November 5, 1905. He attended Pomona College and gained stage experience in amateur dramatics and community plays. He took the male lead in *The Patsy, Laff That Off,* and *The Little Journey.* McCrea made his screen debut in 1932 and appeared in many non-western films during the 1930s and 1940s including *He Married His Wife, Primrose Path, Foreign Correspondent, Sullivan's Travels, The Palm Beach Story* and *The More the Merrier.* He has been married to actress Frances Dee for many years. In recent years McCrea has concentrated almost exclusively on westerns. His appearances include *Virginian, Ramrod, Four Faces West, Outriders, Stars in My Crown, Border River, Black Horse Canyon, Wichita, The Oklahoman, Trooper Hook, Fort Massacre, The Gunfight at Dodge City,* and *Ride the High Country.* In the latter he appeared with Randolph Scott.

Joel McCrea with Ramon Novarro in The Outriders (M-G-M, 1950).

### Tom Mix (1880–1940)

While legend reported that Tom Mix was born near El Paso, Texas, his birthplace was actually a small community in Pennsylvania—Mix Run, near Dubois. He was born on January 6, 1880, and was the son of an Irish captain in the celebrated U. S. Seventh Cavalry. His mother was of Scotch and Cherokee Indian extraction. The man who was to become one of the screen's greatest two-gun, hard-riding cowboys, learned to ride a horse at a very early age, and was an accomplished knife-thrower and lariat spinner. He attended Virginia Military Institute and after leaving VMI, he went to Texas to become a Texas Ranger. At the outbreak of the Spanish-American War in 1898, he enlisted in the army and went to Cuba. He was a scout and courier for General Chaffee, and at the Battle of Cristobal Hill he was wounded in the neck by a Spanish bullet. He also saw service in the Orient during the Boxer Rebellion in China and in the Philippine Insurrection. He later went to South Africa and participated as a non-combatant in the Boer War. After returning to the United States, he served as a guide to Theodore Roosevelt during one of T.R.'s hunting expeditions. He served as sheriff of Montgomery County, Kansas, and later as sheriff of Washington County, Oklahoma, and Two Buttes County, Colorado. Subsequent to that, he became a United States marshal in Montana, Arizona, and New Mexico. During a second term with the Texas Rangers, he single-handedly captured the notorious Shonts Brothers, desperadoes who had terrorized the Texas-Mexico cattle country for years. In 1909, he joined the Miller Brothers "101" Ranch and won numerous rodeo titles throughout the west. In 1918, he became a star at William Fox's Studio and appeared in scores of silent westerns. In all of these pictures and in the many to follow during the 1930s, Mix's companion was his horse, Tony. Mix went to RKO Studios in 1929 after several extensive personal appearance tours through Europe in the mid-1920s. He toured for three years with

*Tom Mix with Noah Beery Jr. in* Rustlers Roundup *(Universal, 1933).*

the Sells-Floto Circus and in 1931 signed a contract with Carl Laemmle for six talking pictures. At one time during his film career, Mix made more than $10,000 a week. In 1932 Mix made *Destry Rides Again,* which was the first of a series of nine westerns for Universal pictures. In 1935, he starred in what was to be his first serial and last motion picture for Mascot entitled *The Miracle Rider.* Tom Mix made nearly 400 movies during his career, but his voice did not fit the new medium of talking films and after 1935 he appeared in road shows. His last years were spent touring with the Tom Mix Circus. On October 12, 1940, he was traveling across the Arizona desert in one of his custom-built roadsters on his way to Hollywood to discuss a movie comeback. The car overturned at a high rate of speed on a dirt road eighteen miles south of Florence, Arizona, and he was killed instantly. His wonder horse, Tony, died in 1944 at the age of 34. In June 1968, the Tom Mix Museum was opened in Dewey, Oklahoma, the site where he first starred in a movie. It features a $250,000 collection that retraces the life and legend of this great western film star.

*Tom Mix.*

### George Montgomery (1916–    )

George Montgomery was born George Montgomery Letz in Brady, Montana, on August 29, 1916. He was educated at the University of Montana. He was one of the five Rangers in Republic's famous serial of 1938, *The Lone Ranger,* where he, along with Bruce Bennett, Lane Chandler, Hal Taliaferro, and Lee Powell were five Texas Rangers who one by one throughout the serial were killed, leaving only Lee Powell as "The Lone Ranger." In 1940 he made his feature film debut in *The Cisco Kid and the Lady* for 20th Century-Fox. Montgomery has made many westerns during his career in films both before and after service in the armed forces in World War II. For many years he was married to singer Dinah Shore. His pictures include *The Cowboy and the Blonde, Riders of the Purple Sage, Last of the Duanes, Roxie Hart, Orchestra Wives, China Girl, Lulu Belle, Belle Starr's Daughter, Texas Rangers, Cripple Creek, Fort Ti, Masterson of Kansas, Robber's Roost,* and *Stallion Trail.*

*George Montgomery in* Canyon River *(Allied Artists, 1936).*

### Clayton Moore (1914–    )

Clayton Moore was born in Chicago on September 14, 1914. His early professional years were spent as a trapeze artist, and as a model for John Robert Powers, 1935–1938. In 1939 he was under contract to Warner Bros., in 1940 with MGM, and in 1941 with Edward Small Productions. From 1943 to 1945 he served in the Air Force. Upon returning to civilian life he made pictures at Columbia, Monogram, R.K.O., and was "King of the Serials" at Republic from 1946 to 1949. In July 1949 he started "The Lone Ranger" role in which he is still active, making personal appearance tours at rodeos and state fairs. Moore is an expert horseman and gun twirler who handled most of his action fight routines throughout his career.

*Clayton Moore.*

*Clayton Moore as* The Lone Ranger *and Jay Silverheels as Tonto.*

### Wayne Morris (1914–1959)

Wayne Morris was born Bert de Wayne Morris on February 17, 1914, in Los Angeles. He attended Los Angeles Junior College and was a graduate of the Pasadena Playhouse, where he was spotted by a Warner Bros. talent scout who was searching for an athletic type to play the lead in *Kid Galahad*. Morris made his screen debut in *China Clipper* in 1936. His role in *Kid Galahad* made him a star overnight. Other films included *Kid from Kokomo,*

*Angel from Texas, Quarterback, I Wanted Wings,* and *Voice of the Turtle.* When World War II began he was one of the first to leave the film capital for military service. He remained five years in the Navy as an aviator and was discharged a lieutenant commander. During his service he was awarded four Distinguished Flying Crosses and two air medals. Rated an ace, he was given credit for shooting down seven Japanese aircraft in aerial

*Wayne Morris, center, with Geraldine Brooks and Robert Hutton in* The Younger Brothers *(Warner Bros., 1949).*

dogfights, sinking a Japanese gunboat and two enemy destroyers, and helping to destroy a submarine. Ironically, Morris's postwar screen heroics were not so spectacular as was his pre-war career. He did, however, make many westerns for Allied Artists in the 1950s. On September 15, 1959, he died of a heart attack while visiting his old squadron commander as he was watching aerial maneuvers on the bridge of the aircraft carrier *Bonhomme Richard,* docked at Oakland, California.

*Wayne Morris with Sally Eilers, Rod Cameron and Kay Buckley in* Stage to Tucson *(Columbia, 1950).*

*Audie Murphy with Joan Evans in* No Name on the Bullet
*(Universal International, 1959).*

## Audie Murphy (1924–1971)

Audie Murphy was born in Kingston, Texas, on June 20, 1924. He was a clerk and service station attendant before entering the service in World War II. He became the most decorated hero of the war and held 24 decorations including the Congressional Medal of Honor, Distinguished Service Cross, Silver Star with Oak Leaf Cluster, and Legion of Merit. He made his screen debut in *Beyond Glory* starring Alan Ladd in 1948. He made many westerns during the 1950s and 1960s including *Sierra, Kid From Texas, Kansas Raiders, Drums Across the River, Destry, Ride a Crooked Trail, The Unforgiven, Six Black Horses, Gunfight at Comanche Creek, Apache Rifles,* and *Gunpoint.* Murphy died in a plane crash in May 1971.

*Audie Murphy with Kipp Hamilton in* The Unforgiven *(United Artists, 1960).*

## James Newill (1911–      )

James Newill was born on August 12, 1911, in Pittsburgh, and spent his boyhood there and in Gardena, California. He left the University of Southern California in 1930 to become a member of the Los Angeles Opera Company. After a season in opera, he joined a traveling tent show known as "Murphy's Comedians" and then jumped into radio as a featured singer on the "Burns and Allen" show. He later became a vocalist with Eddy Duchin, Abe Lyman, and Gus Arnheim. With the latter he signed the show on and off the air nightly with "Say It With Music." A talent scout from Grand National Pictures signed Newill to a contract and he made his film debut in *Something to Sing About* in 1937. Later in the year he signed to do the title role in "Renfrew of the Royal Mounted" series. In 1939–1940 he was in a number of action pictures for Monogram. In 1942 he began the "Texas Rangers" series for PRC which ran through 1944. Some of the titles included *Rangers Take Over, Bad Men of Thunder Gap, West of Texas, Trail of Terror, Return of the Rangers, Gunsmoke Mesa, Pinto Bandit, Spook Town,* and *Brand of the Devil.* In 1947 he made *Shootin' Irons* (a remake of *West of Texas*) and *Thundergap Outlaws* (a remake of *Bad Men of Thunder Gap*) for Eagle-Lion. He retired from films after that and now operates a plastics business in California.

*Jim Newill with Guy Wilkerson and Stanford Jolley in*
Return of the Rangers *(PRC, 1943).*

### Dave O'Brien (1912–1969)

Dave O'Brien was born in Big Springs, Texas, on May 31, 1912. His father was in the boiler works business. As a young man he put on exhibition dances with Imogene Anderson at theatres, fairs, and various other celebrations in and around Abilene, Texas. O'Brien toured with the Harley Sadler Stock Co., singing, dancing, telling jokes, and playing the ukelele. He left Sadler for roles in stage plays in El Paso. His first film experience was as an extra in an Eddie Lambert short in 1929. His first feature film was a no-credit role in *Dawn Patrol* for First National in 1930. His first credited role was in Paramount's film classic *Jennie Ger-*hardt in 1933, and his first starring role was in the serial *Black Coin* in 1936. He worked in many western and non-western films, his first series being the "Renfrew" series, followed by the "East Side Kid" series, and the "Billy the Kid" series. He is perhaps best known for his work in the "Texas Ranger" series for PRC in 1943 and the "Pete Smith Specialties." In the latter he sometimes worked as director and writer. His last film work was in *Desperadoes Are in Town* for 20th Century-Fox and *The Kettles in the Ozarks* for Universal in 1956. In 1955 he turned to TV and worked as Red Skelton's double. For many years he was a writer for Red Skelton and won an Emmy Award for outstanding writing in Comedy in 1961. He died November 9, 1969, after suffering a heart attack.

*Dave O'Brien in the role of "Steve Davis" in* Cowboy from Sundown *(Monogram, 1940).*

*Dave O'Brien with Stanford Jolley in* Frontier Fugitives *(PRC, 1945).*

*George O'Brien with Lee Shumway in Hollywood Cowboy (RKO, 1937).*

*George O'Brien with Hobart Cavanaugh and William Haade in Stage to Chino (RKO, 1940).*

### George O'Brien (1900– )

George O'Brien was born on April 19, 1900, in San Francisco, California. He attended Santa Clara College and then joined the U. S. Navy. As a young man he appeared in many amateur theatricals and entered the motion picture industry in the 1920s as an assistant cameraman, stuntman, double, and finally as an actor. His early pictures include *The Iron Horse, The Man Who Came Back, The Roughneck, The Johnstown Flood,* *Sharpshooters, Honor Bound, Blindfold, Noah's Ark,* and *My Wild Irish Rose.* In the 1930s he joined RKO and became one of their top cowboy stars. He went into the U. S. Navy during World War II. He returned to films in 1946 and retired in 1950. He became a film supervisor for the U. S. government and appeared infrequently in motion pictures. In 1965 he had a small role in *Cheyenne Autumn* for John Ford.

*LOBBY CARD:* Timber Stampede *(RKO, 1939).*

*George O'Brien.*

### Jack Perrin (1896–1967)

Jack Perrin was born on July 25, 1896, in Three Rivers, Michigan, and grew up in Los Angeles. He appeared in some of the Keystone Kops pictures for Mack Sennett before entering the U. S. Navy during World War I. After returning from the service Perrin became a star in dramatic adventure pictures in the 1920s for Pathé, Hodkinson, Universal, Metro, Arrow, FBO, Associated Exhibiters, First National, Aywon, and Rayart. He finished the silent era with a series of westerns at Universal and made an easy transition to talking films. In the early 1930s he starred in a number of independent productions including *Beyond the Rio Grande, Ridin' Law* and *Romance of the West*. He starred in a series of three-reel "Bud n' Ben" westerns with Ben Corbett and a series of six pictures for Astor Pictures in 1933–1934. Featured with Perrin in most of his films was his beautiful white stallion, Starlight, "the wonder horse." Perrin appeared in many westerns in later years and was still active in the 1960s. He died December 17, 1967, from a heart attack.

*Jack Perrin with Ethan Laidlaw in* Rainbow Riders.

*Addison (Jack) Randall.*

### Addison (Jack) Randall (1906–1945)

Addison (Jack) Randall was born on May 12, 1906, in San Fernando, California, the son of famed Associated Press editor Edgar Randall. He was encouraged to enter show business by his brother, Bob Livingston, also a star of westerns. After a Broadway musical and dramatic career in the early 1930s, Randall won an RKO contract in 1935 and had leading roles in several pictures including *His Family Tree, Two in the Dark, Love on a Bet,* and *Follow the Fleet* with Fred Astaire and Ginger Rogers. Blessed with a rich baritone voice, he later starred in a series of musical westerns for Monogram beginning with *Riders of the Dawn* in 1937. He starred in many more westerns in the 1930s and 1940s and after World War II began he entertained troops overseas for two years. In 1945 he was signed by Universal to play the featured villain role in the serial *The Royal Mounted Rides Again.* On location at Iverson's Ranch in Chatsworth, California, on July 16, 1945, Randall suddenly clutched his chest and slumped over in his saddle while filming some riding scenes

*Jack Randall with Ernie Adams in* Riders From Nowhere *(Monogram, 1940).*

and died from a heart attack. Some of his western credits included: *Danger Valley, Gunsmoke Trail, Wild Horse Canyon, Oklahoma Terror, Covered Wagon Trails, Riders From Nowhere,* and *Wild Horse Range.*

### Duncan Renaldo (1904–    )

Duncan Renaldo was born on April 23, 1904, in Spain and his early childhood was spent among agricultural and cattle people in rural districts of Spain and Central Europe. He received his early education at schools in France and later at academies in the United States. In the early stages of his career, Renaldo became an assistant Captain in the Brazilian Merchant Marine. He sailed on ships calling at ports in Turkey, Italy, Greece, Egypt, France, Brazil, and Argentina. He traveled and sailed routes to Africa, Siam, Indo-China, and India. When he returned to the United States he became a portrait painter in New York. He has painted many celebrities such as Florence Reid, Alan Dale, the famous dramatic critic, Jim Tully, the great American author, and many others. He then turned to motion pictures and after playing many bit parts he was given the lead opposite Hope Hampton and Lionel Barrymore in Paramount Picture's *Fifty-Fifty Girl.* He wrote, directed, and acted in a series of Technicolor pictures including *Romany Love, Marchetta, Among My Souve-* nirs, and *Mission Bells.* He played the feature role in *The Bridge of San Luis Rey* for Metro-Goldwyn-Mayer and this box-office smash led to an exclusive contract for Renaldo at MGM. He then co-starred in *Trader Horn.* Renaldo has been a featured player at practically every motion picture studio in Hollywood. His value as a featured actor was demonstrated by his versatility in going from Western pictures at Republic to a featured role in Paramount's *For Whom The Bell Tolls.* In 1946 he was signed by Philip Krasne to play the role of the "Cisco Kid" in a series of featured pictures. When Krasne sold the "Cisco Kid" title to Frederick Ziv in 1948, one of the terms of the sale was that Duncan Renaldo's contract would be included. He not only played the starring role of "The Cisco Kid" for Ziv but he was the Associate Producer of the pictures from 1948 through 1951. This western series was one of the most popular ever released by United Artists. When Ziv decided to convert the series to television, Duncan Renaldo continued in the role.

*Duncan Renaldo as "The Cisco Kid."*

*Duncan Renaldo and Billy Wayne in* The Gay Amigo *(United Artists, 1949).*

*LOBBY CARD:* Roaring Frontiers *(Columbia, 1941).*

*Tex Ritter in* Roaring Frontiers *(Columbia, 1941)*.

## Tex Ritter (1907– )

Woodward Maurice "Tex" Ritter was born on January 12, 1907, in Murvaul, Texas. He graduated with a B.A. from the University of Texas and then attended law school at Northwestern University. He left the law for a show business career and appeared on Broadway in *Green Grow the Lilacs* and *The Roundup*. He also appeared on radio shows including *The Lone Star Rangers, Cowboy Tom's Roundup, Tex Ritter's Campfire* and *Death Valley Days*. Producer Edward Finney signed him in 1936 to star in a series of Westerns for Grand National. Finney put solid production value and good direction behind the films, many of which are still remembered as western classics. Ritter joined the ranks of the *Motion Picture Herald's* top ten Western stars in this 1936 to 1938 series and for some years thereafter. The Grand National films were: *Song of the Gringo, Headin' for the Rio Grande, Arizona Days, Trouble in Texas,*

*Hittin' the Trail, Sing Cowboy Sing, Riders of the Rockies, Mystery of the Hooded Horsemen, Tex Rides with the Boy Scouts, Frontier Town, Rollin' Plains,* and *The Utah Trail.* Changing studios, producer Finney and star Ritter continued to turn out firstrate films from 1938 to 1941 for Monogram. Films such as *Westbound Stage, Rainbow over the Range, Arizona Frontier,* and *Roll Wagons Roll* featured some exceptional production values in the series. In 1941 he starred with Bill Elliott in a Columbia series. In 1942 he starred with Johnny Mack Brown and Fuzzy Knight in a Universal series. In 1944 he starred with Max Terhune in Columbia's *Cowboy Canteen* and starred with Dave O'Brien and Guy Wilkerson in PRC's *Texas Rangers* series. In 1952 his rendition of the "High Noon" ballad won an Academy Award for the song. In recent years he has guest starred on TV and starred in Screen Gems' musical Western TV

*Tex Ritter with Bill Elliott and Virginia Carroll in* Prairie Gunsmoke *(Columbia, 1942)*.

series *Tex Ritter's Ranch Party* in 1959 and is still a noted recording artist. In January 1970, Ritter announced what proved to be an unsuccessful candidacy for the Republican nomination to the U. S. Senate from Tennessee.

### Roy Rogers (1912– )

Roy Rogers was born Leonard Slye on November 5, 1912, in Cincinnati. The "King of the Cowboys" is part Choctaw, German, and Scotch-Irish. He began his career as a radio singer in Los Angeles and was a member of the famous "Sons of the Pioneers." In 1937 he was hired as a singing cowboy at $75.00 a week by Republic Studios and in that year he appeared in *Under Western Stars* and *The Old Barn Dance*. In 1938 and 1939 he appeared in such films as *Billy the Kid Returns, Come On, Rangers, Rough Riders, Round-Up, Frontier Pony Express, Wall Street Cowboy,* and *Sunset Serenade.* From 1943 through 1954 inclusive he was voted the number one Money-Making Western Star in the *Motion Picture Herald* Fame Poll. In 1952 he began producing and acting in TV films with his wife, Dale Evans. By 1956 he had completed 101 of the television shows. In recent years they have devoted themselves to TV specials and nation-wide personal appearance tours. In 1958 Rogers suffered a heart-artery constriction which has confined his activities very little. The Roy Rogers Museum was opened in Apple Valley, California, in June 1967. He and his wife now make recordings, four to five TV specials a year, and perform limited night club engagements in Nevada. Five of their six children are married and they are grandparents twelve times over. Personal tragedy has plagued Rogers's family over the years. One of their children, Eliza-

*Roy Rogers and Dale Evans in* Bells of Rosarita *(Republic, 1945)*.

*Roy Rogers in* Saga of Death Valley *(Republic, 1939)*.

*Roy Rogers.*

*LOBBY CARD:* Utah *(Republic, 1945).*

beth, two years old, died in 1952 from complications following mumps; their adopted daughter, Debbie, a Korean girl, died in a 1964 church bus crash that killed eight; and their adopted son, Sandy, eighteen years old, died during a choking seizure in 1965 while serving with the U. S. Army in Germany. Rogers and his wife are both very religious and their faith has sustained them through these many setbacks. They now live comfortably in Apple Valley, California, 100 miles east of Hollywood.

### Gilbert Roland (1905–     )

Gilbert Roland was born Luis Antonio Damasco Alonso in Chihuahua, Mexico, on December 11, 1905. He was raised in El Paso, Texas. Roland was one of the most successful leading men on the silent screen in the 1920s. In the 1930s, after a successful transition to talking films, he portrayed gangsters repeatedly in films. In the early 1940s he became the third actor to portray the "Cisco Kid" when he began a series for Monogram (Warner Baxter and Cesar Romero preceded him in the role). In 1943 he joined the Air Force. Since World War II, he has been active in many western films.

*Gilbert Roland in* Thunder Trail *(Paramount, 1937).*

### "Reb" Russell (1905– )

"Reb" Russell was born Fay H. Russell on May 31, 1905. He entered films after excelling in sports at Northwestern University, where he was chosen as an All-American fullback in 1930. In 1932 he appeared in a football picture for Paramount appropriately entitled *All-American.* He was then signed by producer Russ Willis Kent to star in a series of independent westerns. He appeared as a star in western films until the late 1930s, mainly for independent companies. He has made his home in Coffeyville, Kansas, in recent years.

*Reb Russell, right, with Chester Gan, Charles Whitaker
and Lucille Lund in* Fighting Through *(Willis Kent, 1934).*

### Fred Leedom Scott (1902–    )

Fred Leedom Scott was born on February 14, 1902, in Fresno, California, and was raised on a ranch. His first acting experience came through the Fresno Community Players and he later studied music in Los Angeles. He went to work for J. Stuart Blackton at the old Vitagraph Studio, and in 1929 went to Pathé where his first part was in *Rio Rita*. He became Helen Twelvetrees's leading man for three years. Other films at Pathé included *The Grand Parade* (a minstrel film and a personal favorite of Scott's), *Swing High, Night Victory,* and *Beyond Victory*. He left films for a short time to sing with the San Francisco Opera Company and appeared in *Salome* with the world famous Maria Jeritza. In 1936 he began a series of singing westerns for Spectrum in which he starred. The series included *Romance Rides the Range, Singing Buckaroo, Melody of the Plains* (Al St. John created the role of "Fuzzy" in this 1937 film, the character he would play for many years to come), *The Fighting Deputy, Moonlight on the Range, Roaming Cowboy* (with Lois January), *The Ranger's Roundup, Knight of the Plains,* and *Songs and Bullets*. In 1938 and 1939 he made *Code of the Fearless, In Old Montana* and *Two-Gun Troubador*. He made *Ridin' the Trail*, a sequel to *Two-Gun Troubador,* for Arthur Ziehm in 1940. In 1942 he starred in *Rodeo Rhythm* in which he wore a mustache to make him look more mature. Scott left films after that for a place as singer and manager for Nils T. Granlund's "Florentine Gardens Revue." He later worked in MGM's sound de-

*Fred Scott with Al St. John in* Songs and Bullets *(Spectrum, 1938).*

partment. In recent years he has been in the real estate business in Hollywood where he lives with his wife in the hills overlooking Universal Studios where they saw at night the production work on "The Virginian," the former TV series. Scott recently commented:

I believe I enjoyed making *Songs and Bullets* about the most of all. It had enjoyable songs written by Don Swander and his wife, June. The Swanders also wrote "Deep in the Heart of Texas." There were a lot of good situations and I think the director Sam Newfield got an awful lot out of this script on this comparatively low budget picture. Al St. John was never better. . . . Westerns I liked best. Coming from farms and ranches, I think I felt most at home. I have been in the manufacturing business and the real estate business for many years. I have two daughters and five grandchildren. My wife was the former Marietta of George White's Scandals. How long ago those days seem. Over the years, I have taken on several pounds in weight,

*Fred Scott in* Ridin' the Trail *(Monogram, 1940).*

which I struggle to hold down. I don't ride anymore. I have a deal with the horses—I don't get on them and they don't sell any real estate.

### Randolph Scott (1903–    )

Randolph Scott was born on January 23, 1903, in Orange County, Virginia. He was educated at the University of North Carolina and had considerable stage experience on the west coast during the 1920s. He made his motion picture debut in *Sky Bride* for Paramount in 1932. Scott appeared in western and non-western roles throughout his career, but since World War II he has appeared mainly in westerns. From 1950 through 1953, he was voted one of the Top Ten Money-Making Stars in the *Motion Picture Herald* Fame Poll. During the 1950s he acted as associate producer with Harry Joe Brown in a number of his films. He is now retired from films. His western films include *The Gunfighters, Albuquerque, Canadian Pacific, The Doolins of Oklahoma, The Nevadan, Sugarfoot, Santa Fe, Fort Worth, Carson City, Hangman's Knot, The Stranger Wore A Gun, Bounty Hunter, Ten Wanted Men, West Bound, Comanche Station,* and his last film was the classic *Ride*

*Randolph Scott in* The Walking Hills *(Columbia, 1949)*

*The High Country.* The latter was a film in which he co-starred with Joel McCrea in 1962. It was directed by Sam Peckenpah.

*Randolph Scott in* Hangman's Knot *(Columbia, 1952).*

*Randolph Scott with Monte Blue and Gail Patrick in* Wagon Wheels *(Paramount, 1934).*

### Charles Starrett (1903–    )

Charles Starrett was born on March 28, 1903, in Athol, Massachusetts. He was the son of Frank and Lena Starrett and the grandson of F. S. Starrett an inventor and founder of the F. S. Starrett Company, producer of precision tools. He was educated at Worcester Academy and Dartmouth College where he graduated in 1926. He was an outstanding collegiate athlete and after his graduation he went to New York and studied at the Academy of Dramatic Arts after which he toured with the Chautauqua circuit and various other stock shows. He joined the Stewart-Walker stock company and played three years in Cincinnati and Indianapolis. Upon returning to Broadway, he appeared in several shows. While still in undergraduate school he

had appeared as an extra with other football players on the Dartmouth squad in support of Richard Dix in *The Quarterback*. In the 1930s he signed a contract for Paramount and appeared in two early sound pictures, *Fast and Loose* and *Royal Family On Broadway*. These were filmed at Astoria, Long Island, and after that Paramount sent him to the west coast where he appeared in many films including *The Sweetheart of Sigma Chi, Murder on the Campus,* and *So Red the Rose*. In 1936 he began starring in westerns for Columbia Pictures. Starrett made westerns for seventeen years and appeared in more than 100 through 1952 including *Riders of the Badlands, West of Tombstone, Lawless Plainsmen,* and *Overland to*

ROARING ACTION!
ROUSING TUNES!

CHARLES STARRETT

as "The Medico" in

THUNDER OVER THE PRAIRIE

with

EILEEN O'HEARN • CLIFF EDWARDS
CARL SHRUM AND HIS RHYTHM RANGERS
Screen play by Betty Burbridge • Directed by Lambert Hillyer    A COLUMBIA Reprint

*LOBBY CARD:* Thunder Over the Prairie *(Columbia, 1941).*

Charles Starrett.

Charles Starrett with an old nemesis, Dick Curtis, in Riders of Black River *(Columbia, 1939).*

*Deadwood.* He was voted one of the top Money-Making Western Stars in the *Motion Picture Herald* Fame Poll in 1942 and 1944 through 1952 inclusive. He recently wrote that "I am happy to be remembered with all the others of my vintage who rode the Hollywood Range during the 1930s and 1940s." His first western film for Columbia, *Gallant Defender,* had Len Slye, later known as Roy Rogers, in the cast. In 1940 Starrett began a series of westerns in which he was known as the *"Durango Kid."* Among the last films that Starrett made were *Junction City, Kid From Broken Gun,* and *Laramie Mountains.* Now retired, he lives in Laguna Beach, California.

*Charles Starrett with Smiley Burnette in* Challenge of the Range *(Columbia, 1949).*

### Bob Steele (1907–    )

Bob Steele was born Bob Bradbury Jr. on January 23, 1907, in Pendleton, Oregon, but he grew up in Los Angeles where his father was a movie director. During their childhood, Bob and his twin brother Bill were photographed by their father during hunting and fishing trips with such good results that the films were edited and sold as a series of "Pathegrams" entitled the "Adventures of Bill and Bob." There were sixteen of these two-reel films made. While still a teenager Steele played roles in several of his father's films, being billed under his real name. With his father's help, Bob changed his name to Steele in 1927 and made his debut as a western star for FBO (later RKO-Radio Pictures). His first starring western was *The Mojave Kid* which was followed by thirteen more starring roles for FBO. Steele made seven westerns for Syndicate Pictures in 1929–1930. The transition to sound films was easy for Steele, who possessed an excellent speaking voice. In 1932–1933 he made eight westerns for Monogram and in 1934 he signed for the first of sixteen westerns produced by A. W. Hackel's Supreme Pictures Corporation. Many of these films were exciting. Although lacking some of the production polish of some of Steele's later films, these had unusual plots, good locations and screenplays, and some were directed by Steele's father. Some of the titles included *Big Calibre, Demon for Trouble, Kid Courageous, Western Justice,* and *Alias John Law.* Steele then made sixteen more films for Supreme from 1936 to

*Bob Steele lays down the law to Jack Ingram in* Trigger Law *(Monogram, 1944).*

1938 which were released by Republic. The last film in this series was *Thunder in the Desert.* In 1938–1939 Steele starred in a series of eight westerns for Metropolitan Pictures, including *El Diablo Rides, Wild Horse Valley,* and *Pinto Canyon.* In 1940 Steele starred in six films for P.R.C. as Billy the Kid. He then went to Republic to star in 13 *3 Mesquiteer* films and after that Monogram signed him for eight films in their *Trail Blazer* series in order to instill some younger blood in the acting for the aging stars Ken Maynard and Hoot Gibson. With the decline of westerns after the war Steele went into major film and TV work. He worked on many TV series and was last seen as "Trooper Duffy" on *F-Troop.* His film credits list more than 150 westerns.

*Bob Steele has a good grip on John Merton's throat in*
The Gun Ranger *(Republic, 1937).*

*Bob Steele with Frank Ellis, Hoot Gibson and Chief Thun-
dercloud in* Outlaw Trail *(Monogram, 1944).*

### Tom Tyler (1903–1954)

Tom Tyler was born Vincent Markowski in Port Henry, New York, on August 9, 1903. His family later moved to Detroit, where he spent much of his boyhood. As a young man, he worked his way across the country and arrived in Los Angeles in 1924 where he soon found work as an extra in films because of his athletic build. He appeared in several silent films including *Let's Go, Gallagher,* released in 1924 and soon followed by *Wyoming Wildcat.* In 1927, he began making westerns for FBO and continued at that studio until 1929. He then signed a contract with Syndicate Pictures for a series of eight silent westerns in 1929–1930. In late 1930, Tyler appeared in his first serial and his first all-talking film, *Phantom of the West,* for

Mascot. His first all-talking feature film was *West of Cheyenne* for Syndicate in 1931. He made his second serial, *Battling With Buffalo Bill,* for Universal shortly thereafter. In the 1931–1932 season, he starred in a series of eight westerns for Monogram Pictures. In 1932–1933, he appeared in several feature films for Freuler Film Associates and made two more serials for Universal, *Clancy of the Mountain* and *Phantom of the Air.* From 1934 to 1936, he made 18 six-reelers for Reliable Pictures Corporation. He also played in more expensive films such as *Gone With The Wind* and *Stagecoach* in 1939 and *The Mummy's Hand* in 1940. His last two serials were *The Adventures of Captain Marvel* made in 1941, and *The Phantom* re-

*Tom Tyler, second from right, with "Black" Jack O'Shea,*
*Bob Steele, Charles King, Jimmy Dodd and Roy Barcroft*
*in* Riders of the Rio Grande *(Republic, 1943).*

*Tom Tyler, left, with Charles (Slim) Whitaker in* The Man From New Mexico *(Monogram, 1932).*

leased in 1943. He then made thirteen pictures as a member of Republic's "Three Mesquiteers." He appeared with Bob Steele in all of the pictures, the first seven included comic sidekick Rufe Davis. Davis was replaced by Jimmie Dodd in the last six. The last film in the series, *Riders of the Rio Grande* was released in May, 1943. Tyler was voted one of the Top Money-Making Western Stars in the *Motion Picture Herald* Poll of 1942. In the late 1940s, Tyler became afflicted with crippling arthritis and was gradually forced to retire from films. In 1952, he returned to Detroit to stay with his sister, Katherine, and on May 1, 1954, he died of a heart attack.

*Jimmy Wakely with Noel Neill in* Gun Runner *(Monogram, 1949).*

### Jimmy Wakely (1914–    )

Jimmy Wakely was born on February 16, 1914, on a farm in Mineola, Arkansas. He became a radio singer in Oklahoma City and signed a Decca recording contract. Wakely has authored numerous hillbilly songs including "Too Late" and "I'll Never Let You Go." He made his screen debut in 1939 in *The Saga of Death Valley*. After 1939 he made westerns for many companies including Paramount, Universal, Monogram, and Republic and in 1949 began producing westerns independently.

*Jimmy Wakely with Lee Phelps, Jane Adams, John James, Edmund Cobb and "Cannonball" Taylor in* Gun Law Justice *(Monogram, 1949).*

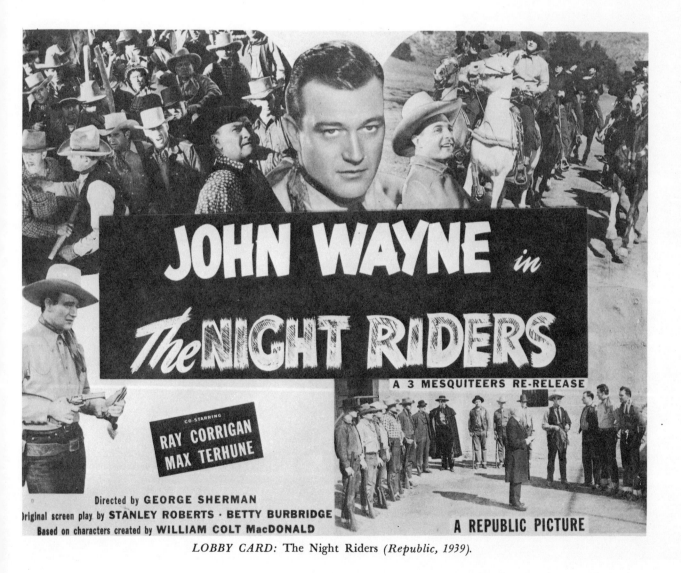

*LOBBY CARD:* The Night Riders *(Republic, 1939).*

## John Wayne (1907–   )

John Wayne was born Marion Michael Morrison on May 26, 1907, in Westerset, Iowa. In terms of longevity he knows no equal as a western star. Much of his early career in the 1930s was in "B" westerns. He was raised in Lancaster and Glendale, California, where he played football. He attended the University of Southern California and was a member of their famous "Wonder Team" as a lineman. While still in college, he met John Ford, who has played an important part in his career. Ford was using some of the U.S.C. football players as extras. In the summer of 1928, Wayne got a job with Fox Studios in the prop department. He was cast in a featured role in *The Big Trail* for Raoul

*John Wayne with Louise Brooks, Ray (Crash) Corrigan and Max Terhune in* Overland Stage Raiders *(Republic, 1938).*

*John Wayne with Sheila Terry in* Haunted Gold *(Warners, 1933).*

*John Wayne with Marsha Hunt in* Boon to the West *(Paramount, 1938).*

Walsh on the recommendation of Ford. *The Big Trail* was a tremendous success but Fox Studios miscast him in a number of leading man parts in non-westerns. Columbia Pictures then co-starred him with Buck Jones in *Range Feud*. He then appeared in a series for Warner Brothers in 1932. In 1933 he began appearing in westerns for Mascot Studios. From 1933 through 1935 he appeared in 13 pictures for Lone Star Productions and when Lone Star became the property of Republic Studios in 1935, in the famous "Three Mesquiteers" series. After his appearance in *Stagecoach* for John Ford in 1939, he began his historic career in major productions.

*And still going strong, John Wayne in his Oscar-winning performance as "Rooster Cogburn" in* True Grit *(Paramount, 1969).*

### "Whip" Wilson (1919–1964)

"Whip" Wilson was born Charles Meyers in Pecos, Texas, on June 16, 1919. He was graduated from Granite City High School in Granite City, Illinois. He became a rodeo star and was the all-around champion at the West Texas Rodeo in 1939. Wilson served in the U.S. Marines from 1942 to 1944. He made his motion picture debut in *Crashin' Thru* for Monogram and made many westerns for them. He died October 23, 1964.

*Whip Wilson.*

*Whip Wilson and Phyllis Coates in* Stage to Blue River *(Monogram, 1951).*

# 2. Sidekicks

### George (Gabby) Hayes (1885–1969)

Cantankerous and lovable would not seem to be compatible, but George (Gabby) Hayes made them seem like synonyms throughout his film career. The crotchety veteran with no teeth gummed his way through more films than most of us can remember. He was a fine actor and brightened many an otherwise dull western with his homespun philosophy and stock phrase, "yore durn tootin'." He was born in Wellsville, New York, on May 7, 1885. After graduating from high school he left home to play stock, vaudeville, and make a name for himself on the stage before entering silent pictures. Having made enough to retire he was forced to go to Hollywood to resume his career after the 1929 stock market crash. He rarely strayed from western films and played both comedy and villainous roles during the early films. He was paired with Gene Autry and John Wayne in early pictures. He became famous for his role of "Windy Halliday," Hopalong Cassidy's sidekick, in 1936 and he kept the role until 1939. He then played "Gabby" with Roy Rogers from 1939 through 1942 and again from 1944 through 1946. He also was the pal of Bill Elliott off and on during and after this period. He left the movies for television in 1950 and had his own television show spinning tales of the old west with film clips of western films. He died February 9, 1969, in Burbank, California of a heart ailment after many years of retirement. His many western roles included: *Border Devils, Riders of the Desert* (1932), *Wild Horse Mesa, Ranger's Code* (1933), *Riders of Destiny, Man from Utah, The Star Packer* (1934),

*Lawless Frontier, Tumbling Tumbleweeds* (1935), *Call of the Prairie, Hopalong Cassidy Returns, Trail Dust* (1936), *North of the Rio Grande, Hopalong Rides Again, Texas Trail* (1937), *Bar 20 Justice, Pride of the West, Sunset Trail* (1938), *Silver on the Sage, The Arizona Kid* (1939), *The Dark Command, Colorado, Young Bill Hickok* (1940), *In Old Cheyenne, Jesse James at Bay* (1941), *Sons of the Pioneers, Ridin' Down the Canyon* (1942), *Calling Wild Bill Elliott, In Old Oklahoma* (1943), *Marshal of Reno, Tall in the Saddle* (1944), *Utah, Along the Navajo Trail* (1945), *Song of Arizona, My Pal Trigger* (1946), *Helldorado, Wyoming* (1947), *Albuquerque, The Untamed Breed* (1948), *El Paso* (1949), *The Cariboo Trail* (1950).

*Gabby Hayes with Bill Elliott in* Calling Wild Bill Elliott *(Paramount, 1938).*

*George (Gabby) Hayes as "Windy Halliday" in Pride of the West (Paramount, 1938).*

*George Hayes as "Gabby," neighbor to ranch foreman, Roy Rogers, in Utah (Republic, 1945).*

### Raymond Hatton (1887–1971)

Raymond Hatton has had one of the longest film careers of any of the western players. He was originally discovered by Cecil B. DeMille and appeared in many of his early films. He was born July 7, 1887, in Bed Oak, Iowa, where his father was a prominent physician. He worked for various stock companies, carnivals, and in vaudeville. He then entered films. He played the sidekick to many of the top western stars. In 1939 he became one of the "Three Mesquiteers" in the long-running western series for Republic with John Wayne and Ray Corrigan. In 1941 he teamed with Buck Jones and Tim McCoy in "The Rough Riders" series. Hatton played "Sandy," a United States Marshal. When Jones lost his life in a tragic fire, Hatton then costarred with Johnny Mack Brown in 45 westerns for Monogram and United Artists. He also costarred with Jimmy Ellison and Russell Hayden in later western films. Mr. Hatton died October 21, 1971, of a heart attack in his Palmdale, California home, at the age of 84. His western films include: *The Girl of the Golden West* (1915), *Romance of the Redwoods* (1917), *The Thundering Herd* (1925), *The Squaw Man* (1931), *Law and Order* (1932), *Terror Trail* (1933), *Thundering Herd* (1934), *Wanderer of the Wasteland* (1935), *The Arizona Raiders* (1936), *The Texans* (1938), *New Frontier* (1939), *Oklahoma Renegades* (1940), *Gunman from Bodie* (1941), *Riders of the West* (1942), *The Ghost Rider* (1943), *Raiders of the Border* (1944), *Flame of the West* (1945), *The Haunted Mine* (1946), *The Law Comes to Gunsight* (1947), *Frontier Agent* (1948), *Colorado Ranger* (1950), *Cow Country* (1953), *Treasure of Ruby Hills* (1955), *Requiem for a Gunfighter* (1965).

*Raymond Hatton, right, with Harry Carey in* Thundering Herd *(Paramount, 1934).*

*Raymond Hatton with John Wayne in* New Frontier *(Republic, 1939).*

*Raymond Hatton, center, as "The Colonel" in* Colorado Ranger *(Lippert Pictures, Inc., 1950). With him are Russell Hayden, Stephen Carr, Jimmy Ellison and Stanley Price.*

*Andy Clyde as "California Carlson," sidekick to Hopalong Cassidy.*

### Andy Clyde (1892–1967)

Andy Clyde was born March 25, 1892, in Blairgowrie, Scotland. His parents were well-known Scottish Players. He moved to the United States in 1912, toured a vaudeville Circuit and in 1919 signed a contract with Mack Sennett. He appeared in many two-reel comedies and often played a Keystone Kop. He is probably best remembered to western fans as "California Carlson," Hopalong Cassidy's sidekick. He was featured in this role from 1940 until 1948. He later played the sidekick of Whip Wilson. He died in Hollywood May 18, 1967, at the age of 75. He was 5 feet 9 inches tall and was known as "the little comic with the big mustache." His brother, David Clyde, who died May 16, 1945, was a featured character actor in many films. His western films included: *Bad Lands* (1939), *Cherokee Strip* (1940), *In Old Colorado, Pirates on Horseback, Border Vigilantes, Twilight on the Trail* (1941), *Hoppy Serves a Writ, Border Patrol, Bar 20, Colt Comrades* (1943), *Riders of the Deadline* (1944), *Unexpected Guest, Plains-*

*Andy Clyde, left, as one of the heirs in his cousin's will, with Earl Hodgins in the suspense western,* Unexpected Guest *(United Artists, 1946).*

*man and the Lady* (1946), *Hoppy's Holiday* (1947), *Silent Conflict* (1948), *Haunted Trails* (1949), *Gunslingers* (1950), *Abilene Trail* (1951), *The Road to Denver* (1955).

### Smiley Burnette (1911–1967)

Smiley (Frog) Burnette was born Lester Alvin Burnette in Summum, Illinois, March 18, 1911. A talented musician he learned to play 52 instruments in high school where he organized his own band. He composed 350 songs, many of which were used in his films. His most popular ones were "It's My Lazy Day," "My Home Town," and "Hominy Grits." He entered films in 1934 and appeared in nearly 200 westerns. His battered hat, checkered shirt, and his white stallion with the black circle around his left eye were trademarks. He appeared as Gene Autry's sidekick in 81 films, Charles Starrett's in 64, and Roy Rogers's in seven. In recent years he was seen on television as the railroad engineer in *Petticoat Junction*. He died February 16, 1967, of leukemia in Encino, California. His western films included: *In Old Santa Fe* (1934), *Tumbling Tumbleweeds* (1935), *The Singing Cowboy* (1936), *Git Along Little Dogies* (1937), *Gold Mine in the Sky* (1938), *Mexicali Rose* (1939), *Gaucho Serenade* (1940), *Back in the Saddle* (1941), *Bells of Capistrano* (1942), *Idaho* (1943),

*Smiley Burnette, left, with Gene Autry in* The Singing Cowboy *(Republic, 1936).*

*Call of the Rockies* (1944), *Terror Trail* (1946), *West of Dodge City* (1947), *Whirlwind Raiders* (1948), *Frontier Outpost* (1949), *Texas Dynamo* (1950), *Ridin' the Outlaw Trail* (1951), *The Rough, Tough West* (1952), *Goldtown Ghost Riders* (1953).

*Smiley Burnette in the Charles Starrett film,* Ridin' the Outlaw Trail *(Columbia, 1951).*

*Biographical Section*

**Pat Brady (1914–    )**

Pat Brady was born Robert Ellsworth Patrick Aloysious Brady of show business parents, December 31, 1914, in Toledo, Ohio. Before entering films he was on the rodeo circuit, riding bareback horses and saddle broncs. He also worked in night clubs as an entertainer, playing the bass fiddle. He broke into films in 1937 with "The Sons of the Pioneers" and was in Charles Starrett films for three years. From there he joined the group on radio for two years. He was in many Roy Rogers films at Republic Studios and he was singled out from the "Sons" to work as a second comic with Gabby Hayes. Pat considers working with a real professional like Gabby as a valuable experience. He later worked as the comic with Roy Rogers both in films and television. His western films include: *West of Cheyenne* (1938), *Man from Sundown* (1939), *The Durango Kid* (1940), *Son of Texas* (1943), *The Golden Stallion, Down Dakota Way* (1949), *Twilight in the Sierras, Trigger Jr.* (1950).

*Pat Brady as "Sparrow Biffle" with Roy Rogers in a lighter
moment from* Down Dakota Way *(Republic, 1949).*

### Leo Carrillo (1880–1961)

Although he was best known as Pancho in "The Cisco Kid" series, Leo Carrillo had a long and varied career. He started as a newspaper cartoonist and then appeared in vaudeville as a monologist in 1913. He made his first Broadway appearance in 1915. He was a descendent of California's first governor and was very interested in strengthening relations with this country and Latin America. He loved parades and at every opportunity he put on his elaborate costumes and rode one of his palominos in various parades. He was also known as Hollywood's greatest host as a result of his lavish parties at his two homes. He died of cancer in Santa Monica, September 10, 1961. His western films included: *Viva Villa!* (1934), *The Gay Desperado* (1936), *The Arizona Wildcat* (1938), *Wyoming* (1940), *The Kid from Kansas* (1941), *Men of Texas* (1942), *Frontier Badman* (1943), *Moonlight and Cactus* (1944), *Under Western Skies* (1945), *The Valiant Hombre* (1948), *The Gay Amigo, The Daring Caballero, Satan's Cradle* (1949), *The Girl from San Lorenzo* (1950).

*Leo Carrillo as Pancho, friend of the Cisco Kid, always in trouble and always with a keen eye for the senoritas. The film is* The Girl from San Lorenzo *(United Artists, 1950).*

### Benny Corbett (1892–1961)

Benny Corbett was born in Ohio February 6, 1892. He moved to Hudson, Illinois, at an early age and received his schooling in that state. He had a long career in western films as a sidekick, comedian, and villain. He doubled in early films for William Duncan and Antonio Moreno and appeared with Hoot Gibson in 26 films. He also appeared with Tim McCoy in his Victory films and teamed with Jack Perrin in "Bud 'n Ben" three-reel westerns for Astor Pictures in 1934. He died May 19, 1961, at the age of 69. His western films included: *The Fearless Rider* (1928), *Forty-Five Calibre War* (1929), *Ridin' Law* (1930), *Partners* (1932), *Strawberry Roan* (1933), *Texas Tornado* (1934), *The Ivory Handled Gun* (1935), *Sunset of Power* (1936), *Texas Trail* (1937), *Gold Mine in the Sky* (1938), *Racketeers of the Range* (1939), *Straight Shooter* (1940), *Arizona Bound* (1941), *Ghost Town Law* (1942), *Marked Trails* (1944), *Enemy of the Law* (1945), *Fool's Gold* (1946), *Thundergap Outlaws* (1947).

### Cliff Edwards (1895–1971)

Cliff Edwards was born in the river town of Hannibal, Missouri. This community was also the boyhood home of one of America's most famous humorists and authors, Mark Twain. "Ukelele Ike," as he was commonly called, played Charles Starrett's sidekick, "Harmony," in many western films. His melodious voice and flair for comedy added much to these films. In the twenties and thirties he had many records that sold over a million and this eventually led to a screen career that began in 1928. He also provided the voice of "Jiminy Cricket" in *Pinocchio* in 1940 and his rendition of "When You Wish Upon a Star" has remained a classic. He died July 17, 1971. His western films included: *Bad Man of Brimstone* (1938), *Thunder over the Prairie, Prairie Stranger* (1941), *West of Tombstone, Lawless Plainsmen, Riders of the Northland, Overland to Deadwood* (1942), *Fighting Frontier, The Avenging Rider* (1943).

*Benny Corbett in an early day pose.*

*Cliff Edwards, left, with Eileen O'Hearn, Charles Starrett and Stanley Brown in* Thunder over the Prairie *(Columbia, 1941).*

### Sterling Holloway (1905–    )

Sterling Holloway has not appeared in many western films, but he did appear as Gene Autry's sidekick, "Pokey," in several films after World War II. He was born in Cedartown, Georgia, January 4, 1905. Ever since he can remember he wanted to be an actor. He left Georgia at the age of 14 for New York City. His bushy shock of carrot colored hair, crazy voice, and natural flair for comedy led to a long film career. His voice has been used in many animated features by Walt Disney and it has also been used for several children's records. He was a regular on *The Life of Riley* and *The Baileys of Balboa* television series. He is a contemporary art collector and has one of the finest collections in the country. Reminiscing over his long career he remembers being "sore in the saddle" from his few western films. He also forgot the very first line he had to say in his first "Talkie." His western films include: *Sioux City Sue* (1946), *Trail to San Antone, Twilight on the Rio Grande, Saddle Pals, Robin Hood in Texas* (1947).

*Sterling Holloway, third from right, as "Pokey" in* Twilight on the Rio Grande *(Republic, 1947). Also featured are Martin Garralaga, Gene Autry and the Cass County Boys.*

### Paul Hurst (1888–1953)

Paul Hurst played the gamut in his film career, switching from one of the most sadistic men on the screen to comedy roles. He first appeared on the stage and later toured with road companies. He moved to Hollywood in the silent era and became a writer and film director. He played many humorous parts in Monte Hale westerns. His last film was *The Sun Shines Bright*. He died in Hollywood, February 27, 1953. His western films included: *The Devil's Saddle* (1927), *California Mail* (1929), *The Big Stampede* (1932), *Robin Hood of El Dorado* (1935), *Bad Lands* (1939), *The Westerner* (1940), *Dakota* (1945), *Angel and the Badman* (1947), *The Arizona Ranger* (1948), *Law of the Golden West, Outcasts of the Trail, Prince of the Plains* (1949), *The Old Frontier, The Vanishing Westerner* (1950).

*Paul Hurst, as Doc Meadowlark, seems perplexed as he plans his next move in* Outcasts of the Trail *(Republic, 1949). Star Monte Hale looks on.*

### Fuzzy Knight (1901–    )

Fuzzy was born John Forrest Knight in Fairmount, West Virginia, on May 9, 1901. His first experience in show business was at the age of 15 when he played an end man in a minstrel show and also played the calliope in the show. He graduated from the University of West Virginia with a law degree, but his classmates urged him to continue entertaining people as he had in college. While playing with the University dance band he invented the "Vo-do-de-o" style of swing singing which led to various stage offers. After graduation he was an immediate hit with a comedy piano and singing act. He has appeared as the comedy relief in many westerns and his singing, slight stutter, and comic ability led to his being voted King of the Cowboy Comedians at one stage of his career. His favorite role was that of "Tater" in *The Trail of the Lonesome Pine*. His western films include: *Sunset Pass* (1933), *Last Round Up* (1934), *Wanderer of the Wasteland* (1935), *Song of the Trail* (1936), *Courage of the West* (1937), *The Cowboy and the Lady* (1938), *Oklahoma Frontier* (1939), *Riders of Pasco Basin, Law and Order*

*Fuzzy Knight and Christine McIntire are puzzled in this scene from* Wanted, Dead or Alive *(Monogram, 1951).*

(1940), *Law of the Range* (1941), *Arizona Cyclone, The Boss of Hangtown Mesa* (1942), *The Old Chisholm Trail* (1943), *Trigger Trail* (1944), *Frontier Gal* (1945), *Gunman's Code* (1946), *Apache Chief* (1949), *Crooked River* (1950), *Wanted: Dead or Alive* (1951), *Kansas Territory* (1952), *Topeka* (1953).

**Emmett Lynn (1897–1958)**

Emmett Lynn is probably best known for his comedy portrayals in the Red Ryder flicks where he provided the laughs with Bill Elliott, Allan (Rocky) Lane and Jim Bannon. He started his career with the Biograph Company in 1913 in *The Imp.* He appeared in legit, vaudeville, burlesque, and radio and reportedly appeared in more than 500 films. He was born February 14, 1897, in Muscatine, Iowa, and died of a heart attack in Hollywood October 20, 1958. His western films included: *Wagon Train* (1940), *Along the Rio Grande* (1941), *Stagecoach Express* (1942), *The Sundown Kid* (1943), *The Laramie Trail* (1944), *Wagon Wheels Westward* (1945), *Man from Rainbow Valley, Stagecoach to Denver* (1946), *West of Sonora* (1948), *Ride, Ryder, Ride!* (1949), *Cowboy and the Prizefighter* (1950), *Badman's Gold* (1951), *Apache War Smoke* (1952), *The Homesteaders* (1953).

*This Red Ryder film* Stagecoach to Denver, *shows Ryder's two sidekicks, Emmett Lynn, right, and Bobby Blake (Republic, 1946).*

*Chris-Pin Martin as "Gordito" in* The Return of the Cisco Kid *(20th Century-Fox, 1939). Warner Baxter starred in the title role.*

### Chris-Pin Martin (1893–1953)

Chris-Pin Martin played the sidekick to Warner Baxter, Gilbert Roland, Cesar Romero, and Duncan Renaldo in "The Cisco Kid" films. He answered to the names of "Gordito" and "Pancho." In later years he made many film appearances as a bartender. He was born Ysabel Ponciana Chris-Pin Martin Piaz in Tucson, Arizona, November 19, 1893. He started in films as an extra and remained in this capacity until his talents were finally recognized. He was then promoted to featured parts. While addressing a Moose lodge meeting he collapsed and died of a heart attack in Los Angeles, June 27, 1953. His western films included: *South of Santa Fe* (1932), *Outlaw Justice* (1933), *The Gay Desperado, The Bold Caballero* (1936), *Boots and Saddles* (1937), *The Texans* (1938), *Stagecoach, Return of the Cisco Kid* (1939), *The Cisco Kid and the Lady, Viva Cisco Kid, Lucky Cisco Kid, the Gay Caballero* (1940), *Ride on Vaquero* (1941), *Tombstone* (1942), *The Ox-Bow Incident* (1943), *San Antonio* (1945), *Robin Hood of Monterey* (1947), *Belle Starr's Daughter* (1948), *The Beautiful Blonde from Bashful Bend* (1949).

*Richard (Chito) Martin with Tim Holt in* Hot Lead *(RKO Radio, 1951).*

### Richard Martin (1917–    )

Richard Martin was born in Spokane, Washington, December 12, 1917. He received his education at California University and made his screen debut in 1941. He became well known to western fans as Tim Holt's sidekick who had a continuing urge for romance. His name in the series was "Chito Jose Gonzales Bustomino Rafferty." He starred in one film, *The Adventures of Don Coyote*, in 1947, which was produced by Buddy Rogers. He spent the rest of his film career in the Tim Holt films.

His western films include, *Nevada, West of the Pecos* (1945), *The Adventures of Don Coyote, Wild Horse Mesa* (1947), *Western Heritage, The Arizona Rangers, Gun Smugglers, Indian Agent* (1948), *Rustlers, Brothers in the Saddle, Masked Raiders, The Mysterious Desperado* (1949), *Rio Grande Patrol, Riders of the Range* (1950), *Saddle Legion* (1951), *Target* (1952), *Desert Passage* (1953).

*Frank Mitchell, center, is concerned about Tris Coffin's hand as Bill Elliott and Ruth Ford watch in* Roaring Frontiers *(Columbia, 1941).*

### Frank Mitchell (1905–    )

Frank Mitchell was born in New York City, May 13, 1905. After graduating from grammar school he entered vaudeville at the age of 14. Two years later he joined the circus as part of an acrobatic troupe that toured Europe. He also doubled as a clown. When he was 18 it was back to vaudeville. After trying a series of partners he became associated with Jack Durant. They became famous as "Mitchell and Durant," playing Broadway in *George White's Scandals* and *Earl Carroll's Vanities*. They also enjoyed great success at the Palladium in London. They parted company in 1935 and Mitchell made his first film at Warners. He was featured at every major studio and then worked for Monogram and Columbia in westerns. His favorite role was as the French Canuck lumberjack in *North of the Rockies* with Bill Elliott and Tex Ritter. Today Mitchell resides with his wife in North Hollywood and looks upon his career with fondness. His many memories contain his first experience in riding a horse in a western film. Mitchell states, "It was a beautiful white stallion. I mounted him and proudly took off in front of the whole cast. Someone with a harmonica started playing 'The Star-Spangled Banner.' The horse stood up with me hanging on for dear life yelling 'Stop the music.' The horse had been purchased from a circus and trained to do this trick." His western films include: *Rhythm of the Rio Grande, West of Carson City* (1940), *The Lone Star Vigilantes, Roaring Frontiers* (1941), *North of the Rockies, Prairie Gunsmoke, Bullets for Bandits* (1942), *Advance to the Rear* (1964).

### Milburn Morante (1887–1964)

Milburn Morante was born April 6, 1887, in San Francisco, California. After attending Nevada State University his early screen work was with Universal, Keystone-Triangle comedies. He appeared in many western films for Monogram and Republic. He died January 28, 1964 at the age of 76. His western films included: *Wizard of the Saddle* (1928), *Vanishing Riders, Wild Mustang* (1935), *Blazing Justice* (1936), *Ghost Town Gold, The Old Corral* (1937), *Gold Mine in the Sky* (1938), *Buzzy and the Phantom Pinto* (1941), *West of the Law* (1942), *The Ghost Rider* (1943), *Drifting Along* (1946), *Ridin' Down the Trail* (1947), *Range Renegade, Hidden Danger, The Fighting Ranger* (1948), *Six Gun Mesa* (1950), *Blazing Bullets* (1951).

*Milburn Morante, center, with House Peters Jr. and Johnny Mack Brown in* Over the Border *(Monogram, 1950).*

### Horace Murphy (1880–    )

Horace Murphy was born May 3, 1880, in Finley, Tennessee, where his father was a physician. He started his career as a child actor on showboats on the Mississippi River. He later played the cornet with a dramatic show complete with band and orchestra. Later he became half owner of the famous showboat, the "Cottonblossom Floating Palace." After two seasons he sold his interest in the "Cottonblossom" and organized a string of dramatic tent shows from New Orleans to Los Angeles witth an orchestra plus a baseball team with each. He sold each one of his shows and built two theatres, one in Los Angeles and one in Burbank. Somehow he found time to enter motion pictures in 1936. He appeared in appromixately 50 westerns with Tex Ritter, Bob Steele, Johnny Mack Brown, Roy Rogers, and Gene Autry. His most famous screen role was that of the talkative "Ananias" in Monogram's Tex Ritter films. He also appeared on radio for four years with Gene Autry and spent two years with Roy Rogers. Retirement is something he has finally managed to do after several previous efforts and he resides today in North Hollywood. His western films include: *Rogue of the Range, Everyman's Law* (1936),

*Horace Murphy, third from left, with Lynton Brent, Tex Ritter, Karl Hackett and Charles King in* Frontier Town *(Grand National, 1938).*

*Trouble in Texas, The Gun Ranger, Border Phantom, Western Gold, Riders of the Rockies* (1937), *Paroled—To Die, Thunder in the Desert, Frontier Town, Stranger from Arizona* (1938), *Song of the Buckaroo, Down the Wyoming Trail* (1939), *Ghost Valley Raiders* (1940), *Arizona Bound, Bad Man of Deadwood* (1941), *Song of Old Wyoming* (1945).

### Bob Nolan (1908–    )

Bob Nolan was born in New Brunswick, New Jersey, April 14, 1908. He graduated from the University of Arizona. The handsome six-footer became the leader of one of the world's most famous singing groups, "The Sons of the Pioneers." Fresh from a stint as a lifeguard he joined Roy Rogers and Tim Spencer in California. They began harmonizing and called themselves "The Rocky Mountaineers." The group folded and started again with the addition of Hugh and Karl Farr, Lloyd Perryman, and later Pat Brady. Radio made them popular and they later appeared in many western films. Bob is the composer of many songs including one of the most famous western ballads, "Tumblin' Tumbleweeds." His western films include: *The Old Homestead* (1935), *The Law of the Plains, West of Cheyenne* (1938), *West of Santa Fe, Spoilers of the Range, Man from Sundown* (1939), *Two-Fisted Rangers, The Durango Kid* (1940), *The Pinto Kid* (1941), *Sunset Serenade* (1942), *King of the Cowboys, Idaho* (1943),

*Bob Nolan, center, with Hugh Farr, Karl Farr and Charles Starrett in* The Stranger from Texas *(Columbia, 1939).*

*Song of Nevada, The Cowboy and the Senorita* (1944), *Utah, Along the Navajo Trail* (1945), *Roll on Texas Moon* (1946), *Bells of San Angelo* (1947), *Under California Skies* (1948).

### Al St. John (1893–1963)

"Fuzzy" St. John was born in Santa Ana, California, and spent his early years in vaudeville and as a circus acrobat. He entered motion pictures in his middle teens appearing in many series of short comedies. He teamed with his uncle, Roscoe (Fatty) Arbuckle, and Buster Keaton in these shorts. He is probably best remembered in this era as a member of the famous Keystone Kops. After he started appearing in westerns he always played the sidekick of the star and created the role of "Fuzzy Q. Jones." He used this characterization alongside almost all of the top western stars of the period. He died of a heart attack in Vidalia, Georgia, on January 21, 1963, while on a personal appearance tour. His western films included: *Riders of the Desert* (1932), *Riders of Destiny* (1934), *Bar 20 Rides Again* (1935), *Hopalong Cassidy Returns* (1936), *Outcasts of Poker Flat* (1937), *Song and Bullets* (1938), *Trigger Pals* (1939), *Texas Terrors* (1940), *Billy the Kid Wanted* (1941), *Arizona Terrors* (1942), *The Mysterious Rider* (1943), *Frontier Outlaws* (1944), *Border Badmen* (1945), *Overland Riders* (1946), *Law of the Lash* (1947), *Son of Billy the Kid* (1949).

*Bewhiskered Al (Fuzzy) St. John is his usual confused self as he is taken by surprise by Bob Kortman in* Border Badmen *PRC, 1945).*

### Max Terhune (1891–     )

Of all the actors that grace the western screen Max Terhune is certainly the most versatile. This master showman has entertained hundreds of thousands of people with his feats of magic, card manipulation, ventriloquism, impersonations, whistling and acting. Ironically he was born in a log cabin on Lincoln's birthday in 1891 near Franklin, Indiana. His show business career started when he won a whistling championship in an old fiddler's contest in Shelbyville, Indiana. The barnyard imitations that he learned as a child plus his many other talents soon attracted national attention and his big break came on *National Barn Dance* during the heyday of radio. This led to his first motion picture in 1936 with Gene Autry in Republic's *Ride Ranger Ride*. Western fans will remember him best as "Lullaby" Joslin and "Alibi" Terhune in Republic's "Three Mesquiteers" productions. With his famous dummy, Elmer, he became the third Mesquiteer and the comedy part of the trio. Max is equally proud of his son, Bob, who is a popular stuntman, riding and doubling for many of the top actors in both films and TV. Looking back on his career Max states, "I loved every minute of it and have many wonderful memories. I have had the opportunity of working with some of the most talented people on earth." Max's own hearty personality has made him one of the beloved members of the acting profession and his talents have earned him a spot in the western Hall of Fame. His western films include: *Ride Ranger Ride, The Three Mes-*

*Max Terhune as "Alibi" with Elmer in scene from* Texas to Bataan *(Monogram, 1942).*

quiteers (1936), *Ghost Town Gold, Roarin Lead, Riders of the Whistling Skull, Range Defenders, Gunsmoke Ranch, The Trigger Trio* (1937), *Wild Horse Rodeo, Call the Mesquiteers, The Purple Vigilantes, Riders of the Black Hills, Santa Fe Stampede, Pals of the Saddle, Overland Stage Raiders* (1938), *The Night Riders, Three Texas Steers* (1939), *The Range Busters, West of Pinto Basin* (1940), *Trail of the Silver Spurs, Wrangler's Roost, Fugitive Valley* (1941), *Texas to Bataan, Boot Hill Bandits* (1942), *Cowboy Commandos, Two-Fisted Justice* (1943), *Sheriff of Sundown* (1944), *Along the Oregon Trail* (1947).

### Ray Whitley ( — )

Ray Whitley was born in Atlanta, Georgia. He was a structural steel worker prior to his musical career. His excellent voice and ability to strum a guitar landed him a job on radio. He and his Six Bar Cowboys made many musical short subjects for RKO from 1937 through 1940. They also appeared in many rodeos in Madison Square Garden. Ray appeared in many RKO features as a star or co-star and also collaborated on many western ballads. His western films include: *Hopalong Cassidy Returns* (1936), *Gun Law* (1938), *Racketeers of the Range* (1939), *Wagon Train* (1940), *Cyclone on Horseback, Along the Rio Grande, The Bandit Trail* (1941), *Six-Gun Gold* (1942), *Boss of Boomtown, Riders of the Santa Fe* (1944), *West of the Alamo* (1946).

*Ray Whitley.*

### Guy Wilkerson (1901–1971)

Born near Katy, Texas, he started his career with Chase Lister Tent Show in 1914 touring the Mid-West. He later switched to minstrel shows, became a juvenile dancer and switched to burlesque and stage plays. He broke into films in 1928 and has many western films to his credit. He created the role of "Panhandle Perkins" in the Texas Rangers films and supplied the comic relief for Dave O'Brien–Jim Newill and then Dave O'Brien–Tex Ritter. One of his better known parts was the role of "Tennessee" in *Sergeant York* (1941). He died July 15, 1971, at the age of 70. His western films included: *Paradise Express* (1937), *Rangers Take Over* (1942), *Bad Men of Thunder Gap, Trail of Terror* (1943), *Boss of the Rawhide, Gunsmoke Mesa, Pinto Bandit* (1944), *Three in the Saddle, Flaming Bullets* (1945), *Great Missouri Raid* (1950), *Shoot Out at Medicine Bend* (1957), *Man of the West* (1958).

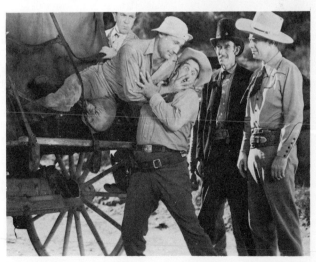

*Guy Wilkerson, second from the right, watches Dave O'Brien give Charles King his usual hard knocks in* Boss of the Rawhide *(PRC, 1944), Billy Bletcher and Jim Newill are the other onlookers.*

*Lloyd (Slim) Andrews: Andrews, center, with Forrest Taylor, Tex Ritter and Fred Burns in* Ridin' the Cherokee Trail *(Monogram, 1941). His western films include:* Pals of the Silver Sage, The Golden Trail, Rainbow over the Range *(1940),* Rolling Home to Texas, Ridin' the Cherokee Trail, Dynamite Canyon, The Driftin' Kid *(1941),* Cowboy Serenade, The Cyclone Kid, The Sombrero Kid *(1942).*

*Don Barclay: Barclay, left, with Bob Baker in* Outlaw Express *(Universal, 1938). His western films include:* Treachery Rides the Range *(1936),* Border Phantom *(1937),* Thunder in the Desert, Outlaw Express *(1938),* Badlands of Dakota *(1941).*

*Bobby Blake: Blake as "Little Beaver" in* Sheriff of Las Vegas *(Republic, 1944). Wild Bill Eliott starred as "Red Ryder". Blake's western films include:* Tucson Raiders, Sheriff of Las Vegas, Marshal of Reno, The San Antonio Kid, Vigilantes of Dodge City, Cheyenne Wildcat *(1944),* Dakota, Phantom of the Plains, Marshal of Laredo, Lone Texas Ranger, Colorado Pioneers *(1945),* In Old Sacramento, Home on the Range, Sun Valley Cyclone, California Gold Rush, Santa Fe Uprising *(1946),* Stagecoach to Denver, Vigilantes of Boomtown, Rustlers of Devil's Canyon *(1947),* Apache War Smoke *(1952),* Three Violent People *(1956),* Tell Them Willie Boy is Here *(1970).*

*Pat Buttram: Buttram with Gene Autry in* Indian Territory *(Columbia, 1950). His western films include:* The Strawberry Roan *(1948),* Riders in the Sky *(1949),* Indian Territory, Mule Train, The Blazing Sun, Beyond the Purple Hills *(1950),* Hills of Utah *(1951),* Night Stage to Galveston, The Old West, Apache Country, Wagon Team *(1952).*

*Jimmy Dodd (1913–1964). His western films included:* Law and Order *(1940),* Shadows on the Sage, Riders of the Rio Grande *(1943),* Moon over Las Vegas, Twilight on the Prairie *(1944).*

*Gordon Jones (1911–1963) with Roy Rogers in* North of the Great Divide *(Republic, 1950). His western films included:* Black Eagle *(1948),* Trigger Jr., Sunset in the West, North of the Great Divide, Trail of Robin Hood *(1950),* Spoilers of the Plains *(1951),* Wagon Team *(1952),* Smoke Signals *(1955).*

*Ralph Peters (1903–1959): Peters, right, as "Scrubby" with Kermit Maynard in* Rough Ridin' Rhythm *(Ambassador-Conn, 1937). His western films included:* Rough Ridin' Rhythm *(1937)*, Outlaws of Sonora *(1938)*, Six-Gun Rhythm, Rovin' Tumbleweeds *(1939)*, Ghost Valley Raiders *(1940)*, Outlaws of the Rio Grande, Across the Sierras *(1941)*, Twilight on the Prairie *(1944)*, Trail to San Antone *(1947)*, Beyond the Purple Hills *(1950)*, Slaughter Trail *(1951)*, Destry *(1954)*.

*Dub "Cannonball" Taylor: Taylor, left, with Claire Whitney and Buddy Swann in* Roaring Westward *(Monogram, 1949). His western films include:* Taming of the West *(1939)*, Pioneers of the Frontier, Prairie Schooners *(1940)*, Across the Sierras, North of the Lone Star, The Son of Davy Crockett *(1941)*, Silver City Raiders, Saddles and Sagebrush *(1943)* Wyoming Hurricane, Saddle Leather Law *(1944)*, Rustlers of the Badlands *(1945)*, Range Renegades *(1948)*, The Bounty Hunter *(1954)*, The Hallelujah Trail *(1965)*, Bandolero! *(1968)*, The Undefeated *(1969)*, A Man Called Horse *(1970)*, Support Your Local Gunfighter *(1971)*.

*Wally Vernon (1905-1970): Vernon, right, with Allan (Rocky) Lane in* Stagecoach to Monterey *(Republic, 1944). His western films include:* Fugitive from Sonora, The Black Hills Express *(1943)*, Outlaws of Santa Fe, Silver City Kid, Stagecoach to Monterey *(1944)*.

*Frank Yaconelli (1898–1965): Yaconelli, right, with Jack Randall in* Wild Horse Canyon *(Monogram, 1939). His western films included:* Strawberry Roan *(1933)*, Western Frontier *(1935)*, Blazing Justice, Romance Rides the Range *(1936)*, Wild Horse Canyon *(1939)*, Pioneer Days, Wild Horse Range *(1940)*, Riding the Sunset Trail *(1942)*, South of Monterey *(1946)*, Riding the California Trail *(1947)*.

*Eddy Waller: Waller, seated, as "Nugget Clark" with Allan (Rocky) Lane in* Powder River Rustlers *(Republic, 1949). His western films include:* Jesse James *(1939)*, Stagecoach War *(1940)*, The Bandit Trail *(1941)*, The Lone Star Ranger *(1942)*, Dakota *(1945)*, Abilene Town *(1946)*, Bandits of Dark Canyon *(1947)*, Oklahoma Badlands *(1948)*, Powder River Rustlers *(1949)*, Vigilante Hideout *(1950)*, Indian Uprising *(1951)*, Montana Territory *(1952)*, El Paso Stampede *(1953)*, Man Without a Star *(1955)*.

# 3. Heavies

## Featured Players

### Roy Barcroft (1902–1969)

Roy Barcroft was crowned "King of the Heavies" and for good reason; he performed in this capacity in over 200 westerns. He was born Howard H. Ravenscroft September 7, 1902, in Crab Orchard, Nebraska. His family were farmers in the area. He worked at a variety of jobs and spent two hitches in the U.S. Army and was a musician before settling for an acting career. Over the years he appeared in many serials and in all of the major television westerns, prior to his death. In the following account, Barcroft wrote about acting, his career, and westerns in general:

I had no desire to become an actor in my youth. The only actors I had seen were in carnivals and circuses and I did not wish to follow in their footsteps. I saw only a few movies and I'm sure my acting experience came from real life experiences. My father died when I was 13 and at 15 I joined the Army in Lincoln, Nebraska. I served in France with the A.E.F., was wounded, returned to the states and was discharged when I was 16. I then spent about four years wandering, working for short periods at any and all types of jobs . . . dishwashing, cook, ranch hand, oil well "roughneck" and gandy-dancer (laborer who works on railroad tracks). I was also a truck driver, driving a moving van (I was the guy who when the boss set a trunk on the tailgate and said "Take this up to the third floor"—I took it). I was a sailor-fireman on a coal burning tramp freighter in Constantinople. It was back in the Army for me in 1923 for a three-year hitch in Hawaii where I spent three of the healthiest years of my life . . . no other choice, no money or time to indulge in the finer things in life. It was swimming, hiking, calesthenics and regular meals. I did find time to read and learn to play a musical instrument, not the ukelele, but the clarinet and saxophone and I played professionally after leaving the Islands in 1926. I played with various bands around Chicago until the Stock Market Crash in 1929 when the curtain came down with a bang. Overnight I left for Cali-fornia, driving a Model A roadster, wife and child and saxophone. We established a residence in Culver City about four blocks from M-G-M, two blocks from Pathe and six blocks from the Hal Roach Studios. I became curious as to what went on behind those high walls. Then came my chance. I joined the American Legion in Culver City and they often furnished well drilled ex-soldiers for scenes in various epics. My chance came in 1931 with *Mata Hari* starring Greta Garbo . . . a soldier at five dollars a day. At last I was inside the forbidden land, but I wasn't interested. Six years later I was an actor in motion pictures. What happened in those intervening years? Nothing much. No music, some selling, radios and cars. Now comes a beautiful era in U.S. History, the Depression. I finally landed a job working in a tunnel for the Metropolitan Water District, bringing water to Los Angeles. I was there two years until the depression finally smoothed out a bit. I went back to the city and started selling again. In order to improve my sales I had to take a course in public speaking. A friend suggested dramatics. I felt very foolish at 35 rehearsing a lot of foolish things on an empty stage. I continued to do one "little theatre" stage play after another until an agent came back stage and said he'd like to represent me in motion pictures. My first picture was a serial at Republic, *S.O.S. Coast Guard*, starring Ralph Byrd in July of 1937 at $66.00 per week. Looking back over my career I would have to say I really do enjoy my work and have enjoyed most of my roles. Of course some days you feel like you've really earned your money. I can look back to some pretty miserable days when it was cold, windy, dirty and dusty and we "chased" all day long. We would wear out 3 or 4 horses. That night it was epsom salt baths, liniment and a half-dozen "belts" (and I don't drink). I think I like the roles best where I could be the dirtiest, meanest, unkempt individual possible. I have a picture in mind called *Night Train to Memphis*. Then again there were a couple of serials where the costumes were quite elaborate, such as *Man Hunt of Mystery Island* and *The Purple Monster Strikes*. I enjoyed doing those very much. There was always

*Roy Barcroft as he appeared in the 1960s.*

a lot of horseplay and tricks going on with a movie crew. One didn't dare lie down on a hot rock for a short nap for fear of getting a "hot foot" or having his spurs wired together or having a nice warm snake released across your chest. I will never forget my first chase. It was a Universal serial. I had thought I was a good horseman. In this particular chase there were about 15 head of horses involved and some of the best old time western actors in the business . . . men like Charlie King, Bob Steele, Kenne Duncan, Karl Hackett, Ethan Laidlaw, and Yakima Canutt. We were on a high hill for the start of the chase. It's funny how the movie horses will just "dog" it on the way back to a starting point and then they come to life like a race horse. The shot was fired, the signal to go. I was in the middle of the pack, down the steep side, across an open grassy prairie, some cactus, prairie dog holes, a couple of ditches, boulders at the edge of the river and into the river. I won't try to tell you what my thoughts were but there was one thing certain, if I wanted to stay alive and in western pictures, I was going to have to learn to really ride, not like a farm kid from Nebraska. I did! I sneaked away many times to practice falls on the sandy beds of a dry creek. It wasn't too long until I was accepted by the old-timers. They were a great bunch of guys. I took in stride their little pranks such as loosening your saddle cinch just before you run out of a saloon for a fast mount and get-away . . . or riding up along side of me in a wide open chase and taking off my horse's bridle and handing it to me. I have always been very happy to be in a business that has the interest of so many others. No matter where I go someone will know me, say "hello" and I will have a friend. They seem to be ready to overlook all the mean, contemptible things I do as the villain who stalks Roy Rogers or Jim Arness. But now that I'm up in years, no more villains, just a crochety gray haired, gray bearded old man and no more fights. I like it like it is now.

Barcroft died of cancer on November 28, 1969, at the Motion Picture Country House. One of his last

*Roy Barcroft as the killer, Jim Judd, battling Monte Hale in* Outcasts of the Trail *(Republic, 1949).*

*Roy Barcroft as "Piute," in a losing battle with Allan (Rocky) Lane in* Captive of Billy the Kid, *a story about hidden gold (Republic, 1952).*

appearances in films was a role as the horserace judge in *The Reivers.* His western films included: *Heroes of the Hills, Stranger from Arizona, The Frontiersman* (1938), *Silver on the Sage, Mexicali Rose, Renegade Trail* (1939), *Rancho Grande, Hidden Gold, Bad Man from Red Butte, Yukon Flight, Stage to Chino, Ragtime Cowboy Joe, Trailing Double Trouble* (1940), *Pals of the Pecos, The Bandit Trail, Jesse James at Bay, The Masked Rider, West of Cimmaron* (1941), *Sunset on the Desert, Romance on the Range, Sunset Serenade, West of the Law, Land of the Open Range* (1942), *The Old Chisholm Trail, Hoppy Serves a Writ, Cheyenne Roundup, Calling Wild Bill Elliott, The Stranger from Pecos, Bordertown Gun Fighters, Wagon Tracks West* (1943), *The Laramie Trail, Hidden Valley Outlaws, Code of the Prairie, Stagecoach to Monterey, Cheyenne Wildcat* (1944), *Bells of Rosarito, Sunset in Eldorado, Dakota, Along the Navajo Trail, Lone Texas Ranger, Marshal of Laredo, The Topeka Terror, Wagon Wheels Westward* (1945), *Home on the Range, Alias Billy the Kid, My Pal Trigger, Night Train to Memphis, Stagecoach to Denver* (1946), *Oregon Trail Scouts, Stagecoach to Reno, Vigilantes of Boomtown, Rustlers of Devil's Canyon, Wyoming, Along the Oregon Trail, Last Frontier Uprising* (1947), *The Bold Frontiersman, Oklahoma Badlands, Eyes of Texas, Grand Canyon Trail, Renegades of Sonora, Desperadoes of Dodge City, Sundown at Santa Fe* (1948), *Sheriff of Wichita, Frontier Investigator, Prince of the Plains, Down Dakota Way, San Antone Ambush* (1949), *Vigilante Hideout, The Vanishing West-*

*Roy Barcroft, right, with Don Costello, corner, and Bill Elliott in* Marshal of Laredo *(Republic, 1945).*

*erner, Surrender, Salt Lake Raiders* (1950), *Night Riders of Montana, Wells Fargo Gunmaster, The Dakota Kid* (1951), *Leadville Gunslinger, Oklahoma Annie, Wild Horse Ambush, Thundering Caravans, Ride the Man Down* (1952), *Marshal of Cedar Creek, Down Laredo Way, Bandits of the West, El Paso Stampede* (1953), *The Desperado,* *Two Guns and a Badge* (1954), *Man Without a Star, The Spoilers* (1955), *Gun Brothers* (1956), *Last Stagecoach West* (1957), *Escort West* (1959), *Six Black Horses* (1962), *Texas Across the River* (1966), *The Way West* (1967), *Bandolero!* (1968).

### Edmund Cobb (1892–    )

Edmund Fessenden Cobb made his first movie in 1911 and has long since quit counting the number of films in which he has appeared. He starred in many westerns in the 1920s and appeared in the first silent serial ever made. He co-starred with Neva Gerber in Arrow's *Days of '49* in 1924. He also played in the first sound serial, his first of many. He was born in Albuquerque, New Mexico, June 23, 1892, and was the grandson of a former governor of the Territory of New Mexico. He played some stock and vaudeville before entering films. During the sound era he became one of the

*Ed Cobb, center, and Dick Curtis, left, rustlers, with two of their gang, Buel Bryant and George Chesebro, are held at bay by Charles Starrett in* The Stranger from Texas *(Columbia, 1939).*

*Ed Cobb struggles with Bill Elliott in* Pioneers of the Frontier *(Columbia, 1940).*

*Ed Cobb is disarmed by Allan (Rocky) Lane in* Stagecoach to Denver *(Republic, 1947).*

lead "heavies" for more than 25 years. He occasionally played a sheriff or character part, but was more comfortable worrying the hero. His western films include: *Riders of the Range* (1923), *Fangs of Destiny* (1927), *Four-Footed Ranger* (1928), *Rider of Death Valley* (1932), *Deadwood Pass* (1933), *Tracy Rides* (1934), *Gunners and Guns* (1935), *Springtime in the Rockies* (1937), *Wild Horse Rodeo* (1938), *Spoilers of the Range* (1939), *Blazing Six Shooters* (1940), *North from the Lone Star* (1941), *Down Rio Grande Way* (1942), *The Stranger from Pecos* (1943), *Outlaws of Santa Fe* (1944), *Law of the Valley* (1945), *Days of Buffalo Bill* (1946), *Oregon Trail Scouts* (1947), *Carson City Raiders* (1948), *The Daring Caballero* (1949), *The Vanishing Westerner* (1950), *Blazing Bullets* (1951), *Broken Lance* (1954), *Hidden Guns* (1956).

## Dick Curtis (1903–1952)

There was never any doubt in the mind of the western fan that Dick Curtis was the "heavy" in the true sense of the word. From the moment he appeared on the screen it was apparent that he was up to no good. As a result of his screen image he was known as "The Meanest Man in Hollywood." Although a member of the Charles Starrett Stock Company, the 6 foot 3 inch Curtis was also the nemesis of many other top western stars during his film career. Born Richard D. Dye in Newport, Kentucky, May 13, 1903, he made his debut in movies in 1918 as an extra in *The Unpardonable Sin*. He left films for the stage, and after building a reputation there he came back to appear in *King Kong*. He was seriously injured during the shooting of the film and was forced to retire for two years. Resuming his career, he made his presence known in fight after fight in countless westerns. He died in Hollywood on January 2, 1953, at the age of 49. His western roles incuded: *Northern Frontier, Code of the Mounted* (1935), *Ghost Patrol* (1936), *Bar Z Bad Men, Two-Gun Law* (1937), *Outlaws of the Prairie, Cattle Raiders, West of Cheyenne, Colorado Trail* (1938), *West of Santa Fe, Spoilers of the Range, Riders of Black River, Stranger from Texas* (1939), *Blazing Six Shooters, Two-Fisted Rangers, Pioneers of the Frontier, Ragtime Cowboy Joe* (1940), *The Roundup, Billy the Kid* (1941), *Arizona Cyclone* (1942), *Pardon My Gun* (1943), *Abilene Town, Santa Fe Uprising* (1946), *Wyoming* (1947), *The Vanishing Westerner* (1950), *Rawhide* (1951).

Dick Curtis, left, as the leader of a band of rustlers is manhandled by U.S. Marshal Charles Starrett in The Stranger from Texas (Columbia, 1940).

Dick Curtis, center, seeks counsel from Kenneth MacDonald as he is again in the grip of Charles Starrett. The film is Two-Fisted Ranger (Columbia, 1940).

*Wild Bill Elliott saves Linda Winters from a fate worse than death in the guise of Dick Curtis in* Pioneers of the Frontier *(Columbia, 1940).*

### Myron Healey (1923–    )

Myron Daniel Healey was born June 8, 1923, in Petaluma, California. His father was a noted proctologist and his godfather was Luther Burbank, world-famed horticulturist. Myron performed as a child singer on radio programs in the 1930s. He also gave concert recitals (violin and piano) during the same period. In 1941 he studied under famed actress Maria Ouspenskaya and in August of 1942 he signed a Metro-Goldwyn-Mayer contract. He served in the Air Force as a navigator and bombardier from 1943 to 1945, and resumed his career in 1946. He has appeared in over 500 television shows in addition to his film career. He also authored two screenplays, *Colorado Ambush* in 1950 and *Lone Star Lawman* in 1951. He is acknowledged as a top-notch western "heavy," usually dying an outlaw's death in the dusty street of a western town. Many of his western characterizations have a suggestion of mental disturbance. His favorite roles are "Andy" in *The Longhorn,* in 1952; the sheriff in *Son of Belle Starr,* in 1953; and "Doc Holiday" in the "Wyatt Earp" TV series in 1957. Today he resides in Simi, California, and is particularly proud of his daughter,

*Myron Healey, the ruthless menace of* Fargo, *starring Bill Elliott (Monogram, 1952).*

Ann, who has won several Oklahoma queen and beauty contests. Of his film career he states: "It has been most rewarding, not by measure of success, but by association with many wonderful co-workers." His western films include: *Gun-Law Justice, Laramie, Across the Rio Grande, Brand of Fear, Range Justice, Haunted Trails* (1949), *I Killed Geronimo, Over the Border, Law of the Panhandle, Outlaw Gold, West of Wyoming* (1950), *Colorado Ambush, Night Riders of Montana, Montana Desperado, Bonanza Town* (1951), *Montana Territory, Apache War Smoke, Fargo, Fort Osage* (1952), *Saginaw Trail* (1953), *Cattle Queen of Montana* (1954), *The White Squaw* (1956), *Shoot-Out at Medicine Bend* (1957), *Apache Territory* (1958), *The Gunfight at Dodge City* (1959), *Journey to Shiloh* (1968), *True Grit* (1969).

*Myron Healey is ready for Johnny Mack Brown in* Over the Border *(Monogram, 1950).*

### Jack Ingram (1902–1969)

Jack Ingram was one of the better "heavies" of the western film, and also was the villain in nearly all of Columbia's serials. He was born in Chicago, November 15, 1902, of Irish parents. He learned to ride and acquired his love for animals on his boyhood vacations at his uncle's farm in Wisconsin. He joined the Army at the age of 15 and was wounded, spending two years in a hospital in France. Although he studied law at the University of Texas, he found that he had the ability to entertain and became a member of a successful traveling minstrel show and later toured the country with the Mae West stage shows. In 1929 he was signed by Paramount and because of his knowledge of horses and his ability to perform difficult stunts and fights, he played the villain. In 1944 he and his wife purchased the Charlie Chaplin 200-acre ranch in the Santa Monica mountains above woodland Hills, California. They turned the area into a motion picture location ranch that eventually consisted of 75 buildings and three different towns. During the next 14 years many westerns and TV films were shot there with Jack simply being able to walk out his front door to be on the set. Many of the "Cisco Kid" and "Lone Ranger" TV films were made there and Jack Ingram's home was the home of Roy Rogers and Dale Evans in all of

*Jack Ingram, center, is a skeptical listener as Bob Steele gives him the word as George Eldredge looks on in* Trigger Law *(Monogram, 1944).*

their TV films. In the late 50s Jack's health began to fail and he sold the ranch and purchased a 55-foot yacht and sailed it up and down the coast. He became restless and rented the boat for sea pictures including TV's *Sea Hunt* starring Lloyd Bridges. Before the cameras Jack Ingram was killed more times than anyone can remember. Off screen he was a congenial man, always ready to laugh and felt it was his duty to set a good example for children. He died February 20, 1969, from a second heart attack at the age of 66. His western films

*Jack Ingram in one of his menacing roles.*

included: *The Lonely Trail* (1936), *Outlaws of Sonora, Riders of the Black Hills, Frontier Scout* (1938), *The Night Riders, Blue Montana Skies, Down the Wyoming Trail, Colorado Sunset* (1939), *Under Texas Skies, Young Bill Hickok* (1940), *Prairie Schooners, Sheriff of Tombstone* (1941), *Men from Cheyenne, Billy the Kid Trapped* (1942), *Lone Star Trail, Silver Raiders* (1943), *Trail of Terror, Arizona Trail, The Pinto Bandit* (1944), *Frontier Gal* (1945), *West of the Alamo* (1946), *Pioneer Justice, Shootin' Irons* (1947), *The Strawberry Roan* (1948), *Law of the West* (1949), *Short Grass* (1950), *Fort Dodge Stampede* (1951), *The Battle of Apache Pass* (1952), *Cow Country* (1953), *Five Guns West* (1955).

### Charles King (1895–1957)

If you grew up in the 1930s or 1940s and attended the Saturday matinees you had an opportunity to see a rather paunchy fellow with a dark moustache get mistreated by nearly every western hero. Of course, he deserved everything he got and more and you were very happy the way things turned out. If you were like most kids you only knew his screen name, "Blackie," "Smokey," or whatever he went by at the moment. Unless you developed an interest in these films as an adult his name was lost forever, but to the true western fan he was none other than Charles King. He was born February 21, 1895, in Hillsboro, Texas. His father was a physician and Charlie was going to follow in his footsteps, but he chose acting instead. He entered films at an early age and was an extra in *Birth of a Nation*. He appeared in many two-reel comedies for Universal called "Mike and Ike," in 1927–1928 and had a definite flair for comedy. He became a film villain in westerns and continued in this role throughout his career. If he ever won a

*Charles King, left, gets his orders from Cy Kendall, center, and is about to draw on George Eldredge in* Outlaw Trail, *(Monogram, 1944).*

*Charles King, second from right, with Dick Cramer, Lynton Brent and Max Terhune in* Trail Riders *(Monogram, 1942). Max's dummy, 'Elmer', is sitting on the bar.*

screen fight, it would be difficult to remember when and he rarely made it to the final reel unless he happened to be the "Big Boss" and then he only lasted a little longer. He was married and had three sons. His hobby was his very complete early day firearm collection. After PRC closed he experienced rather difficult times. In his last years he appeared as an extra on the *Gunsmoke* TV series. His last role was as a corpse in a segment of this series. He died a few minutes after the filming on May 7, 1957, at the age of 62. His western films included: *Honor of the Mounted* (1932), *Son of the Border* (1933), *Mystery Ranch* (1934), *Tumbling Tumbleweeds* (1935), *Sunset of Power, Sundown Saunders* (1936), *A Lawman Is Born, Black Aces* (1937), *Thunder in the Desert* (1938), *Down the Wyoming Trail* (1939), *West of Carson City* (1940), *The Lone Rider in Ghost Town* (1941), *Trail Riders* (1942), *The Ghost Rider* (1943), *Outlaw Trail* (1944), *Marked for Murder* (1945), *Thunder Town* (1946), *Ridin' Down the Trail* (1947), *Olkahoma Blue* (1948).

*Charles King is convinced "hands up" is a good idea as Dave O'Brien holds a gun on him in* Marked for Murder, *(PRC, 1945).*

## Bud Osborne (1884–1964)

Lennie B. (Bud) Osborne was born in Oklahoma Territory, July 20, 1884. After graduating from public schools he became a rancher in Indian Territory. He joined 101 Ranch Wild West Shows and became assistant Arena Director. He then joined Buffalo Bill's Wild West Show, where he remained for over a year. He started his film career with the Thomas Ince company in 1915 and appeared in the first five-reel western starring J. Warren Kerrigan. In most of his films he played the part of a villain, but in his last years was often found playing the sheriff. His greatest talent was the efficiency he displayed in being able to manipulate stagecoaches, buckboards, or any type of wagon, regardless of the number of horses, the

*Bud Osborne, left, and Lee Powell, right, seem to have Bill Elliott at their mercy in* The Return of Daniel Boone, *(Columbia, 1941).*

situation or the countryside. He performed this chore in countless westerns and television shows and did so well into his 70s. He died in Hollywood February 2, 1964. His western films included: *Loser's End* (1925), *Don Desperado* (1927), *The Bronc Stomper* (1928), *On the Divide* (1929), *Mark of the Spur* (1932), *Deadwood Pass* (1933), *Riding Thru* (1934), *Outlaw Deputy* (1935), *Headin' for Rio Grande* (1936), *Western Gold* (1937), *Prairie Moon* (1938), *New Frontier* (1939), *Lone Star Raiders* (1940), *The Return of Daniel Boone* (1941), *Riders of the West* (1942), *The Ghost Rider* (1943), *Range Law* (1944), *Navajo Kid* (1945), *Border Bandits* (1946), *Thundergap Outlaws* (1947), *Gunning for Justice* (1948), *Gun Runner* (1949), *Arizona Territory* (1950), *Nevada Badmen* (1951), *Texas City* (1952), *The Lawless Rider* (1954).

*Bud Osborne at his best in* Trigger Trail *(Universal, 1944).*

### Glenn Strange (1899–      )

Glenn Strange is familiar to most people today as Sam, the bartender in the *Gunsmoke* television series. He has a long career in western films, usually cast as one of the badmen. He was born of Cherokee Indian and Irish parents on August 16, 1899, in Weed, New Mexico. His father was a rancher and prior to films Glenn worked as a cowboy, deputy sheriff, fireman, rodeo performer, and a member of the Arizona Wranglers radio group. In addition to his heavy roles, he also played the sidekick in Dick Foran westerns as well as many sheriff and other assorted parts. He also has portrayed the "Frankenstein Monster" in movies. In looking back over his career he likes to recall the kindness of such stars as his good friend Hoot Gibson who helped him over the rough spots in his first film and Buck Jones insisting he stay in bed on the second day of shooting when Glenn awoke with the flu. Jones put on Glenn's wardrobe and did his rough riding for him. Glenn states, "The stars were not the 'Prima Donna's' some people would have you believe they were." His western films include: *New Frontier* (1935), *Arizona Days* (1937), *Black Bandit, Gun Packer* (1938), *Range War, The Llano Kid* (1939), *Pioneer Days, Stage to Chino* (1940), *Badlands of Dakota* (1941), *Arizona Cyclone* (1942), *Wild Horse Stampede* (1943), *Arizona Trail* (1944), *Frontier Fighters* (1947), *Silver Trails* (1948), *Roll Thunder Roll!* (1949), *The Lawless Breed* (1952), *The Great Sioux Uprising* (1953), *The Vanishing American* (1955).

*Glen Strange as the trigger-happy deputy with Bob Baker in* Honor of the West *(Universal, 1938).*

*Biographical Section*

### Ted Adams (    –    )

Ted Adams's parents were stage performers around the turn of the century. He was born in the dressing room of a theatre and until his retirement spent his entire life on the stage or screen. He was one of the better featured "heavies" in western films and an excellent horseman. For many years he averaged twenty films a year, often appearing in two pictures at the same time. His western films include: *Beyond the Rockies* (1932), *War of the Range* (1933), *Hop-A-Long Cassidy* (1935), *Trail Dust* (1936), *Rustler's Valley* (1937), *Pals of the Saddle* (1938), *Three Texas Steers* (1939), *Gun Code* (1940), *Thunder over the Prairie* (1941), *King of the Stallions* (1942), *The Sundown Kid* (1943), *Red River Renegades* (1946), *Stagecoach to Denver* (1947), *Crossed Trails* (1948), *Gun Runner* (1949), *I Killed Geronimo* (1950), *Night Riders of Montana* (1951).

*Ted Adams, center, as a horse thief named "Barlow", is restrained by rancher Gordon Demaine in* King of the Stallions *(Monogram, 1942). The intended victim on the right is Chief Yowlachie.*

*Richard Alexander, right, prepares to draw his gun on Tom Keene in* Drift Fence *(Paramount, 1936). Keen's dancing partner is Katherine DeMille.*

### Richard Alexander (1902–    )

Richard Alexander certainly was big enough to play a bully and did so in many films of the 1930s and 1940s. He was born November 19, 1902, in Dallas. His film career includes many westerns and he also appeared in many serials including the "Flash Gordon" ones starring Larry (Buster) Crabbe. For a change of pace he occasionally used his bulk to play a slightly deranged character in several other types of films. His western films include: *Two Fisted Law, Law and Order* (1932), *Cowboy Holiday* (1934), *Drift Fence, Wild Brian Kent* (1936), *Where the West Begins, Where Buffalo Roam* (1938), *Son of Roaring Dan* (1940), *Man from Montana* (1941), *Gunsmoke Mesa, Boss of Boomtown* (1944), *Return of the Rangers* (1945), *Rimfire, Trigger Trail* (1949).

### Earl Askam (1898–1940)

Earl Askam was a singer and appeared in many stage musicals before entering films. His film career consisted of character roles far removed from his early voice training in Italy. He appeared as a henchman in western films as well as parts in Flash Gordon serials and ganster films. He was born May 10, 1898, in Seattle, and died April 3, 1940 in Los Angeles of a heart attack while playing golf. His western films included: *Empty Saddles, Trail Dust* (1936), *Red River Range* (1938), *Union Pacific* (1939), *Northwest Mounted Police, Pioneers of the West* (1940).

*Earl Askam, center, watches John Wayne rough up William Royle in* Red River Range *(Republic, 1938). Olin Francis is on the right.*

### Hooper Atchley (1887–1943)

Hooper Atchley was born April 30, 1887, in Ebenezer, Tennessee. After a stage career he entered films during the silent era. In his early westerns he normally was matched against Ken Maynard or Tim McCoy. He shot himself November 16, 1943, in Hollywood. His western films included: *Santa Fe Trail* (1930), *Texas Terror* (1931), *Local Bad Man* (1932), *Fighting for Justice, Drum Taps* (1933), *Outlaw Deputy, The Westerner* (1935), *The Prescott Kid, Bulldog Courage* (1936), *Roarin' Lead* (1937), *Mountain Rhythm* (1939), *The Gay Caballero* (1940), *The Black Hill Express* (1943).

*Hooper Atchley's villainous days are over in this scene with Ken Maynard in* Drum Taps *(World Wide, 1933).*

### Trevor Bardette (1902– )

Trevor Bardette was born in Nashville, Arkansas, November 19, 1902. He moved to Denver at the age of 5 and to Los Angeles when 13. He started his screen career playing "heavies" and has been at it ever since. Although he studied mechanical engineering in college he went to New York to begin a stage career and got his first part in a musical because he could speak Spanish fluently. He is at his best leading a lynch mob, playing a dishonest rancher or leader of a gang of hotheads. Since entering films in 1936 he has been killed on the screen many times. Forms of death include burning at the stake, drowning, hanging, poison, gas, electrocution, gunshots, torture, smothering, strangling, boiling in oil, and having his throat cut. He continued his wicked ways on television in the popular *Wyatt Earp* program where he portrayed "Old Man Clanton." His sayings were put into book form; one of the best: "The best way to stay alive in Tombstone is take the fust stage East." His western films include: *Borderland* (1937), *In Old Mexico* (1938), *The Oklahoma Kid* (1939), *The Dark Command* (1940), *Wild Bill Hickok Rides* (1941), *Apache Trail* (1942), *Marshal of Cripple Creek* (1947),

*Trevor Bardette allows Roy Barcroft to inspect a small lethal weapon in* Fort Dodge Stampede *(Republic, 1951).*

*Sundown at Santa Fe* (1948), *Hellfire, The Wyoming Bandit, The Blazing Trail* (1949), *Hills of Oklahoma* (1950), *Fort Dodge Stampede* (1951), *Montana Territory* (1952), *Bandits of the West* (1953), *Red River Shore* (1954), *The Man from Bitter Ridge* (1955), *Red Sundown* (1956), *The Raiders* (1964).

*Robert Barrat is about to be surprised by a female masked bandit as Richard Lane looks on in* Riders of the Purple Sage *(20th Century-Fox, 1941).*

### Robert Barrat (1891–1970)

Robert Barrat was born July 10, 1891, in New York City. After a career on the New York stage the large and powerful performer entered motion pictures playing a variety of parts ranging from badmen to characterizations of General of the Army Douglas MacArthur whom he resembled He played in many non-western films. He died in Los Angeles January 7, 1970, at the age of 78. His western films included: *Massacre* (1934), *Moonlight on the Prairie* (1935), *Trailin' West* (1936), *The Texans* (1938), *Heritage of the Desert* (1939), *The Man from Dakota* (1940), *Riders of the Purple Sage* (1941), *Dakota, San Antonio* (1945), *Sunset Pass* (1946), *The Fabulous Texan* (1947), *Bad Men of Tombstone* (1948), *Canadian Pacific* (1949), *Riders of the Range* (1950), *Distant Drums* (1951), *The Denver and Rio Grande* (1952), *Cow Country* (1953), *Tall Man Riding* (1955).

*Alfonso Bedoya in a typical pose.*

### Alfonso Bedoya (1904–1957)

Alfonso Bedoya did not appear in many American films, but his first role in *The Treasure of the Sierra Madre* in 1948 assured him of lasting screen immortality. His performance as "Gold Hat," the grinning bandit chief who butchered Humphrey Bogart, was superb. He was born in Vicam, Mexico, and at the age of 14 was sent to Houston to attend school. He quit and found many odd jobs until he returned to Mexico. He became an actor and appeared in many Mexican productions until his Hollywood debut. He died December 15, 1957, of a heart attack. His western films included: *Streets of Laredo, Border Incident* (1949), *California Conquest* (1952), *Sombrero, The Stranger Wore a Gun* (1953), *Border River* (1954), *Ten Wanted Men* (1955).

### Noah Beery Sr. (1884–1946)

Noah Beery Sr. was the villain's villain. He gave the impression that the only fun to be gained out of life had to be obtained by cheating, lying or just plain skullduggery. He was born in Kansas City, Missouri, January 17, 1884. At an early age he took singing lessons, sang in Kansas City and New York, and then appeared in William A. Brady's melodramas. He drifted to Hollywood where he specialized in villainous roles in silents. His portrayal of the ruthless sergeant in *Beau Geste* in 1926 was a masterpiece. He also tortured his screen wives, was a child beater and murdered without conscience in many silent epics. His style of villainy made its way into westerns in the 1930s and 1940s as he appeared in many adaptations of Zane Grey westerns among others. Toward the latter part of his career his roles dwindled in size, but he always made the most of his screen appearances. On April 1, 1946, while at the home of his brother, Wallace Beery, he died of a heart attack. They were rehearsing their roles for the Lux Radio Program on which they were to appear that evening. His western films included: *The Squaw Man* (1918), *The Spoilers* (1923), *The*

*Noah Beery Sr. up to his usual nastiness in Paramount's* Thundering Herd *(Paramount, (1934). With him are Blanche Frederici and Judith Allen.*

*Thundering Herd* (1925), *Riders of the Purple Sage* (1931), *Big Stampede* (1932), *Thundering Herd, Trail Beyond* (1934), *The Bad Man of Brimstone* (1938), *Mexicali Rose* (1939), *Pioneers of the West, The Tulsa Kid* (1940), *A Missouri Outlaw* (1941), *Carson City Cyclone* (1943), *Barbary Coast Gent* (1944).

### Ray Bennett (1895–1957)

Raphael (Ray) Bennett was born March 21, 1895, in Portland, Oregon. Playing primarily in westerns he generally was a villain. His career spanned approximately 20 years. He died in Hollywood of a heart attack, December 18, 1957. His western films included: *Texas Trail, Forlorn River* (1937), *Prairie Moon* (1938), *Knights of the Range* (1940), *Return of Daniel Boone* (1941), *The Renegades* (1943), *Marshal of Gunsmoke* (1944), *Rustlers of the Badlands* (1945), *Galloping Thunder* (1946), *Prairie Raiders* (1947), *Northwest Stampede* (1948), *Red Canyon* (1949), *Apache Drums* (1951), *Waco* (1952), *The Great Sioux Uprising* (1953).

*Ray Bennett, right, corrals drifter Howard Duff in a yarn about wild stallions,* Red Canyon *(Universal-International, 1949).*

*Lyle Bettger takes over the range land and the hero's girl in* Showdown at Abilene *starring Jock Mahoney. (Universal-International, 1956).*

### Lyle Bettger (1915– )

A comparative newcomer to films, handsome Lyle Bettger made his first film in 1950 and his first western in 1952. Since then he has made up for lost time. He was born February 13, 1915, in Philadelphia. After attending the American Academy of Dramatic Art in New York City he started in summer stock and with road companies. He was about to give up his career in 1946 when he had an opportunity for a long run on Broadway.

This led to films and his career was established. His western films include: *The Denver and Rio Grande* (1952), *The Great Sioux Uprising* (1953), *Drums Across the River* (1954), *The Lone Ranger, Showdown at Abilene* (1956), *Gunfight at the O.K. Corral* (1957), *Guns of the Timberland* (1960), *Town Tamer* (1966), *Johnny Reno* (1967).

### Robert Bice (1914–1968)

Robert Bice was born in Dallas on March 4, 1914. After a career as a writer he became a film actor in 1942. During his career he usually performed as a "heavy." He died January 8, 1968. His western films included: *The Red Stallion* (1947), *Canon City* (1948), *Bandit King of Texas* (1949), *Bells of Coronado, Under Mexicali Stars* (1950), *Al Jennings of Oklahoma* (1951), *Night Stage to Galveston, Junction City* (1952), *Bandits of the West, The Star of Texas* (1953), *The Gun That Won the West* (1955).

*Robert Bice, center, is about to get what he deserves from Charles Starrett for tormenting Kathleen Case in* Junction City *(Columbia, 1952).*

### William Bishop (1918–1959)

One of the better looking bad guys of the western film was William Bishop. Although he also played the handsome hero his behavior changed sufficiently for him to portray the leader of the villains in many films. He was born in Oak Park, Illinois, and held a law degree from the University of West Virginia. After graduating from college he was the assistant stage manager for Billy Rose's *Jumbo*. He played Broadway and received a film contract in 1941. He also co-starred on television in 1954 in *It's a Great Life*. He died October 3, 1959, in Hollywood of cancer at the age of 41. His western films included: *Coroner Creek, Adventures in Silverado, Black Eagle, Thunderhoof* (1948), *The Walking Hills* (1949), *Overland Pacific* (1954), *Wyoming Renegades, Top Gun* (1955), *The White Squaw* (1956), *The Oregon Trail* (1959).

*William Bishop as the suave cattle rustler with his eye on the governorship of Wyoming in* The Redhead from Wyoming *(Universal, 1952).*

### Al Bridge (1891–1957)

Al Bridge was born February 26, 1891, in Pennsylvania. He had a long career in films and was particularly adept at playing villains in westerns. He occasionally played a sheriff, sometimes even an honest one. He also appeared in many other type films. He died December 27, 1957, at the age of 66. His western films included: *Galloping Thru* (1932), *Sunset Pass* (1933), *Thundering Herd* (1934), *New Frontier* (1935), *The Lawless Nineties* (1936), *Western Gold* (1937), *Two-Gun Justice* (1938), *The Man from Sundown* (1939), *Pioneers of the Frontier* (1940), *Law of the Range* (1941), *Bad Men of the Hills* (1942), *Tenting Tonight on the Old Camp Ground* (1943), *My Pal Trigger* (1946), *Robin Hood in Texas* (1947), *Silver River* (1948), *The Doolins of Oklahoma* (1949), *Iron Mountain Trail* (1953).

*Al Bridge, second from right, with Charles Starrett, Dick Botiller and Iris Meredith in* The Man from Sundown *(Columbia, 1939).*

*John Cason, center, with Tom Neal, Holly Bane, Jack Holt and Byron Foulger in* Red Desert *(Lippert, 1949).*

### John Cason (1918–1961)

John Cason appeared in westerns primarily for Columbia, PRC, Lippert and Republic. Never seeming to know right from wrong, he continually rode with the band of outlaws during his 20-year career. He was born July 30, 1918, in Texas and was killed in an automobile accident July 7, 1961. His western films included: *Land of the Outlaws* (1944), *Ghost of Hidden Valley, Overland Riders* (1946), *Belle Starr's Daughter* (1948), *The Blazing Trail, Red Desert* (1949), *Colorado Ranger, Rustlers on Horseback, Redwood Forest Trail* (1950), *The Hawk of Wild River, Black Hills Ambush* (1952), *Savage Frontier, Gun Fury* (1953), *Red River Shore* (1954), *Wyoming Renegades* (1955), *Cimarron* (1960).

### George Chesebro (1888–1959)

George Chesebro was born July 29, 1888, in Minneapolis. He started his acting career with a local stock company in 1907. After touring the orient with a musical show in 1911–1913 he came to Hollywood in 1915. He became a regular in westerns and consistently appeared with many studios for 35 years. He also appeared in many serials. He died May 28, 1959, at the age of 70. His western films included: *Mark of the Spur* (1932), *Mystery Ranch, In Old Santa Fe* (1934), *Tumbling Tumbleweeds* (1935), *Trail Dust* (1936), *Two-Fisted Sheriff* (1937), *The Purple Vigilantes* (1938), *Song of the Buckeroo* (1939), *West of Pinto Basin* (1940), *Wrangler's Roost, The Lone Rider Ambushed* (1941), *Two-Fisted Justice* (1948), *Thundering Gun Slingers* (1944), *Colorado Pioneers* (1945), *Two-Fisted Stranger, South of the Chisholm Trail* (1946), *West of Dodge City* (1947), *Check Your Guns* (1948), *Desert Vigilante* (1949), *Trail of Robin Hood*

George Chesebro, center, along with Joe McGuinn and Francis Walker are told to keep their hands up in Roaring Frontiers *(Columbia, 1941). Giving the orders are Bill Elliott and his sidekick, Frank Mitchell.*

(1950), *Night Riders of Montana* (1951), *Montana Territory* (1952), *Winning of the West* (1953).

### Tris Coffin (    –    )

Tris Coffin is probably best known for his television role of Arizona Ranger Captain Tom Rynning in *26 Men,* authentic stories of the Arizona Rangers. He hasn't always worked for the law as the handsome Coffin played the lead heavy in many western films. He was born in Utah in a silver mining community. He became interested in acting at an early age. He traveled with stock companies, pausing long enough to get his degree in speech from the University of Washington. He later became a news analyst and sportscaster. A Hollywood scout heard him broadcast and persuaded him to try films. His western films include: *Overland Mail* (1939), *Arizona Frontier* (1940), *Arizona Bound* (1941), *Dawn on the Great Divide* (1942), *The Vigilantes Ride* (1944), *Under Nevada Skies* (1946), *Trail to San Antone* (1947), *Desperadoes of Dodge City* (1948), *Crashing Thru* (1949), *Short Grass* (1950), *Rodeo King and the*

Tris Coffin, center, and Angela Stevens hold Chris Alcaide at bay as they attempt to make their escape in The Kid from Broken Gun *(Columbia, 1952).*

*Senorita* (1951), *The Kid from Broken Gun* (1952).

*Don Costello is surprised by Bill Elliott in* Marshal of Laredo *(Republic, 1945).*

### Don Costello (1901–1945)

Don Costello entered films in 1939 after his Broadway role in *Come Across*. His Hollywood career only lasted six years, but during that time he appeared in several western films, usually as the bad guy. He died in his sleep October 24, 1945. His western films included: *Last of the Duanes* (1941), *Sundown Jim* (1942), *A Lady Takes a Chance* (1943), *Texas Masquerade* (1944), *Along Came Jones, Marshal of Laredo, Great Stagecoach Robbery* (1945).

### Richard Cramer (1889–1960)

Richard Cramer's features were such that he was immediately cast as a villain. He played mobsters in gangland films and desperadoes in westerns with an occasional switch to the bartender. He was born in Bryan, Ohio, July 3, 1889. After graduation from Ohio State University he started a stage career and spent 10 years on Broadway. He entered films in 1928. He died August 9, 1960, at the age of 71. His western films included: *Painted Desert* (1931), *The Tenderfoot* (1932), *Fourth Horseman* (1933), *Rawhide Mail* (1934), *Riddle Ranch* (1935), *O'Malley of the Mounted* (1936),

*Richard Cramer and Bob Steele are being restrained by a
group of miners in* The Trusted Outlaw *(Republic, 1937).*

*The Trusted Outlaw, Where Trails Divide* (1937),
*Thunder in the Desert* (1938), *In Old Montana*
(1939), *Arizona Frontier* (1941), *Rock River*
*Renegades* (1942), *Two-Fisted Justice* (1943),
*Song of Old Wyoming* (1945).

### Steve Darrell (1904–1970)

Steve Darrell was born J. Stevan Darrell, November 19, 1904, in Osage, Iowa. The acting bug overtook him early in life as he played Abe Lincoln in a grade school tableau. His first professional work was with Galloway Players in Pittsfield, Massachusetts. He came to the West Coast in 1937 at the Pasadena Playhouse. He started his screen career in 1938. He appeared with Buster Crabbe, Johnny Mack Brown, Charles Starrett, Roy Rogers, Allan Lane, Jimmy Wakely and Whip Wilson. He appeared in over 100 films and 200 TV episodes. His favorite movie role was in *Treasure of the Ruby Hills* and his favorite TV role was an episode of *26 Men*. In both he played an ex-lawman. Looking back over a long career Steve wrote: "I enjoyed all kinds of character roles, the more villainous the better." He died on August 14, 1970, of a brain tumor. His western films included: *Lightning Raiders* (1945), *Helldorado, Trailing Danger* (1947), *Overland Raiders, Carson City Raiders* (1948), *Frontier Outpost, Riders in the Sky* (1949), *Under Mexicali Stars* (1950),

*Steve Darrell.*

*Rough Riders of Durango* (1951), *Thunder over the Plains* (1953), *The Law vs. Billy the Kid* (1954), *The Treasure of Ruby Hills* (1955), *Red Sundown* (1956).

### Art Dillard (1906–1960)

Charles (Art) Dillard's was one of the many familiar faces seen in the western film. He was a stuntman and rarely received any official notice for his screen portrayals. He died March 3, 1960, in "Black" Jack O'Shea's Trading Post in Chatsworth, California of a heart attack. His western films included: *Ghost Patrol* (1936), *The Tulsa Kid* (1940), *Santa Fe Uprising* (1946), *Renegades of Sonora* (1948).

*Art Dillard, seated, center, hears approaching horses in* Santa Fe Uprising *(Republic, 1946). Standing center is Tom London and seated right are Lee Reynolds and Forrest Burns.*

### Douglas Dumbrille (1890–      )

Douglas Dumbrille made just as convincing a villain in westerns as he did in other type features. A very talented actor he was constantly in demand by almost every studio. He was born in Hamilton, Ontario, October 13, 1890. While in school he distinguished himself in athletics, particularly in hockey. Prior to and during his career in stock he also had a variety of other professions including that of a bank clerk and farmer. He sold automobile accessories, tea, coffee, insurance, real estate, books, haberdashery and also helped to manufacture plows. He appeared in many important plays on Broadway. After a long stage career he entered films in 1931, appearing in *His Woman* for Paramount. In western films he normally played a corrupt sheriff or businessman, usually impeccably dressed and with a speaking voice to match. His western films include: *Rustler's Roundup* (1933), *End of the Trail* (1936), *Mysterious Rider* (1938), *Rovin' Tumbleweeds* (1939), *Virginia City* (1940), *The Roundup* (1941), *Ride'em Cowboy* (1942), *The Daltons Ride Again* (1945), *Under Nevada Skies* (1946), *The Fabulous Texan* (1947), *Last of the Wild Horses* (1948), *Riders of the Whistling Pines* (1949), *The Savage Horde* (1950), *Apache War Smoke* (1952), *The Lawless Rider* (1954).

*Douglas Dumbrille, center, with Jess Barker, left, and Milburn Stone in* The Daltons Ride Again *(Universal, 1945).*

### Kenne Duncan (1906– )

Kenne Duncan was born Kenneth Duncan MaClachlan in Chatham, Ontario, February 17, 1906. He attended St. Andrew's College in Toronto and the Royal School of Infantry in London, Ontario. He was a gentleman jockey and won several races at Canada's Bluebonnet Tracks. Prior to entering films in 1930 he was an accountant and appeared on the stage. He plays both good guys and bad guys, but prefers the "heavy" roles. One of his biggest thrills was riding the Emperor's white horse while filming in Japan. His western films include: *Man from Wyoming* (1930), *Colorado Kid* (1937), *Frontier Scout* (1938), *Roll Wagons Roll* (1939), *Land of Six Guns, The Kid from Santa Fe* (1940), *A Missouri*

*Kenne Duncan, right, and Denver Pyle as henchmen "Ingo" and "Bowie" await Gene Autry in a copper mine in a scene from* Hills of Utah *(Columbia, 1951).*

*Outlaw* (1941), *Code of the Outlaw* (1942), *The Sundown Kid* (1943), *Outlaws of Santa Fe* (1944), *California Gold Rush* (1946), *Code of the Saddle* (1947), *Gun Runner* (1949), *The Blazing Sun* (1950), *Hills of Utah* (1951), *Pack Train* (1953), *The Lawless Rider* (1954).

### Earl Dwire (1883–1940)

Earl Dwire changed back and forth from white hair and white moustache for elderly roles to black hair and moustache for his villainous portrayals. He was equally at home at both, but made an ideal "heavy" with his rugged features. He was born October 3, 1883, in Rockport, Missouri and died January 16, 1940. His western films included: *Law of the West* (1932), *Riders of Destiny* (1933), *Lucky Texan, Randy Rides Alone, The Star Packer* (1934), *Wagon Trail, Fighting Pioneers, Riders of the Law* (1935), *Roamin' Wild, Sundown Saunders* (1936), *The Gun Ranger, The Trusted Outlaw, Hittin' the Trail* (1937), *The Purple Vigilantes, Two-Gun Justice* (1938), *The Arizona Kid* (1939).

*Earl Dwire, left, is about to be tied up by Bob Steele in* The Gun Ranger *(Republic, 1937).*

### Jack Elam (1917– )

Jack Elam is one of the most convincing screen villains. For many years he played the badman in westerns and a variety of sinister roles in nonwesterns. He then played heroic parts in two television series, *The Dakotas* and *Temple Huston*. He was then very successful in a comedy role in *Support Your Local Sheriff* in 1969 and has followed this pattern since. He was born in Phoenix, Arizona, and after graduating from high school attended junior college. He then entered the business world as an accountant and was promoted to auditor. He then became auditor for the Bel Air Hotel and finally the manager. When the Hotel was sold he worked with independent motion picture companies and developed a budget system that was soon adopted by other companies. Even though he became one of the highest paid auditors he decided to switch to acting. He agreed to obtain financing for two low budget independent films, but only if he could play the heavy in each. This led to a very rewarding career as an actor. His western films include: *High Lonesome, The Sundowners* (1950), *Rawhide* (1951), *Montana Territory, High Noon, Rancho Notorious* (1952), *Moonlighter* (1953), *Cattle Queen of Montana* (1954), *The Man from Laramie* (1955), *Thunder Over Arizona* (1956), *Night Passage* (1957), *the Last Sunset* (1961), *The Rare Breed* (1966), *The Way West* (1967), *Firecreek* (1968), *Support Your Local Sheriff* (1969), *Rio Lobo* (1970), *Support Your Local Gunfighter* (1971).

*Jack Elam as "Shotgun" from* Night Passage *(Universal, 1957).*

### Frank Ellis (1897–1969)

Frank Ellis was born in Oklahoma February 26, 1897. He entered films in the early 1920s and spent most of his career with the band of outlaws, only rarely switching to the side of the law. He died February 23, 1969. His western films included: *Code of the Cow Country* (1927), *Treason* (1933), *Riders of the Whistling Skull, Boothill Brigade* (1937), *Border Wolves* (1938), *Roll Wagons Roll* (1939), *Westbound Stage* (1940), *The Bandit Trail* (1941), *Phantom Killer* (1942), *Black Market Rustlers* (1943), *Law of the Saddle* (1944), *Ambush Trail* (1946), *The Westward Trail* (1948), *Beyond the Purple Hills* (1950).

*Frank Ellis, right, is about to apply the knockout blow to Bill Elliott in* Law Comes to Texas *(Columbia, 1939). Charles (Slim) Whitaker has a good grip on Veda Ann Borg.*

### Franklyn Farnum (1878–1961)

Franklyn Farnum was born June 5, 1878, in Boston. He was not related to William or Dustin Farnum although he had been erroneously reported as a brother. After a stage career of 12 years he entered silent films and starred in several westerns. He played the lead "Silent Joe" in the 1920 serial *Vanishing Trails* as well as starring in a later serial, *Battling Brewster* (1924). In the sound era he could be found in many westerns usually cast as a villain. He became an extra and was president of the screen extras guild for many years. He died of cancer July 4, 1961, in Hollywood. His western films included: *So This Is Arizona* (1922), *Mark of the Spur, The Texas Bad Man* (1932), *Frontier Days* (1934), *Powdersmoke Range* (1935), *Frontier Justice* (1936), *In Early Arizona* (1938), *Saddle Leather Law* (1944).

*Franklyn Farnum as "Spike", one of the baddies of Tombstone, grabs Dorothy Gulliver in* In Early Arizona *(Columbia, 1938).*

### Frank Fenton (1906–1957)

Frank Fenton was born April 9, 1906, in Hartford, Connecticut. He entered films in 1942 in *The Navy Comes Through* and although during his career he played a variety of roles he often found himself cast as the "heavy" in westerns. He died in Los Angeles September 26, 1957. His western films included: *Buffalo Bill* (1944), *Renegades of Sonora* (1948), *The Doolins of Oklahoma, The Golden Stallion, Rustlers* (1949), *Rogue River, Wyoming Mail* (1950), *Streets of Ghost Town* (1950).

*Frank Fenton, right, wants no more of Richard (Chito) Martin's knife throwing prowess in* Rustlers *(RKO, 1948). Tim Holt is in the center.*

### Al Ferguson (1897–    )

Al Ferguson's piercing eyes and sharp nose immediately branded him as a villain, a role he portrayed in most of his films. Very little is known about his life, but he was born in Rosslarre, Ireland, April 19, 1897. He appeared in many silent serials in the 1920s as well as feature films. He also appeared in both in the talkies, many times as an unbilled player. His western films included: *Fangs of Destiny* (1927), *One Way Trail* (1931), *Desert Trail* (1935), *Roamin' Wild* (1936), *North of Rio Grande* (1937), *Law of the Saddle, Outlaw Trail, Sonora Stagecoach* (1944), *Lightning Raiders* (1945), *Overland Riders* (1946), *Prairie Outlaws* (1948).

*Al Ferguson, left, has gained entrance to the safe, but there is trouble behind the door in the form of John Wayne in* Desert Trail *(Monogram, 1935). The girl is Mary Kornman.*

*Douglas Fowley and his gang are rounded up by Rick Vallin and Tim Holt in* Rio Grande Patrol *(RKO, 1950). The cowboy at the right is Forrest Burns.*

### Douglas Fowley (1911–    )

Douglas Fowley played gangster roles very convincingly in the 1930s and in the 1950s. He many times portrayed a bearded, toothless old man. In between he found time to menace the hero with cocksure efficiency in western films. He was born Daniel Vincent Fowley in New York City, May 30, 1911, and aspired to be an actor at an early age. He played in night clubs after completing his education at St. Francis Xavier Miltary Academy in New York. In stock he sang, danced and told a few jokes. He operated a dramatic school, was a barker for theatres, a runner on Wall Street, worked in a shipping department, and was a part time coach at a summer camp before he broke into films. His western films include: *Dodge City* (1939), *Wagons Westward* (1940), *Secrets of the Wasteland* (1941), *Sunset on the Desert* (1942), *Bar 20* (1943), *Along the Navajo Trail* (1945), *Ridin' Down the Trail* (1947), *The Denver Kid* (1948), *Bad Men of Tombstone* (1949), *Rio Grande Patrol* (1950), *Stage to Tucson* (1951), *The Man Behind the Gun* (1952), *Kansas Pacific* (1953), *Red River Shore* (1954), *Texas Lady* (1955), *The Broken Star* (1956).

### Olin Francis (1892–1952)

Olin Francis was one of the charter members of Screen Actor's Guild and his career spanned 40 years. He was a large, broad-shouldered man and specialized in playing the desperado. He was born in Mooresville, Mississippi, September 13, 1892. He graduated from the University of Mississippi with an engineering degree. He performed on the stage prior to entering silent films. He died June 30, 1952, in Hollywood. His western films included: *The Cross Breed* (1927), *Lariats and Six Shooters* (1931), *O'Malley of the Mounted* (1936), *Rough Ridin' Rhythm* (1937), *Two-Gun Justice, Pals of the Saddle, Overland Stage Raiders* (1938), *Riders of Black River* (1939), *Rolling Home to Texas* (1941).

*Olin Francis is under suspicion of having caused the hole in Charles Starrett's hat in* Riders of Black River *(Columbia, 1939).*

### Robert Frazer (1894–1944)

Robert Frazer was born June 29, 1894, in Worcester, Massachusetts. He appeared on the Broadway stage at an early age in such hits as *Ben Hur*. He entered films and played leading roles in silent films. In 1928 he moved to Hollywood and appeared in character parts, mostly heavies, for the next 16 years. He died in Los Angeles, August 17, 1944. His western films included: *Sioux Blood* (1929), *Saddle Buster* (1932), *Fighting for Justice* (1933), *Trail Beyond* (1934), *Black Aces* (1937), *Crashing Thru* (1939), *One Man's Law* (1940), *Pals of the Pecos, Gunman from Bodie* (1941), *Riders of the West* (1942), *Wagon Tracks West* (1943), *Partners of the Trail* (1944).

*Robert Frazer, right, and George J. Lewis, left, tie up Kay Aldridge in* Daredevils of the West, *a serial starring Allan (Rocky) Lane. (Republic, 1943).*

### Terry Frost (1906–    )

Terry Frost was born October 26, 1906, in Bemidji, Minnesota. After graduation from high school he spent the next six years as a miner, lumberjack, cowboy, salesman and jack of all trades. In 1929 he entered vaudeville and went on to appear in stock all over the Midwest. After playing "Killer Mears" in *The Last Mile* in 1941 he entered films. He has authored books, plays, poems, and various articles and is known as a world traveler in addition to his 150 films and 250 television films. His

*Terry Frost, second from left, is taken into custody along with Marshall Reed, second from right, in* West of El Dorado *(Monogram, 1949). Others are Max Terhune, Johnny Mack Brown and William Norton Bailey.*

favorite roles are when he portrays the "heavy." His western films include: *Rustlers' Hideout* (1944), *The Caravan Trail, Moon Over Montana* (1946), *Ghost Town Renegades, Black Hills* (1947), *Oklahoma Badlands* (1948), *West of El Dorado, Son of Billy the Kid* (1949), *Outlaws of Texas* (1950), *Dead Man's Trail, Texas City* (1952), *Utah Blaine* (1957).

### Clem Fuller (1909–1961)

Clem Fuller was a western actor and stuntman for 30 years. He got his start in films when observed by Will Rogers while riding in a rodeo in 1931. He gained his greatest notoriety by playing the bartender in the *Gunsmoke* television series until 1960. After his death he was replaced by Glenn Strange. Fuller was a Purple Heart recipient as a result of being wounded in World War II. His last film was *They Came to Cordura* with Gary Cooper, with whom he frequently appeared. He died May 24, 1961, of cancer. His western films included: *Twilight on the Trail*

(1941), *Gun Runner, Shadows of the West* (1949), *High Lonesome* (1950), *Cave of Outlaws* (1951), *Gunsmoke, The Great Sioux Uprising* (1953), *They Came to Cordura* (1959).

*Clem Fuller, left, as one of the henchmen of rancher John Archer has John Barrymore Jr. in a bind in* High Lonesome *(Eagle-Lion, 1950). The other henchman is Frank Cordell.*

### Bud Geary (1898–1946)

Bud Geary was one of Republic's many stock players during his film career. Although occasionally he took on the part of the sheriff, his features were such that he regularly was on the wrong side of the law. He died in Hollywood, February 22, 1946, as a result of injuries received in an automobile accident. His western films included: *Northwest Mounted Police* (1940), *The Sundown Kid, Calling Wild Bill Elliott, Carson City Cyclone* (1943), *Tucson Raiders, Laramie Trail, Cheyenne Wildcat, Sheriff of Las Vegas* (1944), *Colorado Pioneers, Lone Texas Ranger, Marshal of Laredo, The Topeka Terror* (1945), *Thunder Town, Arizona Skies, Heading West* (1946).

Bud Geary, center, and Kenne Duncan, right, are out-
maneuvered by Bill Elliott in Sheriff of Las Vegas *(Republic, 1944).*

## Leo Gordon (1922–     )

Leo Gordon usually has the audience ready to slit
his throat within the first few minutes of his screen
appearance. Very adept at playing villain roles
with a savage tenacity, applause could be expected
when he finally got what he deserved. He was born
December 2, 1922, in New York City. He worked
with construction and wrecking crews, entered the
Army and after his discharge attended New York's
Academy of Dramatic Arts. This finally paid off
and he made his screen debut in 1953. He also has
authored several movie scripts. His western films
include: *Hondo, Gun Fury* (1953), *Ten Wanted
Men, Santa Fe Passage* (1955), *Red Sundown, Seventh Cavalry* (1956), *The Tall Stranger* (1957),
*Apache Territory* (1958), *Escort West* (1959),
*Noose for a Gunman* (1960), *Mclintock!* (1963).

Leo Gordon, right, battles Jim Davis in Noose for a Gunman *(United Artists, 1960).*

## William Haade (1903–1966)

William Haade was born in the state of New York,
March 2, 1903. He entered films in 1937 and during his career he played "Not So Bright" hoodlums
in gangster films, policemen, many bit parts and
western villains. He died November 15, 1966, at
the age of 63. His western films included: *The
Texans* (1938), *Union Pacific* (1939), *Stage to
Chino* (1940), *Robin Hood of the Pecos* (1941),
*Man from Cheyenne* (1942), *Song of Texas*
(1943), *The Yellow Rose of Texas* (1944), *Phan-*

*tom of the Plains* (1945), *My Pal Trigger* (1946), *Colorado Skies* (1947), *Last of the Wild Horses* (1948), *The Old Frontier* (1950), *Buckaroo Sher-* *iff of Texas* (1951), *Carson City* (1952), *Red River Shore* (1954).

*William Haade, left, is held at gunpoint in an old bauxite mine by Michael Chapin in* Buckaroo Sheriff of Texas *(Republic, 1951).*

### Karl Hackett (1893–1948)

Karl Hackett was born September 5, 1893, in Carthage, Missouri. He entered films in 1936 and his career was primarily in serials and westerns where his presence was felt as a gangleader or henchman. He died October 24, 1948, at the age of 55. His western films included: *Lightnin' Bill Carson, Roarin' Guns* (1936), *Gun Lords of Stirrup Basin,* *Texas Trail* (1937), *Song and Bullets, Starlight over Texas* (1938), *Frontier Crusader* (1940), *Texas Marshal, Riding the Wind* (1941), *Sons of the Pioneers* (1942), *Thundering Trails* (1943), *Mojave Firebrand* (1944), *Rustlers of the Badlands* (1945), *Terrors on Horseback* (1946), *Frontier Fighters* (1947).

*Karl Hackett is captured by "The Three Mesquiteers", Bob Steele, Jimmy Dodd, and Tom Tyler in* Thundering Trails *(Republic, 1943).*

### Don Harvey (1911–1963)

Don Harvey traveled through the Midwest with tent shows and repertory companies. He moved on to Hollywood in 1944 and started in radio with Hedda Hopper. He made the switch to films and usually played a gangster or hoodlum in both films and serials. Born in Kansas in 1911 he died in Hollywood April 24, 1963, of a heart attack. His western films included: *Rimfire* (1949), *Dynamite Pass, Hoedown, Trail of the Rustlers* (1950), *Night Riders of Montana* (1951), *The Old West* (1952), *The Outlaw Stallion* (1954), *Wyoming Renegades* (1955), *Blackjack Ketchum, Desperado* (1956).

*Don Harvey, seated, indicates he expects no funny business from Jock Mahoney in* Hoedown *(Columbia, 1950).*

### Reed Howes (1900–1964)

In the 1920s Reed Howes was acclaimed as America's handsomest man as he posed for Arrow Collar dress shirts on advertisements all over the country. He was born in Washington, D.C., and graduated from the University of Utah. He appeared on the stage and then entered films. The advertisements were for real as he was a dashing figure appearing opposite such leading ladies of the screen as Clara Bow and Marie Prevost. He played in many western films of the 1930s and 1940s, usually playing a desperado. He died August 6, 1964. His western films included: *Dawn Rider* (1935), *Feud of the West* (1936), *Six-Gun Rhythm, Roll Wagons Roll* (1939), *Texas Terrors* (1940), *Fugitive Valley* (1941), *Wild Horse Stampede* (1943), *Outlaw Roundup* (1944), *Under Arizona Skies* (1946), *The Untamed Breed* (1948), *Gunslingers* (1950), *Stage to Tucson* (1951), *Hangman's Knot* (1952), *The Stranger Wore a Gun* (1953).

*Reed Howes, right, as the villain in* Six Gun Rhythm *(Grand National, 1939). With him are Joan Barclay and the hero, Tex Fletcher.*

### Wesley Hudman (1916–1964)

Wesley Hudman had many small parts in westerns. He was usually cast as one of the gang of desperadoes. He left Hollywood for Williams, Arizona, where he owned and operated "Rock Quarries." He was a victim of a slaying in Williams on February 29, 1964 at the age of 48. His western films included: *Satan's Cradle* (1949), *The Girl from San Lorenzo* (1950), *Fort Defiance, Fort Dodge Stampede* (1951), *Leadville Gun Slinger, Black Hills Ambush* (1952), *Pack Train* (1953), *Battle of Rogue River, Masterson of Kansas* (1954), *Blackjack Ketchum, Desperado* (1956), *The Sheepman* (1958).

*Wesley Hudman, left, watches Allan (Rocky) Lane swing into action against his boss, Roy Barcroft in* Fort Dodge Stampede *(Republic, 1951).*

### Victor Jory (1902–    )

Victory Jory often plays the part of a dastardly villain and he relishes this type of role. Even though he has always been in demand in the theatre and for a variety of movie roles he is always at his best in a villainous characterization. He was born in an Alaskan gold rush camp at Dawson City, Alaska, November 23, 1902. His father was a horse trader and his mother one of the few newspaper women in the Alaskan Territory. When he reached school age his parents brought him to Pasadena, California, for formal classroom training. Later he moved to Vancouver, British Columbia, where he attended high school and won the amateur light heavyweight boxing championship of the province. He has appeared in hundreds of television shows, directed, written, and produced plays and films, and had two songs published. He is an expert horseman, golfer, and fly fisherman and owns one of the largest private libraries in Hollywood. His western films include: *Dodge City* (1939), *Knights of the Range, The Light of the Western Stars* (1940), *Border Vigilantes, Bad Men of Missouri* (1941), *Tombstone* (1942), *Hoppy Serves a Writ, Bar 20, The Kansan* (1943), *South of St. Louis* (1949), *The Toughest Man in Arizona* (1952), *Man from the Alamo* (1953), *Blackjack Ketchum, Desperado* (1956).

*Victor Jory in his role of Jared Tetlow, the big cattle baron who tries to take over a peaceful valley in Blackjack Ketchum Desperado (Columbia, 1956).*

### Ian Keith (1899–1960)

Ian Keith was a gifted actor who excelled in Shakespearean roles. He also loaned his talents to horror and western films. He was born in Boston, on February 27, 1899. He gave up his father's engineering business to become an actor. After attending the Sargent School of Drama in New York, he realized his ambition. He was seen on the Broadway stage with William Faversham, Lionel Barrymore, and Nazimova among others. He also played Hamlet. He entered films in 1928 and alternated between the stage and motion pictures. He died of a heart attack March 26, 1960. His western films included: *The Big Trail* (1930), *The Sundown Kid, Wild Horse Stampede, Bordertown Gunfighters* (1943), *Arizona Whirlwind, Cowboy from Lonesome River* (1944), *Under Western Skies, Phantom of the Plains* (1945), *Singing on the Trail* (1946), *Border Feud* (1947).

*Ian Keith is restrained by Virginia Christine in* Phantom of the Plains *starring Bill Elliott (Republic, 1945).*

*Cy Kendall, center, is about to release his grip on Jennifer Holt at the persuasion of Bob Steele in* Outlaw Trail *(Monogram, 1944).*

### Cy Kendall (1898–1953)

The 6-foot, 225-pound Cy Kendall was in demand in the 1930s and 1940s for various vicious roles in many different types of films. His bulk and mannerisms made him ideal as "The Big Boss." The ex-drummer, ex-traveling salesman made his debut at the Pasadena Playhouse, switched to the screen in 1936 and played in more than 100 pictures. He was also radio's first Charlie Chan. He died July 22, 1953, at the Motion Picture Country Home. His western films included: *King of the Pecos, The Lonely Trail* (1936), *Rawhide* (1938), *Prairie Law* (1940), *Robin Hood of the Pecos, Billy the Kid* (1941), *Outlaw Trail* (1944), *The Cisco Kid Returns* (1945).

### Douglas Kennedy (1915–    )

*Douglas Kennedy, left, responsible for an Indian attack due to his lust for gold, is captured by Cavalry Captain George Montgomery in* Indian Uprising *(Columbia, 1952).*

Douglas Kennedy was born September 14, 1915, in New York City. He received his education at Deerfield Academy in Massachusetts and Amherst College. He entered films in 1940, but his career was interrupted by World War II, where he served as a Major in the Signal Corps and worked with the O.S.S. and Army Intelligence. In westerns he many times gives the hero a rough time but has played a variety of roles including many roles as a sheriff. His western films include: *North West Mounted Police* (1940), *The Roundup* (1941), *South of St. Louis, Fighting Men of the Plains* (1949), *Montana, The Cariboo Trail* (1950), *Indian Uprising, Ride the Man Down, Fort Osage* (1952), *San Antone* (1953), *Sitting Bull* (1954), *Wyoming Renegade* (1955), *The Last Wagon* (1956).

### Fred Kohler Sr. (1889–1938)

One of the most contemptible, ill-tempered badmen of the screen was Fred Kohler Sr. The six-foot two-inch Kohler always relished showing a total disregard for the rights of others and if he had any pangs of conscience he never bothered to reveal it. He was born in Kansas City, Missouri, on April 20, 1889, the son of an inventor. He began his career in a local theater and then played stock, vaudeville, tent shows, and one-night stands. He became one of the leading "heavies" in the 1920s and 1930s. He died in his sleep in Hollywood on October 28, 1938, leaving a son, Fred Kohler Jr. to carry on the tradition. His western films included: *The Iron Horse* (1924), *Shootin' Irons* (1927), *Light of the Western Stars* (1930), *Rider of Death Valley, The Texas Bad Man* (1932), *Wild Horse Mesa* (1933), *West of the Pecos, The Last Round Up* (1934), *Trail's End, Wilderness Mail* (1935).

*Fred Kohler Sr. in one of his happier moments.*

"Get out - and get out quick - or ~~~"

*Fred Kohler Sr., center, seems unimpressed as he is ordered to leave by Richard Arlen in Zane Grey's* Light of the Western Stars *(Paramount, 1930). Mary Brian is the interested onlooker.*

## Robert Kortman (1887–1967)

Robert Kortman started early in films working for Ince, Goldstone, Pathé, Paramount, Universal and many other companies during the days of the silent film. He continued on into the talkies as a seedy, unkempt, hungry looking villain willingly taking on any assignment given to him by his current screen boss. He was born in New York State December 24, 1887 and died March 13, 1967, at the age of 79. His western films included: *Hills of Peril* (1927), *The Big Killing* (1928), *Fighting Fool* (1932), *Phantom Thunderbolt* (1933), *Smoking Guns* (1934), *The Ivory-Handled Gun* (1935), *Winds of the Wasteland* (1936), *Ghost Town Gold* (1937), *Law of the Texan* (1938), *Renegade Trail* (1939), *Fugitive Valley* (1941), *The Sundown Kid* (1943), *The Vigilantes Ride* (1944), *Gunning for Vengeance* (1946), *Whispering Smith* (1948), *Streets of Laredo* (1949), *Copper Canyon* (1950).

*Robert Kortman, center, follows MacDonald Carey's orders as he muffles Mona Freeman in* Streets of Laredo *(Paramount, 1949).*

### Ethan Laidlaw (1900–1963)

Ethan Laidlaw was born November 25, 1900, in Butte, Montana. When he was 23 he embarked on his film career. He played primarily villainous roles, usually as one of the gang and certainly looked menacing enough for the part. He died May 25, 1963. His western films included: *The Sonora Kid* (1927), *Little Savage* (1929), *Pardon My Gun* (1930), *Powdersmoke Range* (1935), *Yellow Dust* (1936), *Rhythm of the Saddle* (1938), *Western Caravans* (1939), *Stage to Chino* (1940), *The Lone Star Vigilantes* (1941), *Stagecoach Express* (1942), *The Desperadoes* (1943), *Marshal of Gunsmoke* (1944), *Lawless Empire* (1946), *The Great Missouri Raid* (1951), *Montana Territory* (1952), *Powder River* (1953).

*Ethan Laidlaw, right, as "Tip" and Ed Cobb, left, as "Tex,"*
*a pair of rustlers, capture Sheriff Charles Starrett in* Western Caravans *(Columbia, 1939).*

### Eddie Laughton (1902–1952)

Edward Laughton was born in Sheffield, England, and came to the United States as a child. He received his high school education in Detroit. He worked in stock companies, had his own band, and later entered vaudeville where he met The Three Stooges. He followed them to Hollywood where he had intended to be their straight man, but became a screen villain in both westerns and non-westerns. He died of pneumonia March 21, 1952, in Hollywood. His western films included: *Bullets for Rustlers, Blazing Six Shooters, Texas Stagecoach, West of Abilene* (1940), *Outlaws of the Panhandle* (1941), *Lawless Plainsmen* (1942), *Sundown Valley, Sagebrush Heroes* (1944).

*Eddie Laughton, left, as "Shorty," the bartender with Charles Starrett, in* Bullets for Rustlers *(Columbia, 1940).*

*Rex Lease, right, asks Karl Hackett what to do with the body as John Merton looks on in* Lightnin' Bill Carson *(Puritan Pictures, 1936).*

### Rex Lease (1903–1966)

Rex Lease was born February 11, 1903, in Central City, West Virginia. He studied for the ministry at Ohio Wesleyan College, but entered films instead as an extra. His first starring role was in 1924. He played in many films for FBO and starred in many westerns for various independents. He gradually drifted into character parts, playing mostly villainous roles. He died January 3, 1966. His western films included: *Law of the Range* (1928), *The Utah Kid* (1930), *Lone Trail* (1932), *Man from Guntown* (1935), *Lightnin' Bill Carson* (1936), *Heroes of the Alamo* (1937), *Code of the Rangers* (1938), *South of the Border* (1939), *Under Texas Skies* (1940), *The Phantom Cowboy* (1941), *The Cyclone Kid* (1942), *Dead Man's Gulch* (1943), *Bordertown Trail* (1944), *Frontier Gal* (1945), *Days of Buffalo Bill* (1946), *Hellodorado* (1947), *Singing Guns* (1950), *Ride Vaquero* (1953).

### George Lloyd (1897– )

George Lloyd was born Lloyd Langford in Hobart, Tasmania, September 27, 1897. Prior to his motion picture career he was a vaudeville comedian and dancer. During his career he appeared in many films as a thug, bartender or even a policeman. His western roles were confined mainly to villainous portrayals. His western films include: *The Return of Wild Bill* (1940), *The Wildcat of Tucson* (1941), *The Ox-Bow Incident* (1943), *Home in Oklahoma* (1946), *Vigilantes of Boomtown, Swing the Western Way* (1947), *Under California Stars* (1948), *Laramie* (1949).

George Lloyd as Matt Kilgore, leader of a gang of cattle rustlers, manhandles pretty Iris Meredith in The Return of Wild Bill, *starring Bill Elliott (Columbia, 1940).*

### Arthur Loft (1897–1947)

Arthur Loft was born May 25, 1897, in Ouray, Colorado. He entered films in the early 1930s and played in many non-western films as a swindler, lawyer, politician, banker or gangster. In westerns he normally was cast as the leader of the gang, but behind the scenes was a respected citizen. He died January 1, 1947. His western films included: *Kid Courageous* (1935), *King of the Royal Mounted* (1936), *Paradise Express* (1937), *Rhythm of the Saddle* (1938), *Riders of Pasco Basin* (1940), *North from the Lone Star* (1941), *South of Santa Fe* (1942), *Frontier Badmen* (1943), *Lights of Old Santa Fe* (1944), *Sheriff of Redwood Valley* (1946).

Arthur Loft with Bob Steele in Sheriff of Redwood Valley *(Republic, 1946).*

### Ian MacDonald ( – )

Ian MacDonald was born Ulva Williams Pippy in Helena, Montana. His father was a Methodist minister. In school he was interested in athletics as well as drama and played football and basketball. After graduation from college, where he was president of the drama club, he started working in a bank. He started appearing at the Pasadena Playhouse and entered films in 1941. On the screen he has played the role of an Indian many times in addition to his other henchmen roles. His western films include: *Secrets of the Wasteland* (1941), *Colt .45, The Lawless, Comanche Territory* (1950), *Thunder in God's Country* (1951), *High Noon, Toughest Man in Arizona, Hiawatha* (1952), *The Silver Whip* (1953), *Taza, Son of Cochise, Apache* (1954), *Timberjack* (1955), *Stagecoach to Fury* (1956).

*Ian MacDonald, right, as the town of Hidden Valley's gambling king with Rex Allen in* Thunder in God's Country *(Republic, 1951).*

### Kenneth MacDonald (1901–    )

*Kenneth MacDonald, center, supported by Charles Starrett and Bill Cody, Jr. in* Two-Fisted Rangers *(Columbia, 1940).*

In many of the Charles Starrett westerns in the late 1930s and early 1940s you could see a dapper, black-suited Kenneth MacDonald as the figure behind all the dirtywork. As a gambler or supposedly legitimate businessman he usually hired killers such as Dick Curtis to take care of the ranchers, cattlemen, bankers, and the hero. His plans always went astray and more often than not killing him was the only solution for Starrett. He was born Kenneth Dollins in Portland, Indiana, in September of 1901. He became interested in the theatre at an early age. He discovered the name MacDonald in his family background and changed his name accordingly. He possessed a fine voice and sang tenor solos in various Portland churches. A few years later he had a spectacular career as a high school athlete. After graduation he concentrated on music and acting. He appeared on the American stage in the 1920s and appeared in 3000 performances in this medium. He arrived on the Hollywood scene in the early 1930s and caught on quickly with bit roles in films and later progressed to better roles. He relates that his 12 serials for Columbia, Republic, and Universal were hard, but happy work. He enjoys playing in any film that has entertainment value. In later years he was seen in more than 60 episodes as the judge in the "Perry Mason" television series. In this medium he has ap-

peared on virtually all of the major shows, proving that westerns were only a small measure of his talents. His western films include: *Spoilers of the Range* (1939), *Two-Fisted Rangers, Texas Stagecoach* (1940), *Hands Across the Rockies, Prairie Schooners* (1941), *Riders of the Northland* (1942), *Robin Hood of the Range* (1943), *West of the Rio Grande* (1944), *That Texas Jamboree* (1946), *Frontier Agent* (1948), *The Gay Amigo* (1949), *Border Treasure* (1950), *Law of the Badlands* (1951), *Leadville Gunslinger* (1952), *Marshal of Cripple Creek* (1953), *Southwest Passage* (1954).

*Wallace MacDonald, right, with William Janney in* King of the Wild Horses *(Columbia, 1934).*

### Wallace MacDonald (1896–    )

Wallace MacDonald was born May 5, 1896, in Mulgrave, Nova Scotia. His stage career included stints in San Francisco and Vancouver. He began his screen work with Triangle, Fox, Vitagraph, Goldwyn, and others as a leading man. He starred in several silent serials such as *Breaking Through* in 1921 with Carmel Hyers for Vitagraph and finished this aspect of his career with a starring role in *Whispering Smith Rides* for Universal in 1927.

He became a story editor, then supervisor of writers for Republic, and then turned to producing films for the remainder of his career in films. His western films include: *The Spoilers* (1923), *Drums of the Desert* (1927), *Two-Fisted Law, Texas Cyclone, Riding Tornado* (1932), *Between Fighting Men* (1933), *King of the Wild Horses* (1934).

### Cactus Mack (1899–1962)

Cactus Mack was born Taylor McPeters, August 8, 1899, in Weed, New Mexico. A talented musician he played violin with Ray Whitley's "Six-Bar Cowboys" and guitar with Fred Scott's "The Cimarron Cowboys." He later played villain roles in western films along with other character parts. As he was about to go on location for *The Ugly American*, he died of a heart attack April 17, 1962 in Hollywood. His western films included: *The Fighting Gringo* (1939), *Texas Terrors* (1940), *Shad-*

*Cactus Mack, second from left, with Will Wright and Jack Mower in* Dallas *(Warner Bros., 1950).*

*ows on the Range, Raiders of the South* (1946), *Trailing Danger, Six Gun Serenade* (1947), *The Gallant Legion, Range Renegades, The Rangers Ride* (1948), *The Dalton Gang* (1949), *The Mis-* *sourians, Buckaroo Sheriff of Texas, Twilight in the Sierras, Dallas* (1950), *Old Oklahoma Plains* (1952).

### Barton MacLane (1902–1969)

Noted for his "bad guy" roles in prison and gangster films in the 1930s and 1940s Barton MacLane also found time to appear in many western films. He was one of the noisiest actors ever to lead a prison riot, a role he repeated many times. He was born on Christmas Day 1902 in Columbia, South Carolina. He graduated from Wesleyan University and attended the American Academy of Dramatic Arts in New York. He made his Broadway debut in 1929 and entered films in 1933. He appeared on television as a U.S. Marshal in *The Outlaws* and as a general in *I Dream of Jeannie*. He died of double pneumonia on January 1, 1969, in Santa Monica, California. His western films included: *Thundering Herd* (1934), *Frisco Kid* (1935), *Melody Ranch* (1940), *Western Union* (1941), *Song of Texas* (1943), *Santa Fe Uprising* (1946), *Cheyenne* (1947), *Relentless* (1948), *Best of the Bad Men* (1951), *The Half-Breed* (1952), *Cow Country* (1953), *The Silver Star* (1955), *Hell's Crossroads* (1957), *Gunfighters of Abilene*

*Barton MacLane, right, as the villain being stalked by Robert Young in* Relentless *(Columbia, 1948). Frank Fenton is pictured with MacLane.*

(1959), *Noose for a Gunman* (1960), *Law of the Lawless* (1964), *Town Tamer* (1965), *Arizona Bushwackers* (1968).

### Ted Mapes (1901–    )

Ted Mapes was born November 25, 1901, in St. Edward, Nebraska. He left for California in 1922 and entered films in 1929 through stunt work. From 1935 until his retirement he appeared in all types of features and serials both as a stunt man and an actor specializing in outlaw roles. He doubled and performed stunts for James Stewart in 36 films and Gary Cooper in 17. His western films include: *The Ranger and the Lady* (1940), *Pardon My Gun, Frontier Fury* (1943), *The Last Horseman, Law Men, Dead or Alive* (1944), *Rustlers of the Badlands* (1945), *Roaring Rangers, Two-Fisted Stranger, Texas Panhandle* (1946), *The Wild Frontier, The Stranger from Ponca City* (1947), *The Strawberry Roan, Black Eagle* (1948), *Topeka* (1953).

*Ted Mapes, right, as part of a gang that robs ranch foreman Russell Hayden of $12,000 in scene from* The Last Horseman. *Others are John 'Blackie' Whiteford, Frank La-Rue, Hayden and Nick Thompson. (Columbia, 1944).*

### Leroy Mason (1903–1947)

Leroy Mason looked every bit of the part of "The Big Boss" and he usually was. Through countless films he planned, schemed, and connived his way only to be foiled in the final reel. He started his film career in westerns during the silent era and then switched to leading man roles opposite the stars of the day in 1925. In 1930 he resumed his bad man role and continued until his death. He died of a heart attack in Los Angeles October 13, 1947, on the set of Republic's *California Fire-brand.* His western films included: *Texas Pioneers* (1932), *When a Man Sees Red* (1934), *Northern Frontier* (1935), *Ghost Town Gold, Roundup Time in Texas* (1937), *Outlaw Express, Santa Fe Stampede* (1938), *Wyoming Outlaw, New Frontier* (1939), *The Range Busters* (1940), *Silver Stallion, The Apache Kid* (1941), *The Silver Bullet* (1942), *Blazing Guns* (1943), *Vigilantes of Dodge City, Mojave Firebrand* (1944), *Apache Rose, Bandits of Dark Canyon* (1947).

Big Boss LeRoy Mason is giving orders to his henchmen, Bud Geary, Hal Taliaferro and Kenne Duncan in Vigilantes of Dodge City *(Republic, 1944).*

### Frank McCarroll (1893–1954)

"Just one of the gang" would be the best description of Frank McCarroll. Most "still" shots depict him holding a gun on someone or about ready to. A real cowboy, he was a film stuntman and rodeo rider in addition to his western roles. He died as a result of a fall in his home in Burbank, California March 8, 1954. His western films included: *West of Nevada* (1936), *Code of the Ranger*

(1938), *Fugitive from Sonora* (1943), *Outlaws of Santa Fe, Silver City Kid* (1944), *Rustlers of the Badlands* (1945), *Conquest of Cheyenne* (1946), *Buckaroo from Powder River* (1947), *Brand of Fear* (1949), *Over the Border* (1950), *Captive of Billy the Kid* (1952).

*Frank McCarroll, left, and Tex Terry restrain Gene Autry as he listens to Charles Evans in* Twilight on the Rio Grande *(Republic, 1947).*

*Merrill McCormick, center, explaining his case to Charles Starrett as Frank Ellis watches in* Two-Fisted Sheriff *(Columbia, 1937).*

### Merrill McCormick (1891–1953)

Born William Merrill McCormick he appeared in films for 42 years. Although he played character parts in other films he was usually found unshaven in westerns as one of the gang. He died August 19, 1953, in Hollywood of a heart attack. His western films included: *Born to the Saddle* (1929), *Romance of the Rio Grande* (1930), *Border Devils* (1932), *Deadwood Pass* (1933), *Lawless Border* (1935), *Winds of the Wasteland* (1936), *Two-Fisted Sheriff* (1937), *Outlaws of Sonora* (1938), *Overland Mail* (1939).

### Philo McCullough (1893–    )

Philo McCullough was born June 16, 1893, in San Bernardino, California. He was an original member of the Burbank Stock Company in Los Angeles. After playing stock for eight years he entered films in 1917 with Fox and then First National. He played leads in early films and was featured in several silent serials for Pathé. He portrayed a villain in early sound westerns and later played many unbilled parts in westerns and other type films. His wife, the former Laura Anson, was a leading lady in silents. She died in 1968. His western films include: *Silver Valley* (1927), *Sunset Trail, South of the Rio Grande* (1932), *Wheels of Destiny, Thunder over Texas, Outlaw's Highway* (1934), *Texas Trail* (1937), *Beautiful Blonde from Bashful Bend* (1949), *Dallas* (1950).

*Philo McCullough, right, is surprised by the entrance of Ken Maynard as he struggles with Ruth Hiatt for possession of a pistol in* The Sunset Trail *(Tiffany, 1932).*

### Joe McGuinn (1904–1971)

Joe McGuinn was born in Brooklyn on January 21, 1904. He received his education at Villanova University. He came to California in 1930 and was discovered by a talent scout while playing handball at the Hollywood YMCA. He was a very good horseman and became a stunt man and double for John Boles. He then played mostly heavies in his early westerns and later portrayed sheriffs. Reminiscing on his film career Joe stated of his thirty years, "I liked to work and enjoyed it all." He died September 22, 1971. His western films included: *Marshall of Mesa City* (1939), *Pioneers of the West, Wagons Westward* (1940), *Back in the Saddle, Thunder over the Prairie* (1941), *The Cyclone Kid, Riders of the Northland* (1942), *Jack McCall, Desperado* (1953).

*Joe McGuinn as he appeared in one of his countless roles in the 1940s.*

**Lew Meehan (1890–1951)**

In the 1920s and 1930s James Lew Meehan's features were a familiar sight. His sharp nose that left little room between his moustache and mouth were familiar to audiences even if the name was not. He was one of many regular henchmen who were not usually around at the end of the film. He was born in Minnesota, September 7, 1890, and died August 10, 1951. His western films included:

*Two-Guns of the Tumbleweeds* (1927), *Fighting Pioneers, Unconquered Bandits* (1935), *Roarin' Guns* (1936), *Melody of the Plains, The Gun Ranger, A Roamin' Cowboy, Gun Lords of Stirrup Basin, Arizona Gun Fighter, Ridin' the Lone Trail* (1937), *Thunder in the Desert* (1938), *Roaring Frontiers* (1941).

*Lew Meehan, left, and his henchmen have the drop on Rex Bell and Buzz Barton in* Fighting Pioneers *(Resolute Pictures, 1935).*

### John Merton (1901–1959)

Born John Merton Lavarre, he adopted the name John Merton for his 39-year acting career. He started on Broadway in 1920 and entered films in 1931. Nearly always playing one of the bad guys he rarely made it to the conclusion of the film. His only change of pace was that he sometimes played the big boss instead of one of the henchmen. He died of a heart attack in Los Angeles September 19, 1959. His last three years were spent as a technician at Metro-Goldwyn-Mayer. His son, Lane Bradford, also became a well-known western heavy. His western films included: *The Eagle's Brood* (1935), *Call to the Prairie, Lightning Bill Carson* (1936), *The Gun Ranger, Drums of Destiny* (1937), *Gunman from Bodie* (1941), *Law and Order* (1942), *The Mysterious Rider* (1943), *Texas Masquerade* (1944), *Flame of the West* (1945), *Border Bandits* (1946), *Panhandle Trail* (1947), *Haunted Trails* (1949), *Border Rangers* (1950), *Man from Sonora* (1951), *Trail Guide* (1952).

*John Merton has Smiley Burnette at his mercy in* The Blazing Trail *(Columbia, 1949).*

### Charles B. Middleton (1879–1949)

Charles B. Middleton was best known for his portrayal of "Ming the Merciless" in the "Flash Gordon" serials. In this role, his shaven head, moustache, goatee, and penetrating eyes will be remembered by everyone who ever witnessed a chapter of the serial. His ominous appearance also made him ideally suited for villainous roles in western films. He was born October 3, 1879, in Elizabethtown, Kentucky. He worked with carnivals, circuses, appeared in stock, vaudeville and legit. He entered films in 1927 and was active until his death on April 22, 1949. His western films included: *Mystery Ranch* (1932), *Sunset Pass, Massacre, Lone Cowboy* (1934), *Hop-A-Long Cassidy* (1935), *Song of the Saddle* (1936), *Two-Gun Law* (1937), *Jesse James, Wyoming Outlaw* (1939), *Santa Fe Trail* (1940), *Wild Bill Hickok Rides, Western Union* (1941).

*Charles Middleton, right, with George O'Brien in* Mystery Ranch *(Fox, 1932).*

### John Miljan (1892–1960)

John Miljan was born November 9, 1892, in Lead City, South Dakota. After attending St. Martin's College he became a stage actor in 1908 and continued in this capacity until 1922. He started his film career with Fox in 1922 in *Love Letters*. He was known for his villainous roles throughout his film career. His last appearance was in *The Ten Commandments*. He died January 24, 1960, in Hollywood. His western films included: *Under the Pampas Moon* (1935), *The Plainsman* (1936), *Arizona Mahoney* (1937), *The Oklahoma Kid* (1939), *Young Bill Hickok* (1940), *Texas Rangers* (1941), *Stampede* (1949), *Mule Train* (1950).

*John Miljan, second from left, as a European agent out to seize western territory in* Young Bill Hickok *(Republic, 1940). Participating in the poker game are Marshal Monte Blue, Monte Montague, and Fred Burns.*

### Walter Miller (1893–1940)

Walter Miller was best known for his starring roles in silent serials for Pathé. From 1925 through 1929 he escaped death by inches in 12 of these thrillers for Pathé and one for Mascot. Allene Ray was consistently his leading lady. He was born March 9, 1893, in Dayton, Ohio. He was educated in Brooklyn and went on the stage at the age of 17. He started his film career several years later. He played in early D. W. Griffith films at Biograph Studios, was one of the first screen actors to be paid

$1000 a week, and was at one time a leading man with Mary Pickford. He became a western heavy during the last few years of his film career. He died March 30, 1940, while performing a fight scene in a Gene Autry western at Republic Studios. His western films included: *The Utah Kid* (1930), *Ridin' for Justice, Ghost City* (1932), *Gun Justice, Smoking Guns, Rocky Rhodes* (1934), *The Ivory-Handled Gun, Valley of Wanted Men* (1935), *The Fugitive Sheriff, Ghost Patrol, Heart of the West* (1936), *Boss of Lonely Valley* (1937), *Wild Horse Rodeo* (1938), *Home on the Prairie* (1939), *Bullet Code* (1940).

*Walter Miller, right, and Wheeler Oakman, left, are captured by Tim McCoy in* Ghost Patrol *(Puritan, 1936).*

*James Millican, right, with Dick Foran, Dan Duryea, and Louis Jean Heydt as the Jennings Brothers in* Al Jennings of Oklahoma *(Columbia, 1951).*

### James Millican (1910–1955)

James Millican's excellent voice and serious approach to his work were ingredients that made him a top notch heavy during his 22-year screen career. He was born in Palisades, New York, and attended the University of Southern California. In addition to his film career he also collaborated with Bill Elliott in staging rodeos. He died in Los Angeles November 24, 1955, at the age of 45. His western films included: *Last of the Wild Horses* (1948), *The Gal Who Took the West* (1949), *Winchester '73* (1950), *Rawhide* (1951), *Carson City, Springfield Rifle* (1952), *Cow Country* (1953), *Riding Shotgun* (1954), *Chief Crazy Horse, The Man From Laramie, Top Gun* (1955).

### Jack Montgomery (1891–1962)

Jack Montgomery was one of many of the regular members of a gang of rustlers whose name rarely appeared in the cast. He did have one distinction that the others did not have. He was the father of "Baby Peggy," the famous child star of the Universal silents in the 1920s. He was born November 14, 1891, in Nebraska and died January 21, 1962. His western films included: *The Arizonian* (1931), *Outlaw Deputy* (1935), *Border Wolves, Black Bandit* (1938), *Pursued* (1947), *Colorado Territory* (1949).

Jack Montgomery, left, and Bob Baker are about to meet in Black Bandit *(Universal, 1938).*

### Dennis Moore (1908–1964)

Dennis (Smoky) Moore was born Dennis Meadows in Ft. Worth, Texas, January 26, 1908. After a career in stock and on the legitimate stage he entered films in 1936. He was also a commercial pilot and a physical director at an athletic club. He played leading roles in many "B" films and also starred in some western films. He rode with the desperadoes in many of his films during the last 10 years of his career. He died March 1, 1964. His western films included: *Overland Mail* (1939), *Rainbow over the Range* (1940), *Pals of the Pecos* (1941), *Raiders of the Range* (1942), *Black Market Rustlers* (1943), *Arizona Trail, Oklahoma Raiders* (1944), *Rainbow over the Rockies* (1946), *Frontier Agent* (1948), *Haunted Trails* (1949), *Marshal of Heldorado* (1950), *Fort Defiance* (1951), *Canyon Ambush* (1952).

Dennis Moore, center, with the rest of the gang—Carl Mathews, Tom Tyler, John Cason and Bud Osborne—in Marshall of Heldorado *(Lippert, 1950).*

### Lee Morgan (1902–1967)

Lee Morgan was born June 12, 1902, in Texas. He appeared mainly in outlaw roles in westerns with the majority of his films being for Eagle Lion Studios. He died January 30, 1967, at the age of 64. His western films included: *Return of the Lash,* *Shadow Valley, Stage to Mesa City* (1947), *Black Hills, The Westward Trail* (1948), *The Younger Brothers, Roll Thunder Roll!, Rio Grande* (1949), *Raiders of Tomahawk Creek* (1950).

*Lee Morgan, center, and Tom Tyler, right, entice female outlaw Janis Paige to aid them in their plot against The Younger Brothers in the film of the same name (Warner Bros., 1949).*

### "Black" Jack O'Shea (1906–1967)

"Black" Jack O'Shea was billed throughout his movie and television career as "The Man You Love to Hate." He entered films in the 1930s and was a veteran of over 200 movie and television productions. In addition to his villainous chores, he also did stunt work for Lou Costello and doubled for Leo Carrillo and Orson Welles. He made many personal tours with Bob Steele, Tim Holt, Sunset Carson, and Lash LaRue. The tours featured a fistfight and gunfight, with "Black" Jack losing as usual. He was born Jack Rellaford April 6, 1906, in San Francisco. He operated antique shops in Chatsworth and Paradise, California, during the last years of his life. He died October 1, 1967, in Paradise, California. His western films included: *The Big Show* (1937), *The Tulsa Kid* (1940), *Sons of the Pioneers* (1942), *Wagon Tracks West* (1943), *The San Antonio Kid* (1944), *Rough Riders of Cheyenne* (1945), *The Caravan Trail, Overland Riders* (1946), *King of the Bandits* (1947), *Ride, Ryder, Ride* (1949), *Star of Texas* (1953).

"Black" Jack O'Shea, left, as the killer "Keno" is foiled in his attempt to kill Steve Pendleton, second from left, in Ride, Ryder, Ride *(Eagle Lion, 1944). Holding the gun is Jim Bannon as Red Ryder, Emmett Lynn, and Don Kay Reynolds.*

### William Pawley (1905–1952)

William Pawley rarely played a "good guy" on the screen. In addition to westerns he appeared in many gangster roles. He began his acting career on the stage and appeared in several Broadway productions. He was born in Kansas City, Missouri, in 1905 and died in New York, June 15, 1952.

His western films included: *Robbers Roost* (1933), *Prairie Moon* (1938), *Union Pacific*, *Rough Rider's Roundup* (1939), *West of Abilene*, *The Return of Frank James* (1940).

*William Pawley, left, with Charles Starrett, William A. Kellogg, and Don Beddoe in* West of Abilene *(Columbia, 1940).*

### House Peters, Jr. (1916–    )

House Peters Jr. was born January 12, 1916, in New Rochelle, New York. His father, who died in 1967, was a silent screen star from 1913 until 1928. House Peters Jr. has appeared in many serials, westerns and other type films in many character parts. He has appeared in approximately 200 features and 250 television shows during his 30-year career. Unusual as it may seem, his favorite role is when he is given the opportunity to play a drunk. His western films include: *Public Cowboy No. 1* (1937), *Oklahoma Badlands, Desperadoes of Dodge City, Renegades of Sonora* (1948), *Son of Billy the Kid* (1949), *Border Treasure* (1950), *Spoilers of the Plains* (1951), *The Old West* (1952), *Winning of the West* (1953), *Overland Pacific* (1954).

*House Peters Jr., third from left, as second in command in* Border Treasure *(RKO, 1950). Others are Tom Monroe, Robert Peyton, gangleader John Doucette, and Jane Nigh.*

### George Plues (1895–1953)

Rarely receiving billing George Plues played in films for 35 years. He normally executed the role of one of the countless henchmen in many horse operas. He died August 16, 1953, at the Motion Picture Country Home in Los Angeles. His western films included: *Overland Stage Raiders* (1938), *Ragtime Cowboy Joe, Law and Order* (1940).

*George Plues, center with hat, and George Sherwood are caught by John Wayne and Ray Corrigan in* Overland Stage Raiders *(Republic, 1938).*

**Warner Richmond (1886–1948)**

Warner Richmond was born in Culpeper County, Virginia, January 11, 1886. He attended Virginia Military Institute and the University of Virginia. He had a long and distinguished career as a stage player and entered films in 1922. He played leading parts in many silent films. In 1940 he suffered a bad fall from a horse during a Monogram picture. He never fully recovered and this hampered his film career. He died June 19, 1948, in Los Angeles of a coronary thrombosis. His western films included: *New Frontier, Smokey Smith, The Singing Vagabond* (1935), *Song of the Gringo, Headin' for Rio Grande* (1936), *Riders of the Dawn, Where Trails Divide* (1937), *Six Shootin' Sheriff* (1938), *Wild Horse Canyon* (1939), *Rhythm of the Rio Grande, The Golden Trail, Rainbow Over the Range* (1940), *Outlaw Trail* (1944), *Colorado Serenade* (1946), *Prairie Outlaws* (1948).

*Warner Richmond, right, plotting with Al Bridge in* New Frontier *(Republic, 1935).*

### Walter Sande (1906–    )

Walter Sande hasn't had an opportunity to ply his trade in most of his films. An accomplished musician, his roles usually include just about everything but this. He was born in Denver, Colorado, in 1906, and started studying music at the age of six. At 30 he could play any musical instrument. He toured with a band and later became a musical director for the Fox West Coast theatres. His first film was in 1938 and he has been active since. In westerns he usually divided his time between the law and the lawless. His western films include: *The Singing Sheriff* (1944), *The Daltons Ride Again* (1945), *Canadian Pacific, Rim of the Canyon* (1949), *Dakota Lil* (1950), *Rawhide, Fort Worth* (1951), *The Duel at Silver Creek* (1952), *The Great Sioux Uprising* (1953), *Overland Pacific* (1954), *Wichita* (1955), *The Maverick Queen* (1956), *Oklahoma Territory* (1960).

*Walter Sande, seated right, Milburn Stone and Thomas Gomez, as land grabbers in* The Daltons Ride Again *(Universal, 1945).*

### Ray Spiker (1901–1964)

Ray Spiker was born Ray Faust and was a professional boxer before he entered films in 1929. He became a stuntman and actor specializing in western films. He died in Hollywood February 23, 1964. His western films included: *Nevada* (1944), *San Antonio* (1945), *Shane* (1953), *Thunder Over Arizona* (1956).

Ray Spiker, second from left, as "Rebel White," with Dan White, gangleader Paul Kelly, Charles Stevens and Al Hill in San Antonio (Warners, 1945).

## Milburn Stone (1904–    )

Milburn Stone was born in Burrton, Kansas, July 5, 1904. After graduation from high school he turned down an appointment at the U.S. Naval Academy at Annapolis for an acting career. He followed the usual path of stock and Broadway before entering films, stopping momentarily as a song and dance man in vaudeville. His family moved to California and this gave him an opportunity for a motion picture career. He was a leading man for awhile, starring in several films and in 1939 co-starred in several "Tailspin Tommy" films for Monogram. He played in many westerns and often found himself the scoundrel in Republic and Universal films. His long running characterization of kindly but gruff "Doc Adams" in television's *Gunsmoke* has won a new generation of admirers. His western films include: *The Three Mesquiteers* (1936), *California Frontier* (1938), *Crashing Thru* (1939), *Colorado* (1940), *The Phantom Cowboy* (1941), *Twilight on the Prairie* (1944), *The Daltons Ride Again* (1945), *Michi-*

Milburn Stone, left, being held at gunpoint by one of the Dalton Brothers, Noah Beery Jr. in The Daltons Ride Again (Universal, 1945).

*gan Kid* (1947), *Calamity Jane and Sam Bass* (1949), *Branded* (1951), *The Savage* (1952), *Arrowhead* (1953), *The Siege at Red River* (1954), *White Feather* (1955).

## Hal Taliaferro (1895–    )

Hal Taliaferro was born Floyd T. Alperson in Sheridan, Wyoming, November 13, 1895. He played in countless films as a "heavy" and in other character parts from 1937 until his retirement. He was born on a ranch and his superb horsemanship landed him work in films as an extra in 1915. He was given a chance to star in westerns in the mid 1920s under the name of "Wally Wales" and appeared in many films. He starred for 10 years for various film companies prior to changing his name to Hal Taliaferro for the remainder of his motion picture career. His western films include:

*Galloping On, The Roaring Rider* (1926), *The Soda Water Cowboy, The Meddlin' Stranger* (1927), *Saddle Mates* (1928), *Deadwood Pass, Fighting Texans* (1933), *Fighting Through* (1934), *Powdersmoke Range* (1935), *Hair Trigger Casey* (1936), *Rootin' Tootin' Rhythm* (1937), *Pioneer Trail* (1938), *Saga of Death Valley* (1939), *Hi'Yo Silver* (1940), *Law of the Range* (1941), *Sons of the Pioneers* (1942), *Silver Spurs* (1943), *The Yellow Rose of Texas* (1944), *Utah* (1945), *Plainsman and the Lady* (1946), *Ramrod* (1947), *Red River* (1948), *The Savage Horde* (1950).

*Hal Taliaferro, center, with Monte Blue and Frankie Marvin in* Rootin' Tootin' Rhythm *(Republic, 1937).*

### Ray Teal (1902–    )

Ray Teal was born in Grand Rapids, Michigan, January 12, 1902. He attended Grand Rapids Junior College, the University of Texas, and graduated from the University of California. An accomplished musician he used his skill as a saxophone player to work his way through college and from 1931 until 1936 had his own musical show throughout the south. He entered films in 1938 and has played more than his share of bad guy roles. He became a regular on the popular *Bonanza* television program as "Sheriff Roy Coffey" and has gained his greatest recognition on this show. His western films include: *Western Jamboree* (1938), *Cherokee Strip* (1940), *Outlaws of the Panhandle, Wild Bill Hickok Rides* (1941), *Apache Trail* (1942), *Michigan Kid* (1947), *Whispering Smith* (1949), *The Kid from Texas* (1950), *The Redhead and the Cowboy* (1951), *Hangman's Knot* (1952), *Apache Ambush* (1955), *The Burning Hills* (1956), *Posse from Hell* (1961), *Cattle King* (1963).

### Frank M. Thomas (1889–    )

Frank M. Thomas was born in St. Joseph, Missouri, in 1889. He played in stock in his home town and later toured the country before ending up on Broadway. He entered films in 1934 and in the late 1930s and 1940s was one of the most steadily employed actors in Hollywood. His son, Frankie Thomas, played juvenile leads in many films including parts in "The Dead End Kids" films. His western films include: *The Last Outlaw* (1936), *Outcasts of Poker Flat* (1937), *Saga of Death Valley* (1939), *Brigham Young* (1940), *Wyoming Wildcat* (1941), *Apache Trail, Sunset on the Desert, Sunset Serenade* (1942).

*Ray Teal.*

*Frank M. Thomas and Jack Ingram in* Saga of Death Valley
*(Republic, 1939).*

### Guy Usher (1883–1944)

Guy Usher was in films for only 11 years, but during this time made many films. He made his screen debut in 1933 and played many fatherly roles in feature films. He also portrayed policemen, attorneys, district attorneys and similar parts. In western films he was often cast as a businessman, both honest and otherwise. He was a railroad engineer and started his acting career in stock in Denver, Colorado. He was born May 9, 1883, in Mason City, Iowa, and died at his ranch near San Diego, California, June 16, 1944. His western films included: *Law Beyond the Range, Justice of the Range* (1935), *Boots and Saddles, The Old Wyoming Trail* (1937), *Under Western Stars* (1938), *Rough Riders' Roundup, Rovin' Tumbleweeds* (1939), *Ridin' on a Rainbow, The Bandit Trail* (1941), *Bad Men of the Hills* (1942), *Lost Canyon* (1943).

*Guy Usher, center, seeks protection from Dick Curtis as George Chesebro looks on in* The Old Wyoming Trail *(Columbia, 1937).*

### Lee van Cleef (1925– )

Lee van Cleef was born in Somerville, New Jersey, January 9, 1925. After graduation from high school he joined the Navy where he served on subchasers and minesweepers. After a brief accounting career he became a film actor. His menacing features were ideally suited for the part of the paid killer or hired gunman, a role he has played in countless films and television shows. After years in "B" westerns he received second billing in *For a Few Dollars More* in 1967. This led to leading roles in several Italian-Spanish films, and now he has earned star billing. Van Cleef states that his favorite role is the one he is playing at the moment and that he is always trying to find something new to add to the part he is playing. His western films include: *High Noon* (1952), *The Nebraskan* (1953), *Rails into Laramie* (1954), *Ten Wanted Men* (1955), *Tribute to a Badman* (1956), *Gunfight at the O.K. Corral* (1957), *Day of the Badman* (1958), *Ride Lonesome* (1959), *Posse from*

*Lee Van Cleef with Dan Duryea in* Rails into Laramie *(Universal, 1954).*

*Hell* (1961), *The Man Who Shot Liberty Valance* (1962), *For a Few Dollars More* (1967), *The Big Gundown* (1968), *Death Rides a Horse* (1969), *El Condor* (1970).

*Wally West, left, is disarmed by Bob Steele as Ray Henderson and Al St. John look on in* Billy the Kid's Fighting Pals *(PRC, 1941).*

### Wally West ( – )

Wally West has been a stuntman for over 35 years participating in bar room brawls, driving the runaway stage, being shot from his horse, and doubling for many of the top stars. He was born Theo Wynn in Texas and learned trick riding while working on a ranch in his home state. He first entered films in 1926, left for awhile, and returned for good in 1931. Unlike many of his fellow stuntmen Wally even starred in a western.

This was Denver Dixon's 1936 film *Desert Mesa*. He has played many character and heavy parts since. His western films include: *Desert Trail* (1935), *Roamin' Wild, Outlaws of the Range, Ambush Valley, Desert Mesa* (1936), *Fighting Texan, The Trusted Outlaw* (1937), *Westbound Stage, Straight Shooter* (1940), *Billy the Kid's Fighting Pals* (1941), *Death Valley Rangers* (1943).

### Charles "Slim" Whitaker (1893–1960)

Movie fans of the twenties, thirties, and forties will remember that Charles (Slim) Whitaker played in hundreds of westerns and fit the pattern of the no good, yellow-bellied polecat in most of his films. He was typical of the henchman, but occasionally rose above these heights to the big boss of the villainy. He was born Charles Orbie Whitaker in Missouri on July 29, 1893, and died in Los Angeles June 27, 1960. The last year of his life was spent as a cook in a Los Angeles cafe. His western films included: *The Soda Water Cowboy, Roaring Broncs, The Obligin' Buckaroo* (1927), *Saddle Buster* (1932), *War of the Range* (1933), *Terror of the Plains* (1934), *Tumbling Tumbleweeds* (1935), *Roamin' Wild* (1936), *Law of the Ranger* (1937), *Phantom Gold* (1938), *New Frontier* (1939), *Bullet Code* (1940), *Hands Across the Rockies* (1941), *The Silver Bullet* (1942), *The Mysterious Rider* (1943), *The Laramie Trail* (1944), *Overland Raiders* (1946), *The Westward Trail* (1948).

*Charles (Slim) Whitaker, left, and Harry Woods are up to their usual bad deeds in* In Early Arizona *(Columbia, 1938).*

### Frank Wilcox (1907– )

Frank Wilcox was born March 13, 1907, in De Soto, Missouri. His father was a physician and he also intended to become one, but decided upon an acting career instead. He began his career as an actor-director in the Kansas City Civic Center after graduating from the University of Kansas.

He traveled to California with intentions of becoming a salesman, but organized the Pomona Theatre Guild in 1937. The next stop was the Pasadena Playhouse and it was there that a talent scout noticed his resemblance to Henry Clay. He was cast in a short entitled "The Monroe Doc-

trine" in 1939. The six-foot three-inch actor has remained in films ever since with the exception of a stint in the U.S. Navy during World War II. His western films include: *Virginia City* (1940), *Wild Bill Hickok Rides* (1941), *The Mysterious Desperado, Masked Raiders* (1949), *The Kid from Texas* (1950), *The Half-Breed* (1951), *The Treasure of Lost Canyon* (1952), *The Black Dakotas* (1954), *Seventh Cavalry* (1956), *Man from God's Country* (1958).

*Frank Wilcox, center, as a scheming land agent with sheriff Kenneth MacDonald and Tim Holt in* The Mysterious Desperado *(RKO, 1949).*

*Robert Wilke, left, with Robert Clarke, in* Pistol Harvest *(RKO, 1951).*

### Robert Wilke ( – )

Robert Wilke got his start in 1935 as a stuntman. He was virtually unnoticed until 1944 when he started playing in "B" westerns. Nearly always a badman, he emerges as one of the finest with a toothy chuckle similar to Richard Widmark. He has now advanced to feature roles in major productions and makes many television appearances. He was born in Cincinnati and prior to entering films was a lifeguard at a Miami hotel. His western films include: *The San Antonio Kid* (1944), *Sheriff of Cimarron* (1945), *Out California Way* (1946), *Law of the Canyon* (1947), *West of Sonora* (1948), *Laramie* (1949), *Outcast of Black Mesa* (1950), *Pistol Harvest* (1951), *High Noon* (1952), *Powder River* (1953), *Two Guns and a Badge* (1954), *Smoke Signal* (1955), *The Lone Ranger* (1956), *Night Passage* (1957), *Man of the West* (1958), *The Long Rope* (1961), *The Gun Hawk* (1963), *The Hallelujah Trail* (1965), *A Gunfight* (1971).

### Roger Williams (1895– )

One of the busiest bandits of the screen in the mid-thirties was Roger Williams. In 1935 alone he appeared in over 35 western films. He was born in Berlin, Germany, in 1895. In 1913 he attended the Denver School of Mines. He entered the Army during World War I and was decorated three times while serving in battle. He was a direct descendent of General "Mad Anthony" Wayne, famous Revolutionary War hero. He entered films with the Selig Polyscope Company and in addition to his acting career was a technical advisor and production supervisor. His western films include: *Trouble Busters* (1933), *Rustler's Paradise, Wagon Trail, The Pecos Kid, Cheyenne Kincaid* (1935), *Frontier Justice, The Cattle Thief, The Riding Avenger* (1936), *Aces Wild, Come on Cowboys!, Riders of the Whistling Skull* (1937), *Code of the Rangers, Call the Mesquiteers* (1938), *Mountain Rhythm* (1939).

*Roger Williams in black hat, in* The Pecos Kid *(Coe, 1935). Others visible from left to right are Hal Taliaferro, Jack Evans, Fred Kohler Jr., Francis Walker, Ed Cassidy, Rose Plummer, Clyde McClary, Robert Walker, and Budd Buster.*

### Norman Willis (1903– )

Born in Chicago in 1903, Norman Willis entered films in 1935. His perpetual sneer made him ideally suited for villainous parts in both westerns and serials. Although sometimes relegated to henchman roles, he normally assumed the duties of the head man behind the cattle rustling, gambling enterprises, or theft of the gold shipment. His western films include: *Secret Valley* (1936), *Outlaws of the Prairie* (1938), *Legion of the Lawless, The Bad Man from Red Butte* (1940), *Beyond the Sacramento, Outlaws of the Panhandle, Twilight on the Trail* (1941), *Down Rio Grande Way, Overland to Deadwood* (1942), *The Avenging Rider, King of the Cowboys* (1943), *Heading West* (1946), *Bandits of Dark Canyon* (1947).

*Norman Willis, left, as "Faro Jack Vaughn" with Frances Robinson and Jack Low in* Outlaws of the Panhandle *(Columbia, 1941).*

## Grant Withers (1904–1959)

Grant Withers was born January 17, 1904, in Pueblo, Colorado. He attended Kemper Military School in Boonville, Missouri. He traveled to Los Angeles where he was a salesman for an oil company. He then became a reporter and his first assignment was covering the funeral of the silent matinee idol, Wallace Reid. He started his movie career as an extra in a Douglas McLean film and then became a leading man in the 1930s. He later became a villain and character actor in many films including westerns. He married Loretta Young when she was only 17 as they eloped to Yuma, Arizona. She was the second of his five marriages. He took his own life by an overdose of sleeping pills March 27, 1959. His western films included: *Apache Trail* (1942), *In Old Oklahoma* (1943), *The Yellow Rose of Texas* (1944), *Utah* (1945), *In Old Sacramento* (1946), *Wyoming* (1947), *Fort Apache* (1948), *Rio Grande* (1950), *Spoilers of the Plains* (1951), *Captive of Billy the Kid* (1952), *Iron Mountain Trail* (1953), *The White Squaw* (1956), *Last Stagecoach West* (1957).

*Grant Withers gets a gun from the safe as he is cautiously watched by Roy Barcroft in* Last Stagecoach West *(Republic, 1957).*

## Harry Woods (1889–1968)

Harry Lewis Woods certainly looked the part of the "big boss," a role he played so often in countless westerns. A diversified actor he also played in many feature productions, but was still normally cast as a "heavy." Casting aside his military business in 1921 he broke into films in the Ruth Roland serials. He also appeared in several of the top silent features of the day. After a 40-year career he retired in 1961 due to illness. He died December 28, 1968, in Hollywood of uremia. His western films included: *Cyclone of the Range* (1927), *Desert Rider* (1929), *Law and Order* (1932), *Haunted Gold* (1933), *Lone Rider* (1934), *Heroes of the Range* (1936), *Range Defenders* (1937), *Hawaiian Buckaroo* (1938), *In Old California* (1939), *Bullet Code* (1940), *Sheriff of Tombstone* (1941), *Down Texas Way* (1942), *The Ghost Rider* (1943), *Silver City Kid* (1944), *West of the Pecos* (1945), *Sunset Pass* (1946), *Wyoming* (1947), *Indian Agent* (1948), *Colorado Territory* (1949), *Short Grass* (1950), *Law of the Badlands* (1951), *Lone Star* (1952).

*Menacing Harry Woods, left, waits for his prey in scene from* Silver City Kid *(Republic, 1944). With him are Peggy Stewart and Glenn Strange.*

### Clifton Young (1917–1951)

Clifton Young received his introduction to show business early in life as he appeared in vaudeville at the age of five with his parents. At the age of seven he played a juvenile villain in the "Our Gang" screen comedies. A few years later he entered radio and after World War II returned to the screen mostly as a western villain. On September 10, 1951, he apparently fell asleep while smoking and died of asphyxiation at the age of 34. His western films included: *Blood on the Moon* (1948), *Calamity Jane and Sam Bass* (1949), *Trail of Robin Hood, Bells of Coronado, Salt Lake Raiders* (1950).

*Clifton Young, left, and Roy Barcroft, right, have Allan (Rocky) Lane, right where they want him in* Salt Lake Raiders *(Republic, 1950).*

*Holly Bane: Bane, center, being securely tied by Tim Holt and Richard (Chito) Martin in* Storm Over Wyoming *(RKO Radio, 1950). His western films include:* Hoppy's Holiday *(1947),* Carson City Raiders, Overland Trails *(1948),* Brand of Fear *(1949),* Storm Over Wyoming *(1950),* Montana Belle *(1952),* Bitter Creek *(1954),* Rage at Dawn *(1955),* Frontier Gun *(1958).*

*Dick Botiller: Botiller, second from left, with Al Bridge, Charles Starrett, Forrest H. Dillon, and Clem Horten in* The Man from Sundown *(Columbia, 1939). His western films included:* Wild Mustang, Outlaw Deputy *(1935),* Treachery Rides the Range, West of Nevada *(1936),* The Californians *(1937),* California Trail *(1938),* West of Santa Fe, The Man from Sundown *(1939),* The Pinto Kid, Wild Bill Hickok Rides *(1941),* Bad Men of the Hills *(1942),* The Vigilantes Ride *(1944).*

Lane Bradford: Bradford, center, watches Whip Wilson square off at Leonard Penn in Wanted: Dead or Alive (Monogram, 1951). His western films include: Overland Raiders (1946), Prairie Raiders, Riders of the Lone Star (1947), Frontier Agent, The Hawk of Powder River (1948), Roll Thunder Roll! (1949), The Old Frontier, Frisco Tornado (1950), Wanted: Dead or Alive, Lawless Cowboys (1951), Texas City, Rose of Cimmaron (1952), Savage Frontier (1953), Ride Clear of Diablo, Drums Across the River (1954), Showdown at Abilene (1956), The Phantom Stagecoach (1957), Toughest Gun in Tombstone (1958).

Henry Brandon: Brandon, left, with Jacqueline Wells, Charles Baldra and Roy Rogers in The Ranger and the Lady (Republic, 1940). His western films include: Marshal of Mesa City, The Ranger and the Lady, Under Texas Skies (1940), Bad Man of Deadwood (1941), Old Los Angeles (1948), War Arrow, Pony Express (1953), Vera Cruz (1954), Comanche (1956), Two Rode Together (1961).

*Steve Brodie: (1919–   ): Brodie is restrained by Stanley Andrews and Tim Holt in* Brothers of the Saddle *(RKO Radio, 1949). Emmett Vogan is seated at the left. His western films include:* Badman's Territory, Sunset Pass *(1946),* Trail Street, Code of the West *(1947),* The Arizona Ranger, Return of the Badmen *(1948),* Massacre River, Brothers of the Saddle *(1949),* Winchester '73 *(1950),* Only the Valiant *(1951),* The Charge at Feather River *(1953),* The Far Country *(1955).*

*Stephen Chase: Chase, right, with Keith Richards and Roy Rogers in* North of the Great Divide *(Republic, 1950). His western films include:* Cowboy Millionaire *(1935),* Rogue of the Range *(1936),* Under Western Stars *(1938),* Gun Code *(1940),* The Lone Rider in Ghost Town *(1941),* The Daring Caballero *(1949),* Frisco Tornado, North of the Great Divide *(1950),* Cavalry Scout *(1951),* Old Oklahoma Plains, The Lawless Breed *(1952),* The Great Sioux Uprising *(1953).*

*Steve Clemente (1885–1950): Clemente, left, with Richard Alexander and Dewey Robinson in* Law and Order *(Universal, 1932). His western films included:* Law and Order *(1932),* King of the Arena *(1933),* The Hills of Old Wyoming, It Happened Out West *(1937).*

*Harry Cording (1891–1954): Cording, center, with Robert Bice, Judy Nugent, and Virginia Huston, in* Night Stage to Galveston *(Columbia, 1952). His western films included:* Texas Cyclone *(1932),* Fighting for Justice *(1933),* Painted Desert *(1938),* Texas Stagecoach, Stage to Chino, Law and Order *(1940),* Riders of the Badlands *(1941),* Fugitive from Sonora *(1943),* San Antonio *(1945),* The Marauders *(1947),* Bad Men of Tombstone *(1949),* Al Jennings of Oklahoma *(1951),* Night Stage to Galveston *(1952).*

*Jim Corey: Corey, left, has the upper hand on sheriff Roy Rogers in* Robin Hood of the Pecos *(Republic, 1941). His western films include:* Cheyenne's Pal *(1917),* The Phantom Riders *(1918),* The Last Outlaw *(1927),* Terror Trail *(1933),* The Last Round Up *(1934),* Guns and Guitars *(1936),* Guns in the Dark *(1937),* Gold Mine in the Sky *(1938),* Silver on the Sage, Rough Riders Round-Up *(1939),* Prairie Stranger, Robin Hood of the Pecos *(1941),* Down Rio Grande Way *(1942).*

*Ted Decorsia (1905–    ): His western films include:* The
Outriders *(1950),* Vengeance Valley, New Mexico *(1951),*
The Savage *(1952),* Ride Vaquero *(1953),* Man with the
Gun *(1955),* Mohawk, Showdown at Abilene *(1956),* Okla-
homa Territory, Noose for a Gunman *(1960),* The Quick
Gun, Blood on the Arrow *(1965),* Five Card Stud *(1968).*

*John Doucette: Doucette, second from right, with Richard (Chito) Martin, Kenneth MacDonald, and Tim Holt in* Border Treasure *(RKO Radio, 1950). His western films include:* Canon City, Station West *(1948),* Broken Arrow, Border Treasure *(1950),* Cavalry Scout *(1951),* The Treasure of Lost Canyon *(1952),* Goldtown Ghost Riders *(1953),* The Forty-Niners *(1954),* Ghost Town *(1955),* Frontier Scout *(1956),* The Lawless Eighties, Gunfire at Indian Gap *(1957),* The Sons of Katie Elder *(1965),* Nevada Smith *(1966),* Journey to Shiloh *(1968),* True Grit *(1969),* Big Jake *(1971).*

*Curley Dresden: Dresden, center, with Cliff Parkinson and Olin Francis in* Rough Ridin' Rhythm *(Ambassador-Conn, 1937). His western films include:* Rough Ridin' Rhythm *(1937),* Gun Packer, Pals of the Saddle *(1938),* Ghost Valley Raiders, Under Texas Skies *(1940),* Billy the Kid's Fighting Pals *(1941),* Carson City Cyclone, Wagon Tracks West *(1943),* Law of the Saddle, Westward Bound *(1944).*

*George Eldredge: Eldredge, right, with Bob Steele in* Trigger Law *(Monogram, 1944). His western films include:* The Lone Star Trail *(1943)*, Sonora Stagecoach, Outlaw Trail, Trigger Trail, Song of the Range, The Old Texas Trail *(1944)*, Rustlers of the Badlands, Frontier Gal *(1945)*, Sierra Passage *(1951)*, California Conquest, The Duel at Silver Creek *(1952)*, The Man from the Alamo *(1953)*, Overland Pacific *(1954)*.

*Robert Fiske (1889–1944): Fiske, left, with Arthur Loft, Julie Duncan, Don (Red) Barry, and Al St. John in* Texas Terrors *(Republic, 1940). His western films included:* Drums of Destiny *(1937)*, The Purple Vigilantes, Cassidy of Bar 20, Colorado Trail *(1938)*, West of Santa Fe, Racketeers of the Range *(1939)*, Texas Terrors, Law and Order *(1940)*, Along the Rio Grande, The Apache Kid *(1941)*, Cyclone Prairie Rangers *(1944)*.

*Herman Hack (1899–1967): Hack, second from left, with Walt LaRue, Victor Cox, Gene Autry, Steve Darrell, Kenny Cooper and Jock Mahoney in* Cow Town *(Columbia, 1950). His western films included:* Western Caravans *(1939),* The Lady Takes a Chance, The Kansan *(1943),* Two-Fisted Stranger *(1946),* The Valiant Hombre *(1948),* Over the Border, Cow Town *(1950),* The Redhead from Wyoming *(1952).*

*Chick Hannon: Hannon, second from left, with Bob Wilke, Weldon Heyburn, Neal Hart and Jack Kirk in* Bordertown Trail *(Republic, 1944). His western films included:* The Trusted Outlaw *(1937),* Robin Hood of the Pecos *(1941),* Bordertown Trail, Land of the Outlaws *(1944),* Six Gun Serenade, Code of the Saddle *(1947),* Vigilante Hideout *(1950).*

*Al Haskell (     –1969): Haskell, second from right, back row, with an impressive lineup of western players, reading left to right, Foxy Callahan, Jim Massey, Marshall Reed, Bill Elliott, Rose Plummer, Bill Wolfe, Gabby Hayes, Jim Mitchell, Harry Woods, Buck Bucko, Neal Hart and Frosty Royce. The film is* Bordertown Gunfighters *(Republic, (1943). His western films included:* The Man from Sundown, Mexicali Rose, Rough Riders Round Up *(1939),* Texas Terrors *(1940),* In Old California *(1942),* Bordertown Gunfighters *(1943),* Roaring Westward *(1949),* Man in the Saddle *(1951),* Vigilante Terror *(1953).*

*John James (     –1960): James, center, with George Baxter and Marion Colby in* Son of Billy the Kid *(Screen Guild, 1949). His western films included:* Westward Ho, The Sombrero Kid *(1942),* The Laramie Trail, Hidden Valley Outlaws, Bordertown Trail *(1944),* Great Stagecoach Robbery *(1945),* The Wild Frontier, Ridin' Down the Trail *(1947),* The Valiant Hombre, Range Renegades *(1948),* Son of Billy the Kid *(1949),* Topeka *(1953).*

*Ray Jones: Jones, second from right, with I. Stanford Jolley, Raymond Hatton, Fuzzy Knight and Jimmy Ellison in* Fast on the Draw *(Lippert, 1950). His western films include:* Prairie Gunsmoke *("1942)*, Wagon Tracks West *(1943)*, Trigger Trail *(1944)*, Under Western Skies *(1945)*, Code of the Saddle *(1947)*, The Fighting Redhead, Riders of the Dusk, Gun Law Justice *(1949)*, Hostile Country, Fast on the Draw *(1950)*.

*Fred Kohler Jr.: Kohler is about to be surprised by Charles Starrett in* Texas Stampede *(Columbia, 1939). His western films include:* Toll of the Desert *(1935)*, Texas Stampede *(1939)*, Two-Gun Sheriff, Nevada City *(1941)*, The Lone Star Ranger, The Boss of Hangtown Mesa *(1942)*, Calling Wild Bill Elliott *(1943)*, The Big Bonanza *(1945)*, Loaded Pistols *(1949)*, Twilight in the Sierras *(1950)*, Spoilers of the Plains *(1951)*.

*Jack Lambert: Lambert as "Ringo" with his boss, George Brent in* Montana Belle *(RKO Radio, 1952). His western films include:* Abilene Town *(1945)*, The Vigilantes Return *(1947)*, Belle Starr's Daughter *(1948)*, Brimstone *(1949)*, Dakota Lil, West of the Great Divide *(1950)*, Bend of the River, Montana Belle *(1952)*, Vera Cruz *(1954)*, At Gunpoint *(1955)*, Canyon River *(1956)*, Day of the Outlaw *(1959)*, Four for Texas *(1963)*.

*George J. Lewis (1904–     ): Lewis, right, with Linda Sterling, Jay Kirby and Bill Elliott in* Wagon Wheels Westward *(Republic, 1945). His western films include:* Outlaws of the Desert *(1941),* The Black Hills Express *(1943),* The Laramie Trail *(1944),* Wagon Wheels Westward *(1945),* Under Nevada Skies *(1946),* Twilight on the Rio Grande *(1947),* Silver Trails *(1948),* Bandits of El Dorado *(1949),* Colorado Ranger *(1950),* Al Jennings of Oklahoma *(1951),* Wagon Train *(1952),* Cow Country *(1953),* Border River *(1954),* The Sign of Zorro *(1960),* The Comancheros *(1961).*

*Carl Mathews (1900–1959): Mathews, second from left, with Frank McCarroll, Bud Osborne, Gail Davis and Steve Clark in* West of Wyoming *(Monogram, 1950). His western films included:* Melody of the Plains *(1937),* Rangers Roundup, Frontier Scout *(1938),* Six-Gun Rhythm, Code of the Fearless *(1939),* Wild Horse Range, The Kid from Santa Fe *(1940),* Fugitive Valley *(1941),* Rock River Renegades *(1942),* The Rangers Take Over *(1943),* Song of the Range *(1944),* Law of the Lash, Shadow Valley *(1947),* Range Renegades *(1948),* West of Wyoming *(1950).*

*Art Mix: Mix, right, as "Santos," hired killer, with Dick Curtis and Kenneth MacDonald in* Spoilers of the Range *(Columbia, 1939). His western films include:* The Bronc Stumper *(1928),* King of the Wild Horses *(1933),* Powdersmoke Range *(1935),* Swifty *(1936),* Two-Fisted Sheriff *(1937),* Outlaws of the Prairie, West of Cheyenne, Call of the Rockies *(1938),* Spoilers of the Range *(1939),* The Westerner *(1940),* Hands Across the Rockies *(1941),* Prairie Gunsmoke *(1952),* Riding Through Nevada *(1943).*

*Chuck Morrison: Morrison, left, as "Bart" and George Lloyd as "Matt" taunt Luana Walters in* The Return of Wild Bill *(Columbia, 1940). His western films include:* Wagon Trail, Fighting Pioneers, Rustler's Paradise, Saddle Aces, Wild Mustang *(1935),* Aces Wild *(1937),* The Return of Wild Bill, Rainbow over the Range *(1940),* North from the Lone Star *(1941),* Code of the Outlaw *(1942).*

*Zon Murray: Murray, right, with Jimmy Wakely in* Gun Law Justice *(Monogram, 1949). His western films include:* Terror Trail, The El Paso Kid, Ghost of Hidden Valley *(1946),* West of Dodge City, Law of the Canyon *(1947),* Crossed Trails, Blood on the Moon *(1948),* Gun Law Justice *(1949),* Dallas, Outlaws of Texas, The Kid from Texas *(1950),* Night Riders of Montana, The Longhorn *(1951),* Cripple Creek *(1952),* Down Laredo Way *(1953),* Bitter Creek *(1954),* The Lone Ranger *(1956).*

*Ted (Squint) Palmer: Palmer, left, with Charles (Slim) Whitaker and Hal Taliaferro in* Pioneer Trail *(Columbia, 1938). His western films include:* Westward Ho *(1935),* Pioneer Trail *(1938),* Colorado *(1940),* Rock River Renegades, Westward Ho *(1942),* Wild Horse Stampede *(1943),* The Hawk of Powder River *(1948).*

*Cliff Parkinson (1898–1950): Parkinson, right, prepares to disarm Kermit Maynard as Olin Francis guards him in* Rough Ridin' Rhythm *(Ambassador-Conn, 1937). His western films included:* Rough Ridin' Rhythm *(1937),* Rawhide *(1938),* Border Patrol, Calling Wild Bill Elliott, The Kansan, Riders of the Deadline *(1943),* The San Antonio Kid, Bordertown Trail *(1944),* Bad Men of the Border *(1945),* Ramrod *(1947).*

*Leonard Penn: Penn with Christine McIntyre in* Wanted: Dead or Alive *(Monogram, 1951). His western films include:* Girl of the Golden West *(1937),* Hoppy's Holiday, Outlaw Brand *(1947),* Six Gun Mesa, Silver Raiders, Gunfire *(1950),* Wanted: Dead or Alive, Law of the Badlands *(1951),* Outlaw Woman *(1952).*

*Hugh Prosser (1906–1952): Prosser, left, with Johnny Mack Brown and Milburn Morante in* Outlaw Gold *(Monogram, 1950). His western films included:* Hands Across the Rockies, West of Cimarron *(1941),* The Boss of Hangtown Mesa *(1942),* Lost Canyon *(1943),* Riders of the Deadline, Range Law, Land of the Outlaws *(1944),* Prairie Raiders *(1947),* Outlaw Gold *(1950),* Canyon Ambush *(1952).*

*Hugh Sanders (1911–1966): Hugh Sanders with Rosemarie Bowe in* The Peacemaker *(United Artists, 1956). His western films included:* Only the Valiant, Along the Great Divide, Sugarfoot *(1951),* Indian Uprising, Montana Territory, Last of the Comanches *(1952),* Thunder over the Plains, City of Bad Men *(1953),* Silver Lode *(1954),* The Last Command, Top Gun *(1955),* The Peacemaker *(1956),* The Phantom Stagecoach *(1957).*

*Jack Rutherford: Rutherford, right, with Al Bridge and Frank Ellis in* The Cowboy Counsellor *(Allied Pictures, 1933). His western films include:* The Cowboy Counsellor *(1933),* Justice of the Range *(1935),* Three on the Trail, The Oregon Trail, Heart of the West *(1936),* North of Rio Grande, Hopalong Rides Again *(1937),* Trailing Double Trouble *(1940),* Rolling Home to Texas *(1941),* Utah *(1945),* Untamed Fury *(1947).*

*Carl Sepulveda: Sepulveda, second from left, watches Dick Curtis backhand Charles Starrett in* Spoilers of the Range *(Columbia, 1939). Art Mix holds his gun on Hank Bell. His western films include:* Fangs of Destiny *(1927)*, Four-Footed Ranger *(1928)*, Spoilers of the Range *(1939)*, Bordertown Gun Fighters, Black Market Rustlers *(1943)*, Stagecoach to Monterey *(1944)*, Rustlers of the Badlands *(1945)*, Rainbow over the Rockies *(1946)*, Song of the Sierras *(1947)*, Best of the Badmen *(1951)*.

*Tex Terry: Terry, right, with Tom London, Peggy Stewart and Russ Whiteman in* Alias Billy the Kid *(Republic, 1946). His western films include:* Rough Riders of Cheyenne *(1945)*, The El Paso Kid, Alias Billy the Kid, Rio Grande Raiders *(1946)*, Apache Rose, Twilight on the Rio Grande *(1947)*, The Gallant Legion *(1948)*.

*Francis Walker:* Walker, left, seems to have the best of Charles Starrett *in* Bullets for Rustlers *(Columbia, 1940). His western films include:* Vanishing Riders *(1935),* The Riding Avenger *(1936),* Galloping Dynamite *(1937),* Bullets for Rustlers, Texas Stagecoach, The Man from Tumbleweeds *(1940),* The Pinto Kid, The Return of Daniel Boone *(1941),* Riders of the Northland, Overland to Deadwood *(1942).*

*John P. (Blackie) Whiteford (1889–1962):* Whiteford, left, with Guy Usher, Ray Jones, and Dick Curtis *in* The Old Wyoming Trail *(Columbia, 1937). His western films included:* Man from New Mexico, Mark of the Spur *(1932),* Deadwood Pass *(1933),* West of the Divide *(1934),* Toll of the Desert *(1935),* The Last of the Warrens *(1936),* The Old Wyoming Trail *(1937),* Union Pacific *(1939),* Riding West *(1944),* Tough and Ready *(1945),* Santa Fe *(1951).*

*Harry Worth: Worth, right, with Charles King, Jimmy Dodd, Roy Barcroft, Tom Tyler, "Black" Jack O'Shea, Bob Steele and Jack Ingram in* Riders of the Rio Grande *(Republic, 1943). His western films include:* Bar 20 Rides Again *(1935)*, Lightning Bill Carson, The Cowboy and the Kid *(1936)*, Hopalong Rides Again *(1937)*, The Leano Kid *(1940)*, Kansas Cyclone, Cyclone on Horseback *(1942)*, Riders of the Rio Grande *(1943)*.

*Carleton Young: Young, in* Gene Autry and the Mounties *(Columbia, 1950). His western films include:* Git Along Little Dogies *(1937)*, Cassidy of Bar 20 *(1938)*, El Diablo Rides *(1939)*, Pals of the Silver Sage *(1940)*, Badlands of Dakota *(1941)*, Code of the Outlaw *(1942)*, Gene Autry and the Mounties *(1950)*, Best of the Bad Men *(1951)*, Last of the Comanches *(1952)*, Goldtown Ghost Riders *(1953)*, Bitter Creek *(1954)*.

# 4. Indians

**Monte Blue (1890–1963)**

Monte Blue was a part Cherokee Indian who started his screen career as a silent star and played many character parts during the sound era. He was born in Indianapolis, January 11, 1890, grew up in an orphan's home, and held a variety of jobs prior to becoming a script clerk and stuntman for D. W. Griffith in 1915. He appeared in such screen classics as *Intolerance, The Birth of a Nation* and *Orphans of the Storm.* In westerns the affable Blue played every conceivable part from a renegade Indian to the gentle sheriff. Many of Blue's parts were in Warner Brothers films and in later years Jack L. Warner personally made sure he appeared in character roles. He died in a Milwaukee hospital of a heart attack February 18, 1963, while working as an advance agent for the Hamid-Morton Circus. His western films included: *The Squaw Man* (1918), *The Black Diamond Express* (1927), *Thundering Herd, Wagon Wheels* (1934), *Wanderer of the Wasteland* (1935), *Desert Gold* (1936), *Thunder Trail* (1937), *Born to the West* (1938), *Geronimo* (1939), *Young Bill Hickok* (1940), *Texas Rangers* (1941), *San Antonio* (1945), *Cheyenne* (1947), *Silver River* (1948), *South of St. Louis* (1949), *Montana* (1950), *Warpath* (1951), *Hangman's Knot* (1952), *Apache* (1954).

*Monte Blue in* Thundering Herd *(Paramount, 1934).*

*Monte Blue with Gail Patrick in* Wagon Wheels *(Paramount, 1934).*

### Iron Eyes Cody ( – )

Iron Eyes Cody, Cherokee Indian, was born in Oklahoma. He learned to ride at an early age and he accompanied his father, Thomas Long Plume, who toured the country with the wild west show. He became expert at Indian lore and sign language. When he was 16, Cody left home, traveled throughout the world, and appeared with the Miller Brothers 101 Wild West Show and the Al G. Barnes Circus. In 1921 he arrived in Hollywood, armed with a letter of introduction to a film director at Paramount Studio. He was given a small part in a picture, and this led to a great deal of work in other silent pictures. He traveled with rodeos between films, including the Buck Jones Wild West Show. He was the star dancer with the show in 1934 and 1935, and toured Australia for the Sydney Royal Agriculture Show. During the Melbourne Centenary in September, 1934, he demonstrated his Indian dancing before the King and Queen of England. After his return to America he returned to films but his old friend, Colonel Tim McCoy, persuaded him to tour with the Ringling Brothers Circus for a year in 1937. During his career he has appeared in countless numbers of westerns, both "A" and "B" pictures. From 1948 to 1950 he appeared on the Tim McCoy TV show, then had his own show for one year, 1951–52. In recent years, he has become a

*Iron Eyes Cody.*

*Iron Eyes Cody as "Long Knife" in* Cherokee Uprising *(Monogram, 1950).*

Angeles. Both boys are champion Indian ropers, both are life scouts, and Robert is blood brother in The Order of the Arrow. Iron Eyes Cody's one hobby is photography, but he also is an avid collector of any rare Indian object, book or painting. He has written many articles for newspapers and magazines. His life in many ways belies the image of American Indians who are a misunderstood minority in American life. His western films include: *King of the Stallions* (1942), *The Paleface, Indian Agent* (1948), *Sand, Massacre River* (1949), *Broken Arrow, Cherokee Uprising* (1950), *Fort Defiance, Son of Paleface* (1951), *Fort Osage, Night Raiders* (1952), *Sitting Bull* (1954), *Westward Ho the Wagons!* (1956), *The Great Sioux Massacre* (1965), *A Man Called Horse* (1970).

star on TV commercials. He has appeared in advertisements for many sponsors. He has also appeared on television in *Here's Lucy, Then Came Bronson,* and *A Woman for Charley.* He has appeared in many Walt Disney productions for TV. He is married to the daughter of the famous Indian anthropologist, Dr. Arthur C. Parker of New York. Mrs. Cody for many years was affiliated with the Southwest Museum of Los Angeles doing archaeological and ethnological research. She has written many articles on California Indians and other tribes. Cody's latest pictures are *A Man Called Horse* and *El Condor.* Active in civic affairs in Los Angeles, Cody has two sons; Robert, or Iron Eyes Jr., is 18 years old, six feet ten-inches, a basketball star, and is attending Bacone College in Bacone, Oklahoma; Arthur, or Little Eagle, is 16 years old and is a junior at Marshall High School in Los

*Iron Eyes Cody, center, with Whip Wilson and Steve Clark in* Night Raiders *(Monogram, 1952).*

## Biographical Section

### Chief John Big Tree (1875–1967)

Chief John Big Tree was a six-foot two-inch Seneca Indian who started his film career in 1915. He played minor roles in more than 100 films in his career. He was born Isaac Johnny John and has been assured of a certain amount of everlasting fame as he posed for the 1912 Indian Head nickel. In his films he had an air of nobility about him and normally played the Indian chief. He died

July 5, 1967, at the age of 92 on the Onandaga, New York, Indian Reservation. His western films included: *The Frontiersman* (1927), *Sioux Blood* (1929), *Last of the Mohicans* (1932), *Hills of Old Wyoming* (1937), *Stagecoach, Drums Along the Mohawk* (1939), *Brigham Young* (1940), *Western Union* (1941), *She Wore a Yellow Ribbon* (1949), *Devil's Doorway* (1950).

*Chief John Big Tree as the war weary chieftain, "Pony-That-Walks" in John Ford's classic western* She Wore a Yellow Ribbon *(RKO, 1949). George O'Brien, Mildred Natwick, and Joanne Dru are also shown.*

### Frank Lackteen (1894–1968)

Frank Lackteen was born August 29, 1894, in Kubber-Ilias, Asia Minor. After attending an American school in his native country he spent five years in Massachusetts, traveled through many countries, and then returned to the United States to live. He found film work in Canada, then in New York. His early screen work was with Pathé, Paramount, PDC, and First National. His greatest fame came in silent serials in the 1920s. The dusky, rawboned Lackteen, with his intimidating stare, spooked heroines, heroes, and audiences alike. His 15th serial for Pathé in 1927 is considered his best by many. It was titled *Hawk of the Hills* and Lackteen had the title role. He played many Indian parts in talkies, but also portrayed just about every type of villain throughout the rest of his

*Frank Lackteen, second from right, as part of a bandit gang in* Under Western Skies *(Universal, 1945). Others are Jack Ingram, bandit chief Leo Carrillo, and Jack Casey. The bartender is Guy Wilkerson.*

career. He died July 8, 1968, at the age of 73 after being in poor health for several years. His western films included: *The Last Frontier, Desert Gold* (1926), *Texas Pioneer* (1932), *Rustlers Roundup* (1933), *The Kansas Terrors* (1939), *Stagecoach* *War* (1940), *Frontier Badmen* (1943), *Moonlight and Cactus* (1944), *Under Western Skies* (1945), *Oregon Trail Scouts* (1947), *Son of a Bad Man* (1949), *Dakota Lil* (1950), *Northern Patrol* (1953).

### Chief Many Treaties (1875–1948)

Although he was known on the screen as Chief Many Treaties his real name was William Hazlett. Prior to entering films he performed in wild west shows and rodeos. He was a member of the Blackfoot tribe and a graduate of Carlisle University. He died in Hollywood on February 29, 1948 at the age of 73. His western films included: *Drums of Destiny* (1937), *Outlaw Express* (1938), *Go West, Young Lady* (1941), *King of the Stallions* (1942), *Sundown Riders* (1944).

*Chief Many Treaties, second from left, with formidable line-up of Indians in* King of the Stallions *(Monogram, 1942). Others, reading left to right are George Sky Eagle, Chief Yowlachie, Charles Brunner, Joe W. Cody, Iron Eyes Cody, and Willow Bird.*

### Rodd Redwing (1905–1971)

One of the most amazing performers on the screen was Rodd Redwing. The full-blooded Chickasaw Indian taught the stars how to shoot for over 30 years. He was acknowledged as the "Quick Draw" Champion and his most famous stunt was throwing a knife, drawing his revolver and shooting a hole in the wall where the knife blade stuck. The talented Redwing supervised gunfight scenes, taught the actors how to handle their guns, did most of the actual fancy shooting, and also taught knife throwing, fencing, and whip fighting. He died of a heart attack on May 30, 1971, in Los Angeles at the age of 66. His western films included: *Apache Chief* (1949), *Little Big Horn* (1951), *Buffalo Bill in Tomahawk Territory*, *Rancho Notorious* (1952), *Winning of the West*, *Conquest of Cochise* (1953), *Cattle Queen of Montana* (1954), *The Tin Star* (1957).

*Rodd Redwing in* Riders of the Pony Express *(Screencraft).*

*Jay Silverheels, right, as Cajou, Cree blood brother of mountie, O'Rourke, played by Alan Ladd in* Saskatchewan *(Universal, 1954).*

### Jay Silverheels (1919–    )

Jay Silverheels gained his greatest popularity as "Tonto" on the popular *Lone Ranger* television series. He also played the role in several Lone Ranger westerns starring Clayton Moore as well as other varied Indian parts in movies. A full-blooded Mohawk Indian, he was born May 26, 1919, on the Six Nations Indian Reservation in Ontario, Canada. In 1936 he became a professional Lacrosse player and became the best in Canada. When his family moved to Buffalo, New York, he became a champion middleweight boxer. Comedian Joe E. Brown was responsible for Jay's becom-ing an actor. He spotted him in a Lacrosse game and encouraged him to try acting. Bit parts in early films established Jay until he became well known. He now resides with his wife and family in the San Fernando Valley. His western films include: *Yellow Sky* (1948), *Lust for Gold, Cowboy and the Indians* (1949), *Broken Arrow* (1950), *Red Mountain* (1951), *Brave Warrior* (1952), *Jack McCall, Desperado* (1953), *Black Dakotas* (1954), *Vanishing American* (1955), *Lone Ranger and Lost City of Gold* (1958), *Alias Jesse James* (1959).

### Charles Stevens (1893–1964)

Charles Stevens specialized in sneaky, villainous roles throughout his film career that began in 1915 when he first appeared in D. W. Griffith's *Birth of a Nation*. An Apache, he was the grandson of Geronimo. In addition to his acting career he was an authority on Indian history and folklore. In the silents he appeared in most of Doug Fairbanks' films and in some, with changes of makeup, played as many as six different roles. He was born May 26, 1893, in Solomonsville, Arizona, and died August 22, 1964, in Hollywood. His western films included: *Mystery Ranch* (1932), *California Trail* (1933), *The Bold Caballero* (1936), *Forbidden Valley* (1938), *Desperate Trails* (1939), *Kit Carson* (1940), *The Bad Man* (1941), *Tombstone* (1942), *Marked Trails* (1944), *San Antonio* (1945), *Border Bandits* (1946), *Fury at Furnace Creek* (1948), *Roll, Thunder, Roll* (1949), *The Showdown* (1950), *Smoky Canyon* (1952), *Jubilee Trail* (1954), *The Vanishing American* (1955).

*Charles Stevens, right, has some tall explaining to do to Charles Middleton and James Blaine in serial* Flaming Frontiers *(Universal, 1938).*

### Nipo Strongheart (1884–1966)

Nipo Strongheart was an Indian, who in his younger days traveled with the Buffalo Bill Show. He was also under contract to David Belasco and Cecil B. DeMille. The veteran Yakima Indian entered motion pictures close to their very beginning. In addition to his acting chores he was a famed lecturer, a technical director and an authority on Indian films. He died in Hollywood on December 30, 1966. His western films included: *Across the Wide Missouri, Westward the Women* (1951), *Lone Star, Pony Soldier* (1952).

*Nipo Strongheart, second from right, as the Cree medicine man with Tyrone Power, Frank Dekova, Adeline Dewalt Reynolds, and John War Eagle in* Pony Soldier *(20th Century-Fox, 1952).*

### Jim Thorpe (1889–1953)

Jim Thorpe's athletic prowess is legendary as he was one of the greatest athletes of all time. On the screen he usually portrayed an Indian Chief, renegade Indian, or henchman. A member of the Sac and Fox tribe, he attended Carlisle University and during the 1912 Olympic games in Stockholm, won both the decathlon and pentathlon championships. Disclosure of his participation in professional baseball in 1910 deprived him of the honor. He later participated in both professional baseball and football. Upon his retirement from sports he entered films. He died of a heart attack March 28, 1953 in Los Angeles. He was portrayed by Burt Lancaster in 1951 in a film entitled *Jim Thorpe— All American.* His western films included: *White Eagle* (1932), *Wild Horse Mesa* (1933), *Code of the Mounted, Wagon Wheels* (1934), *Wanderer of the Wasteland* (1935), *Treachery Rides the Range, Wildcat Trooper* (1936), *Arizona Frontier, Prairie Schooners* (1940), *Outlaw Trail* (1944).

*Jim Thorpe, second from left, with Hoot Gibson, Al Fergu-son, Frank Ellis and Chief Thundercloud in* Outlaw Trail *(Monogram, 1944).*

### Chief Thundercloud (1899–1955)

Chief Thundercloud will be best remembered as "Tonto" in the Lone Ranger films. In many of his other roles he was cast as a heavy. He was born Victor Daniels, the oldest of nine children, April 12, 1899, in Muskogee, Oklahoma. He was a full-blooded Cherokee Indian. He received his public schooling in Texas and Arizona. He studied mining for two years at the University of Arizona. Prior to entering films he worked on cattle ranches, drove a stagecoach, was a mining foreman, a guide, boxer, rodeo performer and presented a program of Indian songs and dances on a regular circuit. He entered films as a stunt man in 1929 and doubled for many of the top stars. He died of cancer at a Ventura County Hospital in California November 30, 1955. His western films included: *Geronimo* (1939), *Hi-Yo Silver* (1940), *Western Union* (1941), *King of the Stallions* (1942), *Out-*

*Chief Thundercloud in* Outlaw Trail *(Monogram, 1944).*

law Trail, Sonora Stagecoach (1944), Badman's Territory (1946), Ambush, Colt .45, I Killed Geronimo (1950), Santa Fe, The Half-Breed (1951), Buffalo Bill in Tomahawk Territory (1952).

## Chief Yowlachie (1890–1966)

Chief Yowlachie was born in 1890 on the Yakima Indian Reservation in Washington. His father was the head chief of the reservation. He had an outstanding bass-baritone voice and went to California to study after his schooling at the Government's Indian Trade School. He later journeyed to New York where he studied under Pasquale Amato, noted Metropolitan Opera star. In the early 1920s he returned to Hollywood where he appeared in many films. He sang at many music festivals and with the Los Angeles Philharmonic orchestra. In 1930 he returned to New York and spent several years singing on stage and radio. He died March 7, 1966, at the age of 75. His western films included: *King of the Stallions* (1942), *Bowery Buckaroos* (1947), *Prairie Outlaws, Red River, Yellow Sky* (1948), *El Paso, The Cowboys and the Indians* (1949), *A Ticket to Tomahawk, Cherokee Uprising* (1950), *Buffalo Bill in Tomahawk Territory* (1952), *Yellowstone Kelly* (1959).

*Chief Yowlachie with Anne Baxter in* A Ticket to Tomahawk *(20th Century-Fox, 1950).*

*Noble Johnson: Johnson, center, with Iron Eyes Cody, Keith Richards and Roy Rogers in* North of the Great Divide *(Republic, 1950). His western films include:* The Renegades *(1930),* Mystery Ranch *(1932),* Frontier Pony Express *(1939),* The Ranger and the Lady *(1940),* The Plainsman and the Lady *(1946),* She Wore a Yellow Ribbon *(1949),* North of the Great Divide *(1950).*

*John War Eagle: John War Eagle with Jeff Chandler in*
The Great Sioux Uprising *(Universal-International, 1953).*
*His western films include:* Broken Arrow *(1950)*, Tomahawk
*(1951)*, Laramie Mountains, Last of the Comanches *(1952)*,
The Great Sioux Uprising *(1953)*, They Rode West *(1954)*.

# 5. Assorted Players

*Featured Players*

### Hank Bell (1892–1950)

Although very few people knew his name, Hank Bell was a familiar sight in westerns for many years. His moustache was his trademark and it could not be matched by anyone else on the screen. He usually played the sheriff, but was also seen as a ranchhand, one of the townspeople or the sourdough sidekick. He was born Henry Branch Bell in Los Angeles January 21, 1892, and died of a heart attack February 4, 1950, in Holly-wood. His western films included: *Law of the West* (1932), *Terror Trail* (1933), *Westward Ho* (1935), *Two-Gun Law* (1937), *Outlaws of the Prairie* (1938), *Texas Stampede, West of Santa Fe, Spoilers of the Range* (1939), *The Pinto Kid* (1941), *The Law Rides Again* (1943), *Flame of the Barbary Coast* (1945), *Red Desert* (1949), *Over the Border* (1950).

*Hank Bell, right, as the sheriff assists Charles Starrett round up a group of hired killers in* Spoilers of the Range *(Columbia, 1939).*

*Hank Bell, center, with Charles Starrett and Ernie Adams in* The Pinto Kid *(Columbia, 1941).*

### Ward Bond (1905–1960)

When John Ford was directing a film in 1929 called *Salute* he included the entire University of Southern California football team. Members of the team that year were John Wayne and Ward Bond. They were both given small speaking roles and the career of both began. This formed a lasting allegiance, for every John Ford film that had John Wayne in it also had Bond. Ward Bond played many roles from bit parts to featured ones. He played assorted parts, but was best as a heavy in his earlier westerns. Off the screen he was a man of deep convictions. He was a true patriot, detested Communism, was an active participant in national and international politics and would argue with almost anyone about any issue. He gained his greatest fame as Major Seth Adams on

the *Wagon Train* television series. He started with the show in 1957 and continued until his death from a heart attack on November 5, 1960, in Dallas. His western films included: *Sundown Rider* (1933), *Frontier Marshal* (1934), *Justice of the Range* (1935), *The Cattle Thief* (1936), *Law West of Tombstone* (1938), *Dodge City* (1939), *Kit Carson* (1940), *Wild Bill Hickok Rides* (1941), *Cowboy Commandos* (1943), *Tall in the Saddle* (1944), *Dakota* (1945), *Canyon Passage* (1946), *Fort Apache* (1948), *Three Godfathers* (1949), *Wagonmaster* (1950), *The Great Missouri Raid* (1951), *Hondo* (1953), *Johnny Guitar* (1954), *The Long Gray Line* (1955), *The Searchers* (1956), *The Halliday Brand* (1957), *Rio Bravo* (1959).

*Ward Bond as "Garvey" is skeptical of John Wayne in* Tall in the Saddle *(RKO, 1944).*

### Harry Carey (1878–1947)

Harry Carey was born January 16, 1878, in New York City. He started his career as an author of melodramas in 1906. His film career began in 1908 and he became a western star in the tradition of William S. Hart. He started with Biograph making westerns for director D. W. Griffith. He moved to Hollywood in 1911 and became a favorite of director John Ford; he starred in many western films for him and many others. He played a variety

of character parts in later films and returned to the Broadway stage in the 1940s for several appearances. His son, Harry Carey Jr., followed in his father's footsteps as an actor and his wife, the former Olive Golden, was also a silent screen actress and also appeared in the sound era. He died in Brentwood, California, of a heart attack September 21, 1947. His western films included: *Straight Shooting* (1917), *The Phantom Riders*

*Ward Bond as "Wiggs", the wagonmaster, in* Wagonmaster
*(RKO, 1950). With him is Ben Johnson.*

(1918), *Riders of Vengeance* (1919), *Desperate Trails* (1921), *Night Riders* (1922), *The Fox* (1924), *The Prairie Pirate* (1925), *Trail of '98* (1928), *Law and Order* (1932), *Sunset Pass* (1933), *Thundering Herd* (1934), *Rustler's Paradise* (1935), *The Last Outlaw* (1936), *Aces Wild* (1937), *Law West of Tombstone* (1938), *The Spoilers* (1942), *Duel in the Sun* (1946), *Angel and the Badman* (1947), *Red River* (1948).

*Harry Carey with Raymond Hatton in* Thundering Herd *(Paramount, 1934).*

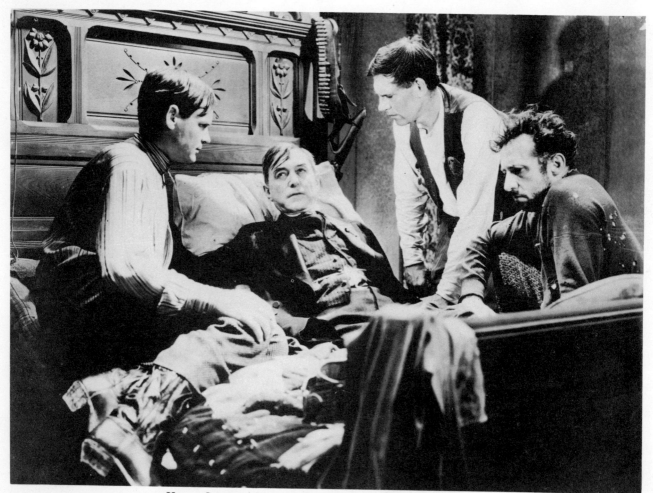

*Harry Carey with Russell Hopton, Walter Huston, and Raymond Hatton in* Law and Order *(Universal, 1932).*

## Tom London (1889–1963)

Tom London was one of the busiest players over a long career that covered almost a half century. He switched back and forth from a badman to lawman many times during his career, but he is probably best remembered for his portrayal of the honest sheriff. Born Leonard Clapham in Louisville, Kentucky, August 24, 1889, he began his film career in 1917. He appeared in many serials, both silent and sound. Under his real name of Leonard Clapham he appeared in *The Lion's Claw* (1918) and *The Lion Man* (1919) and *Nan of the North* (1922). Somewhere around 1924 he adopted the name of Tom London. His other silent serials included *Snowed In* (1926), *The Re-*

*Tom London, center, is not so amused as he instructs sheriff Jack Kirk as to the disposition of Bill Elliott in* Cheyenne Wildcat *(Republic, 1944).*

*Tom London, left, is amused in this scene from* Brand of Fear *(Universal, 1949). Also pictured are Gail Davis, Jimmy Wakely, Dub Taylor, and Frank McCarroll.*

turn of the Riddle Rider, The Mystery Rider (1927), and The Yellow Cameo (1928). In The Mystery Rider he was up to the task of the villain by portraying "The Claw," which came from having a deformed hand in the film. He also appeared in many sound serials. His western films included: The Devil's Twin (1927), Bronc Stumper (1928), Border Wildcat (1929), Arizona Terror (1931), Night Rider (1932), Outlaw Justice (1933), Mystery Ranch (1934), Tumbling Tumbleweeds (1935), Border Patrolman (1936), Springtime in the Rockies (1937), Six Shootin' Sheriff (1938), The Renegade Ranger (1939), Ghost Valley Raiders (1940), Dude Cowboy (1941), West of Tombstone (1942), Shadows on the Sage (1943), Vigilantes of Dodge City (1944), Sunset in Eldorado (1945), Santa Fe Uprising (1946), Saddle Pals (1947), Riders in the Sky (1949), Rough Riders of Durango (1950), Hills of Utah (1951), The Old West (1952), Pack Train (1953), The Saga of Hemp Brown (1958).

*Biographical Section*

### Eddie Acuff (1908–1956)

Eddie Acuff used to call himself a Missouri hick. He was born in Caruthersville, Missouri, and at the age of 16 had embarked on an acting career as a professional playing a 70-year-old man. He

*Eddie Acuff, center, with Eddy Waller and Willard Parker in* Renegades *(Columbia, 1946).*

went to Broadway via stock and entered films in 1935. He worked primarily with Warner Brothers and Columbia studios. At Columbia he played the mailman in the "Blondie" series. He died December 17, 1956, in Hollywood of a heart attack. His western films included: *Guns of the Pecos* (1937), *Rhythm of the Saddle* (1938), *Rough Riders' Round-Up* (1939), *Shooting High* (1940), *Robin Hood of the Pecos, Texas Rangers Ride Again* (1941), *Helldorado, Renegades* (1946), *Swing the Western Way* (1947), *Song of Idaho* (1948).

### Ernie Adams (1885–1947)

Equally at home running with a band of outlaws or defending law and order, Ernie Adams appeared with great regularity in western films. He also appeared in other features and was especially proficient when it came to playing a "Stoolie" in prison films such as *San Quentin* in 1937. His name in the film was a dubious one, "Fink." He appeared in many stage musicals before entering films in the 1920s. He was born June 18, 1885, in San Francisco, and died November 26, 1947. His western films included: *Nevada* (1927), *Beyond the Rockies* (1932), *Ranger's Code* (1933), *Trail's End* (1935), *Hopalong Cassidy Returns* (1936), *The Gun Ranger* (1937), *Thunder in the Desert* (1938), *Trigger Pals* (1939), *The Man from Tumbleweeds* (1940), *The Pinto Kid* (1941), *Stagecoach Buckaroo* (1942), *Beyond the Last Frontier* (1943), *Marshal of Gunsmoke* (1944), *The Fighting Frontiersman* (1946), *Robin Hood of Monterey* (1947).

*Ernie Adams, left, and Bob Steele, right, find the body of Frank Ball in* The Gun Ranger *(Republic, 1937).*

### Stanley Andrews (1892–1969)

Stanley Andrews was best known as "The Old Ranger," narrator of the *Death Valley Days* television series. On the show he told stories of the old west as it really was supposed to be. In the days of radio he could be heard as "Daddy Warbucks" on the *Little Orphan Annie* program and was also a regular on "Fu Manchu." In western films he sometimes played the big boss, sheriff, rancher or father. He died in Hollywood June 23, 1969. His western films included: *Nevada* (1936), *Mysterious Rider* (1938), *Hi-Yo Silver* (1940), *The Ox-Bow Incident* (1943), *Tucson Raiders* (1944), *The Michigan Kid* (1947), *Northwest Stampede* (1948), *The Valiant Hombre* (1949), *Al Jennings of Oklahoma* (1950), *Saddle Legion* (1951), *Kansas Territory* (1952), *El Paso Stampede* (1953), *Treasure of Ruby Hills* (1955).

*Stanley Andrews, second from left, as the sheriff in Michigan Kid (Universal, 1947). Against him at the moment are Leonard East, Milburn Stone, Rita Johnson, Jon Hall, and William Ching.*

### Morris Ankrum (1897–1964)

Morris Ankrum was born August 27, 1897, in Danville, Illinois. He received a law degree from the University of Southern California. He became interested in acting while an associate professor of economics at the University of California and he founded the Little Theatre there. He became director of the Pasadena Playhouse in 1930. He appeared on Broadway in many plays and made his film debut in 1940. He worked for most of the major and independent screen companies in a variety of roles. He died of trichinosis in Pasadena, California September 2, 1964. His western films included: *Hopalong Cassidy Returns* (1936), *Hills of Old Wyoming* (1937), *Knights*

*Morris Ankrum, right, with Lon Chaney, Jr. in Silver Star (Lippert, 1955).*

of the Range (1940), *In Old Colorado, Border Vigilantes, The Bandit Trail* (1941), *The Omaha Trail* (1942), *Bad Men of Tombstone* (1948), *Short Grass* (1950), *The Redhead and the Cowboy* (1951), *Fort Osage* (1952), *Devil's Canyon* (1953), *Cattle Queen of Montana* (1954), *Chief Crazy Horse, The Silver Star* (1955), *Fury at Gunsight Pass* (1956), *The Saga of Hemp Brown* (1958).

### Roscoe Ates (1895–1962)

This veteran comedian with the mobile face, pop eyes and long drawn out stutter portrayed town and ranch roustabouts in many western films during a long career. Born in Grange, Mississippi, January 20, 1895, he had intended to be a concert violinist, but Ates played for 15 years in vaudeville and repertory shows before entering the movies in 1930. He had actually cured himself of stammering at the age of 18 through diligent practice in front of a mirror, but put this trait to good use in his films. He was well known as a scene stealer. Roscoe Ates died March 1, 1962, of lung cancer in Hollywood. His western films included: *Billy the Kid* (1930), *The Rainbow Trail, Cimarron* (1931), *Cheyenne Kid* (1933), *Riders of the Black Hills* (1938), *Three Texas Steers* (1939), *Rancho Grande* (1940), *Robin Hood of the Pecos* (1941), *Tumbleweed Trail* (1946), *Black Hills* (1947), *The Westward Trail* (1948).

Roscoe Ates, center, as "Soapy", friend of the hero, Eddie Dean, right. Sheriff Lee Morgan completes the threesome in Shadow Valley *(PRC, 1947)*.

### Irving Bacon (1893–1965)

Irving Bacon was usually willing to take any role that came along and as a result appeared in hundreds of films in a variety of parts. He was at his best when the film had a rural atmosphere. He was born in St. Joseph, Missouri, September 6, 1893. He attended Santa Clara College in San Jose, California, and launched his career with Mack Sennett in 1913. His career spanned 50 years and he played the postman in several "Blondie" movies and also the television series of the same name. He died in Hollywood February 5, 1965. His western films included: *Lone Cowboy* (1934), *Powdersmoke Range* (1935), *Drift Fence* (1936), *Arizona Mahoney* (1937), *The Texans* (1938), *The Return of Frank James* (1940), *Western Union* (1941), *The Desperadoes* (1943), *Under Western Skies* (1945), *Saddle Pals* (1947), *Albuquerque* (1948), *Son of New Mexico* (1950), *Fort Ti* (1953), *Dakota Incident* (1956).

*Irving Bacon as lawyer Thaddeus Bellweather is more interested in fishing than tending to Gene Autry's affairs in* Saddle Pals *(Republic, 1947). On the left is Tom London.*

## William Norton Bailey (1886–1962)

William Norton Bailey went to Hollywood in 1912, found it to his liking and stayed. He became an early day film director, working primarily for Cosmopolitan pictures. He later became an actor and played a variety of character parts. He died in Hollywood November 8, 1962. His western films included: *Fighting for Justice* (1933), *Thunder Mountain* (1935), *Code of the Saddle* (1947), *Silver Trails* (1948), *Brand of Fear, Trail's End* (1949), *Lightning Guns* (1950), *Al Jennings of Oklahoma* (1951).

*Sheriff William Norton Bailey is restrained by Johnny Mack Brown in* Trail's End *(Monogram, 1949).*

### Vince Barnett (1902–      )

Vince Barnett is a professional "ribber." His father, Luke Barnett, was an internationally known comedian. Vince has been in demand for banquets and social events for years where he poses as a headwaiter, doctor, lawyer, banker or foreign correspondent. His gift for dialects, makeup and patter has enabled him to fool many of the leading personalities of the world. He started as a stand-in for his father after he left Carnegie Tech, where he was studying aeronautical engineering. He worked with "Earl Carroll Vanities" in 1927, then went to Hollywood where he entered films. He has appeared in over 350 films. One of his favorite roles was that of "Charleston" in *The Killers* with Burt Lancaster. He appeared in seven Zane Grey westerns with Randolph Scott in the early 1930s. He was born July 4, 1902, in Pittsburgh. He has two brothers who are physicians. He has had an exciting life in addition to his acting career, and has been a licensed pilot since 1921. He was one of the first pilots to fly the mail between Pittsburgh and Cleveland in 1927. In 1931 he drove a supercharged Cord Phaeton cross-country in 58 hours. In 1963 he flew an Air Force jet at twice the

*Vince Barnett, left, with Sheila Ryan, Gene Autry, and Pat Buttram in* Mule Train *(Columbia, 1950).*

speed of sound, one month before his 61st birthday. His western films include: *Heritage of the Desert, Sunset Pass* (1933), *Overland Trail* (1939), *Heroes of the Saddle* (1940), *The Virginian* (1946), *Loaded Pistols* (1949), *Mule Train, Border Treasure* (1950), *Carson City, Springfield Rifle* (1952).

### Noah Beery Jr. (1915–      )

Noah Beery Jr. was born August 10, 1915, in New York City. He traveled with his parents in a stock company and appeared in the Douglas Fairbanks silent classic, *The Mark of Zorro,* in 1920. He entered films seriously in 1929 and his boyish charm allowed him to both star and co-star in various westerns. He has also supported many heroes through the years and only occasionally changed his character to go against the law. His western films include: *Rustlers Roundup* (1933), *Trail Beyond* (1934), *Forbidden Valley* (1938), *Bad Lands* (1939), *The Light of Western Stars, The Carson City Kid* (1940), *Frontier Badmen* (1943), *The Daltons Ride Again, Under Western Skies* (1945), *Red River* (1948), *The Doolins of Oklahoma* (1949), *The Savage Horde* (1950), *The Last Outpost* (1951), *The Black Dakotas* (1954), *White Feather* (1955), *The Fastest Gun Alive* (1956), *Guns of the Timberland* (1960), *The Cockeyed Cowboys of Calico County* (1970).

*Noah Beery Jr.*

### James Bell (1891–     )

James Bell was born in Suffolk, Virginia, December 1, 1891. He attended Virginia Polytechnic Institute and made his stage debut in 1921. He entered films in 1932 with a bit in *I Am a Fugitive from a Chain Gang*. The softspoken Bell did not seriously enter the western field until 1948 and since that time has appeared in many as a lawman or rancher. His western films include: *Black Eagle* (1948), *Streets of Laredo* (1949), *Buckaroo Sheriff of Texas, The Dakota Kid, Arizona Manhunt* (1951), *Wild Horse Ambush, Ride the Man Down* (1952), *Devil's Canyon* (1953), *Riding Shotgun* (1954), *Texas Lady, A Lawless Street* (1955), *Posse from Hell* (1961).

*Sheriff James Bell is wounded as Eilene Janssen comes to his aid in* Arizona Manhunt *(Republic, 1951).*

### Clem Bevans (1880–1963)

Clem Bevans was a definite asset to any film in which he appeared. He was at home in any role, but particularly so when seen as an old prospector or friend of the law or lawless. He always had a twinkle in his eye and seemed to have a slight touch of larceny in his heart. He was born in Cozaddale, Ohio, and after several amateur shows, made his way through vaudeville, legit, and musical comedies. He entered films in 1935. He died August 11, 1963, at the Motion Picture Country Hospital in Woodland Hills, California. His western films included: *Rhythm on the Range* (1936), *Tombstone* (1942), *The Woman of the Town*, *The Kansan* (1943), *Streets of Laredo*, *The Gal Who Took the West*, *Rim of the Canyon*, *Loaded Pistols* (1949), *Man in the Saddle*, *Silver City Bonanza* (1951), *Captive of Billy the Kid*, *Hangman's Knot* (1952), *The Stronger Wore a Gun* (1953), *Ten Wanted Men* (1955).

*Clem Bevans, center, demonstrates his finesse at the plate to the enjoyment of Billy Kimbley and Rex Allen in* Silver City Bonanza *(Republic, 1951).*

### Walter Brennan (1894–    )

Walter Brennan has given many memorable performances during his long career. This accounts for his three Oscars for best supporting actor. His seeming indestructibility can be attributed to his playing elderly parts even when a young man, which has given him the illusion of agelessness. He was born July 25, 1894, in Swampscott, Massachusetts. He graduated from college with an engineering degree but preferred vaudeville and musical comedy. He served in World War I, was

*Walter Brennan as Roy Bean, "The Hanging Judge", in* The Westerner, *starring Gary Cooper (United Artists, 1940).*

badly gassed on the front lines, and was not in good health when discharged in 1919. He had no desire to return to the stage and went to Guatemala where he bought a pineapple plantation. This was a successful venture for four years. He moved to Los Angeles in 1923 for his health and lost his savings in real estate in 1925. He sought extra work in the movies, appeared in many films, but did not get his big break until 1935. His Academy Award performances were for *Come and Get It* in 1936, *Kentucky* in 1938, and *The Westerner* in 1940. He endeared himself to a vast television audience, starring in *The Real McCoys* (starting in 1957), as the cantankerous, gimpy Grampa McCoy. He also starred in two later series, *The Tycoon* and *The Guns of Will Sonnett.* His western films include: *Ridin' Rowdy* (1927), *Smilin' Guns* (1929), *Law and Order* (1932), *Fighting for Justice* (1933), *Law Beyond the Range* (1935), *The Three Godfathers* (1936), *The Texans* (1938), *The Westerner* (1940), *Dakota* (1945), *My Darling Clementine* (1946), *Red River* (1948), *Curtain Call at Cactus Creek* (1950), *Along the Great Divide* (1951), *Return of the Texan* (1952), *Drums Across the River* (1954), *The Far Country* (1955), *The Way to the Gold* (1957), *Rio Bravo* (1959), *How the West Was Won* (1962), *Support Your Local Sheriff* (1969).

### Lynton Brent (1903–    )

Lynton Brent was born August 2, 1903, in Chicago. He appeared in a variety of roles in all types of films including many westerns where he played rustlers, sheriffs, and ranchers. He authored many stories that appeared in popular magazines of the 1930s and gained recognition as a painter. In World War I he served as a cavalry captain. His western films include: *Texas Bad Man* (1932), *The Old Corral* (1937), *Frontier Town* (1938), *Gunman from Bodie, Red River Valley* (1941), *Trail Riders, Overland to Deadwood* (1942), *Calling Wild Bill Elliott* (1943), *Partners of the Trail, Raiders of the Border* (1944), *The Haunted Mine* (1946).

*Lynton Brent, left, with John King, Max Terhune and David Sharpe in* Trail Riders *(Monogram, 1942).*

### Charles Brinley (1880–1946)

Charles E. Brinley was born November 15, 1880, in Yuma, Arizona. He got an early start in films and appeared in many silent serials in the early 1920s. In western films he sometimes played an outlaw and other times was a law abiding citizen. He died February 17, 1946. His western films included: *The Dawn Trail* (1930), *Spirit of the West* (1932), *Treason* (1933), *Fighting Code, Dawn Trail* (1934), *Crimson Trail, Outlaw Deputy* (1935), *Two-Fisted Sheriff* (1937), *Texas Stampede, Western Caravans* (1939).

*Charles Brinley, left, with Charles Starrett in* Western Caravans, *a story of ranchers vs. nesters (Columbia, 1939).*

### Rand Brooks (1918– )

Rand Brooks was born September 21, 1918, in Los Angeles. After graduation from college he was granted an interview with M-G-M's casting director, studied acting for a year and then was signed for a film career. His screen debut was in 1938 in *Dramatic School*. His biggest break was his role as Scarlett O'Hara's first husband in *Gone With the Wind* in 1939. He appeared in several Hopalong Cassidy films and also appeared with Whip Wilson in several westerns. He now devotes most of his time to ranching. His western films include: *Cowboy Serenade* (1942), *Unexpected Guest* (1946), *Hoppy's Holiday* (1947), *Sundown at Santa Fe* (1949), *The Wyoming Bandit* (1949), *The Vanishing Westerner* (1950), *Heart of the Rockies* (1951), *Montana Incident* (1952), *Comanche Station* (1960).

*Rand Brooks, right, with Whip Wilson in* Montana Incident *(Monogram, 1952).*

### Edgar Buchanan (1903– )

Edgar Buchanan was born in Humansville, Missouri, on March 21, 1903. His father was a dentist and he followed in his footsteps after attending the University of Oregon and graduating from the North Pacific Dental College, where he met his wife who was also a dentist. In 1939 he moved his practice to Altadena, California, and he joined the Pasadena Community Playhouse. In 1940 he appeared in his first western film, *Arizona*, Columbia's. He enjoys roles where he can be un-

*Edgar Buchanan, right, with Hugh Marlowe in* Rawhide *(20th Century-Fox, 1951).*

shaven and slightly cynical. He appeared as "Uncle Joe" for many years on television in the popular *Petticoat Junction* show. His western films include: *Arizona* (1940), *Texas* (1941), *Tombstone, The Town too Tough to Die* (1942), *The Desperadoes* (1943), *Buffalo Bill* (1944), *Abilene Town* (1946), *Coroner Creek* (1948), *Red Canyon* (1949), *Rawhide* (1951), *Toughest Man in Arizona* (1952), *Shane* (1953), *Destry* (1954), *Wichita* (1955), *The Sheepman* (1958), *Cimarron* (1960), *The Comancheros* (1961), *Ride the High Country* (1962), *McLintock* (1963), *The Rounders* (1965), *Gunpoint* (1966).

*Fred Burns, right, with Lina Basquette and Ken Maynard in* Arizona Terror *(Tiffany, 1931).*

### Fred Burns (1878–1955)

Fred Burns had a long career in western films. He appeared in Vitagraph serials in the teens and early twenties as well as silent and sound features well into the late forties. In the sound films he usually played a sheriff or one of the townspeople. His brother, Robert E. Burns, also played in westerns for over 40 years. He was born April 24, 1878, in Ft. Keough, Montana, and died July 18, 1955. His western films included: *Arizona Terror* (1931), *The Saddle Buster* (1932), *The Mysterious Rider, Flaming Guns* (1933), *Texas Tornado, Men Without Law* (1934), *Too Much Beef* (1936), *Springtime in the Rockies* (1937), *The Arizona Kid* (1939), *Colorado* (1940), *Ridin' the Cherokee Trail* (1941), *Sons of the Pioneers* (1942).

### Robert E. Burns (1884–1957)

Robert E. (Bob) Burns was born November 21, 1884, in Montana. He had a long screen career in western films and also played in silent serials. He usually played a good guy and during the last few years of his screen career could be seen as one of the townspeople, rarely receiving billing. His son, Forrest Burns, also appeared in many western films and he was the brother of another screen pioneer, Fred Burns. He died March 14, 1957, at the age of 72. His western films included: *Border Law* (1931), *Ride Him Cowboy* (1932), *Sagebrush Trail* (1933), *Singing Vagabond* (1935),

*Bob Burns, third from left, with Frank Rice and Buck Jones in* Border Law *(Columbia, 1931).*

*Guns and Guitars* (1936), *Guns of the Pecos* (1937), *Gun Law* (1938), *Prairie Schooners* (1940), *Lumberjack* (1944), *Twilight on the Rio* *Grande* (1947), *Dallas, The Missourians, Rough Riders of Durango, Twilight in the Sierras* (1950).

### Budd Buster (1891–1965)

Budd Buster was born in Colorado Springs June 14, 1891. He made his debut in stock at the tender age of six and from 1907 through 1913 he appeared in vaudeville and dramatic roadshows. He started his motion picture career shortly thereafter with the Powers Co., but quit in 1915. He returned to the screen in 1934 and appeared in many western films until 1949. He died December 21, 1965, at the age of 74. His western films included: *Cyclone Ranger* (1935), *Desert Guns, The Riding Avenger* (1936), *The Gun Ranger, The Trusted Outlaw* (1937), *Thunder in the Desert, Frontier Scout* (1938), *Covered Wagon Trails* (1940), *Texas Marshal, The Lone Star Vigilantes* (1941), *Billy the Kid Trapped* (1942), *The Old Chisholm Trail* (1943), *The Pinto Bandit* (1944), *Border Badmen* (1945), *Home on the Range* (1946), *The Wild Frontier* (1947), *The Westward Trail* (1948).

*Budd Buster, left, with Tex Ritter and Virginia Carpenter in* The Lone Star Vigilantes *(Columbia, 1941).*

### Yakima Canutt (1895–    )

Yakima Canutt is acknowledged as the greatest stuntman ever to appear in films. He has performed some of the most daring stunts ever attempted. He was born Enos Edward Canutt November 29, 1895, in Colfax, Washington. His father was a rancher. In his teens "Yakima" became a very good horse breaker. He won the northwest championship as a bronc rider before his seventeenth birthday. He entered the rodeo field and became the world's champion. He won the Police Gazette Belt for the all around championship for the years 1917, 1919, 1920, and 1923. He won many of the championship bronc riding contests from 1917 through 1923. He also won many firsts in bulldogging. The publicity he received opened the door into motion pictures. He was featured in a great number of silent westerns. After the talkies came in he also took acting parts, many times playing the heavy. He specialized in stuntwork and also created and wrote action into the scripts. He became a director and filmed many action sequences in non-westerns such as *Ben Hur, El Cid,* and *Helen of Troy.* He is still active in this field. His western films include: *Two-Fisted Justice, Cheyenne Cyclone* (1932), *Telegraph Trail, Via Pony Express* (1933), *Lucky Texan, Blue Steel, Randy Rides Alone* (1936), *Ghost Town Gold, Riders of the Whistling Skull* (1937), *Stagecoach, Wyoming Outlaw* (1939), *Pioneers of the West* (1940), *Gauchos of El Dorado* (1941), *Shadows on the Sage* (1943), *Hidden Valley Outlaws* (1944).

*Yakima Canutt during a break in the shooting.*

*Harry Carey Jr., right, and Ben Johnson as two horse traders who end up leading a wagon train in* Wagonmaster *(Argosy-RKO, 1950).*

### Harry Carey Jr. (1921–    )

Harry Carey Jr. was born in Saugus, California, May 16, 1921. He received his education at the Newhall Public School in Newhall, California, and Black Fox Military Academy in Hollywood. He participated in summer stock with his famous father and was a page boy for NBC. After serving in the U.S. Navy from 1941 until 1946 he made his film debut in 1947. The good-natured youthful-appearing Carey was a favorite of director John Ford during the early years of his film career. His western films include: *Pursued* (1947), *Red River* (1948), *She Wore a Yellow Ribbon* (1949), *Copper Canyon, Wagonmaster* (1950), *San Antone* (1952), *Silver Lode* (1954), *Seventh Cavalry* (1956), *From Hell to Texas* (1958), *Escort West* (1959), *Noose for a Gunman* (1960), *Two Rode Together* (1961), *The Raiders* (1964), *Alvarez Kelly* (1966), *The Way West* (1967), *Bandolero!* (1968), *The Undefeated* (1969), *Dirty Dingus Magee* (1970), *Big Jake* (1971).

### Horace B. Carpenter (1875–1945)

Horace B. Carpenter entered films as a member of the Famous Players-Lasky Co. He was a favorite of Cecil B. DeMille and had leading parts in many of DeMille's early films. His acting career spanned 50 years. He also wrote scenarios for Douglas Fairbanks Sr. He portrayed many minor bit parts in western films until his death May 21, 1945, of a heart attack. His western films included: *Riders of the Desert* (1932), *Smokey Smith* (1935), *Range Defenders, Gunsmoke Ranch* (1937), *Spoilers of the Range* (1939), *Thunder Over the Prairie* (1941), *Outlaws of Pine Ridge* (1942).

*Horace B. Carpenter smiles as he contributes to Iris Meredith's needy cause in* Spoilers of the Range *(Columbia, 1939). Also donating are Hank Bell, Charles Brinley and Joe Weaver.*

### Ed Cassidy (1893–1968)

Ed Cassidy bore a strong resemblance to Teddy Roosevelt and as a result played the Rough Rider several times in films. In most western films, however, he played a rancher, sheriff, or citizen and was one of the busiest in the 1930s and 1940s. He was born in Illinois March 21, 1893, and before turning to the stage graduated from McGill University in Canada with a degree in optometry. He died January 19, 1968. His western films included: *Toll of the Desert* (1935), *Feud of the West* (1936), *Come on Cowboys!* (1937), *Cassidy of Bar 20* (1938), *Wild Horse Canyon* (1939), *Riders of Pasco Basin* (1940), *Wyoming Wildcat* (1941), *Pirates of the Prairie* (1942), *The Avenging Rider* (1943), *The Pinto Bandit* (1944), *Colorado Pioneers* (1945), *The El Paso Kid* (1946), *Stage Coach to Denver* (1947), *Desperadoes of Dodge City* (1948), *Roughshod*

(1949), *Trail of Robin Hood* (1950), *Buckaroo Sheriff of Texas* (1951), *Desperadoes Outpost* (1953).

*Ed Cassidy is mortally wounded as Bill Elliott is already contemplating his next move in* Colorado Pioneers *(Republic, 1945). Behind Elliott is Cliff Parkinson.*

*Jess Cavin, standing, second from left, with Duke Taylor, Noah Beery Sr., Horace B. Carpenter, and Emmett Lynn in* Outlaws of Pine Ridge *(Republic, 1942). Seated are Don (Red) Barry, Duke Green, and Wheaton Chambers.*

### Jess Cavin (1885–1967)

Jess Cavin was an early day film player who doubled for Wallace Beery for many years, Primarily an extra he appeared in many western films. He died July 20, 1967, at the age of 82. His western films included: *The Desert Rider* (1929), *The Plainsman* (1936), *Valley of the Giants* (1938), *Texas Stampede* (1939), *Outlaws of Pine Ridge* (1942), *The Daltons Ride Again* (1945).

### Lane Chandler (1899–    )

Lane Chandler has had an interesting career in motion pictures. In the late twenties he starred opposite such leading ladies as Greta Garbo, Clara Bow, Esther Ralston and Betty Bronson. He starred in many westerns of the twenties and early thirties. He has played a large variety of character parts ranging from the bad guy to the train conductor as he did in *Union Pacific* for Cecil B. DeMille. He was born Robert Oakes June 4, 1899, in Walsh County, North Dakota, where his father raised horses. They soon moved to Northern Montana cattle country. While working as a mechanic in a garage in Los Angeles he was signed by Paramount in 1927 and his film career began. Lane states, "Even though I starred in Willis Kent westerns my favorite roles were the ones I played for Cecil B. DeMille even though they were small. Mr. DeMille was a perfectionist. My own career has been interesting due to the many diversified parts I have played." His western films include: *Open Range* (1927), *Hurricane Horseman* (1931), *Cheyenne Cyclone* (1932), *Via Pony Express* (1933), *Texas Tornado* (1934), *Idaho Kid* (1936), *Law of the Ranger* (1937), *Two-Gun Justice* (1938), *Outpost of the Mounties* (1939), *Hy-Yo Silver* (1940), *Sundown Jim* (1942), *Tenting Tonight on the Old Camp Ground* (1943), *Sagebrush Heroes* (1944), *Two-Fisted Stranger* (1946), *The Vigilantes Return* (1947), *Northwest Stampede* (1948), *Montana* (1950), *The Charge at Feather River* (1953), *The Indian Fighter* (1955), *The Lone Ranger* (1956), *Noose for a Gunman* (1960), *Requiem for a Gunfighter* (1965).

### Tom Chatterton (1881–1952)

Tom Chatterton was born in Geneva, New York, February 12, 1881. He toured in stock from 1907 through 1912 when he joined the New York Motion Picture Company. He starred in silent films until 1918, when he returned to the stage. He returned to films in 1933 and played in many westerns as a sheriff, heroine's father, or rancher. Occasionally he would take a villain's role. He died at his Hollywood home August 17, 1952. His western films included: *Boss Rider of Gun Creek* (1936), *Under Western Stars* (1938), *Covered Wagon Days* (1940), *Desert Bandit* (1941), *Raiders of the Range* (1942), *Cheyenne Wildcat* (1944), *Lone Texas Ranger* (1945), *Alias Billy the Kid* (1946), *Stage Coach to Denver* (1947), *Marshal of Amarillo* (1948), *Gun Law Justice* (1949).

*Tom Chatterton comforts Helen Talbot as Alice Fleming looks on in this scene from* Lone Texas Ranger, *starring Bill Elliott (Republic, 1945).*

*Lane Chandler in a recent character part.*

### Cliff Clark (1893–1953)

Cliff Clark was one of the many underrated Hollywood actors who because of their ability to play their parts convincingly never lacked for screen roles. Starting in vaudeville he made his way to Hollywood and played character parts his entire career. In westerns he often was cast as the sheriff. In other films he was adept as the police captain, inspector, mayor, town councilman, army officer, newspaper editor, or businessman. He died in Hollywood of a heart attack February 8, 1953. His western films included: *Wagon Train* (1940), *False Paradise* (1948), *Vigilante Hideout* (1950), *Warpath, Desert of Lost Men, Saddle Legion, Cavalry Scout* (1951), *Cripple Creek* (1952).

*Wounded Cliff Clark is being administered to by doctor Dorothy Malone in* Saddle Legion *(RKO, 1951). Roving cowboys Richard (Chito) Martin and Tim Holt look on.*

### Steve Clark (1891–1954)

Steve Clark was born in Indiana, February 26, 1891. The kindly Clark was a familiar face to western audiences through the years as he played ranchers, sheriffs, fathers and similar roles. He played for every studio throughout his long career. He died June 29, 1954, at the age of 63. His western films included: *Silent Men* (1933), *Man Trailer* (1934), *Square Shooter* (1935), *West of Nevada* (1936), *Gun Lords of Stirrup Basin* (1937), *Paroled—To Die* (1938), *Roll Wagons Roll* (1939), *Land of Six Guns* (1940), *Tumbledown Ranch in Arizona* (1941), *The Stranger from Pecos* (1943), *Saddle Leather Law* (1945), *Flame of the West, Under Arizona Skies* (1946), *West of Dodge City* (1947), *Range Renegades* (1948), *West of Wyoming* (1949), *Six Gun Mesa* (1950), *Abilene Trail* (1951), *Night Raiders* (1952), *Cow Country* (1953).

*Steve Clark, right, with Johnny Mack Brown in* West of Wyoming *(Monogram, 1950).*

### George Cleveland (1886–1957)

George Cleveland began his career on the stage in 1899. He also directed such stars as Leo Carrillo, Marjorie Rambeau and May Robson on the New York stage. He was born in Sydney, Nova Scotia, in 1886. He came to Hollywood in 1934 to appear with Noah Beery Sr. in *Mystery Liner* and stayed to appear in many screen productions. He played ranchers, the heroine's father, derelicts, and a va-

riety of roles, but he was best known as "Gramps" on the *Lassie* television series. He died of a heart attack in Burbank, California, July 15, 1957. His western films included: *Blue Steel, The Star Packer* (1934), *Rio Grande Romance* (1936), *Rose of the Rio Grande* (1938), *Overland Mail* (1939), *Blazing Six Shooters, West of Abilene* (1940), *Sunset in Wyoming* (1941), *The Spoilers* (1942), *The Man from Music Mountain* (1943), *The Yellow Rose of Texas* (1944), *Dakota* (1945), *Albuquerque* (1948), *Home in San Antone* (1949), *Trigger Jr.* (1950), *Cripple Creek* (1952), *San Antone* (1953), *The Outlaw's Daughter* (1954).

*George Cleveland is listening to Charles Starrett tell of a silver deposit found on the line separating two ranches in* Blazing Six Shooters *(Columbia, 1940).*

*Tex Cooper, right, and Dub Taylor, left, harmonize much to Bill Elliott's discomfort in* North of the Lone Star *(Columbia, 1941).*

### Tex Cooper (1877–1951)

Tex Cooper was one of the most picturesque characters in westerns due to his strong resemblance to Buffalo Bill. A bit player, he could often be spotted in many scenes of townspeople through his 35-year film career. He toured with Buffalo Bill and also performed with the Miller Brothers 101 Ranch Shows before entering films. He died at the age of 74 March 29, 1951, in Hollywood and was survived by his wife who was a former circus midget. His western films included: *Two-Fisted Sheriff, The Old Wyoming Trail* (1937), *The Oklahoma Kid* (1939), *North of the Lone Star* (1941), *Thundering Trails* (1943), *Border Badmen* (1945), *Return of the Frontiersman, Colt .45* (1950).

### Rufe Davis (1908– )

Rufe Davis was born Rufus Eldon Davidson, December 2, 1908, in Dinson, Oklahoma, one of 11 children. He began his acting career in amateur shows, winning almost all he entered. Prior to entering films he was with the Dubinsky Brothers Stock Company, The Weaver Bros. and Elviry, Larry Rich, The Radio Rubes, and finally his own act. He was brought to Hollywood in 1937 and has appeared in nearly 50 films. One of his favorite roles was that of "Lullaby Joslin" in the famed "Three Mesquiteers" series. He performed in this capacity in 14 of these films in 1940, 1941 and 1942. His imitations of barnyard animals and other noises are legendary. He played engineer "Floyd Smoot" on *Petticoat Junction* on television for several years. His western films include: *Under Texas Skies, The Trail Blazers, Lone Star Raiders* (1940), *Prairie Schooners, Pals of the Pecos, Gangs*

*Rufe Davis, right, with Lloyd Nolan and Gladys Swarthout in* Ambush *(Paramount, 1938).*

*of Sonora, Outlaws of the Cherokee Trail* (1941), *Code of the Outlaw, Westward Ho* (1942), *The Strawberry Roan* (1948).

### Edgar Dearing (1893– )

Edgar Dearing was born May 4, 1893, in Ceres, California. He appeared with stock companies from 1907 through 1909. He later became a stage and vaudeville performer. He appeared in the classic *Intolerance* in 1916. In World War I he was a master gunner with the U.S. Army artillery. He appeared in many films, often performing as a policeman. He made many film appearances before making his first western and in the early 1950s appeared in several Charles Starrett westerns. His western films include: *Don't Fence Me In* (1945), *Lightning Guns, Raiders of Tomahawk Creek* (1950), *Pecos River* (1951), *The Kid from Broken Gun* (1952).

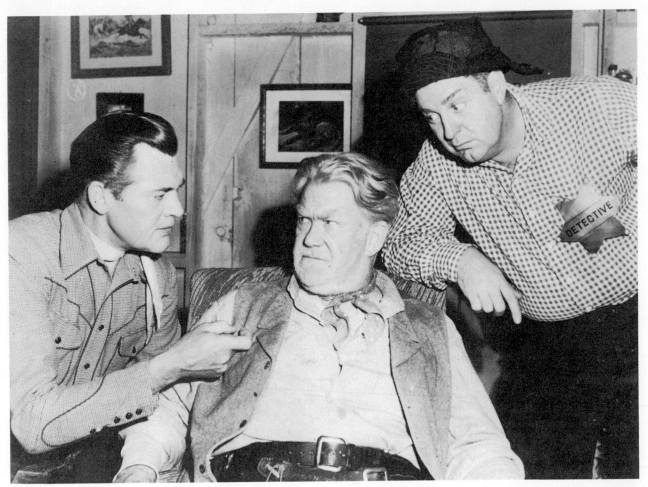

*Edgar Dearing, center, is interrogated by Charles Starrett and Smiley Burnette in* Raiders of Tomahawk Creek.

### William Desmond (1878–1949)

William Desmond was born in Dublin, Ireland, January 23, 1878. He came to the United States at a very early age. After completing his education in New York he became interested in acting and appeared in many stock productions. He did not enter motion pictures until 1915 and despite his age he became a star in silent serials and one of the sure box-office draws. His serials include *Beast of Paradise* (1923), *The Riddle Rider* (1924), *Strings of Steel* (1926), and The Vanishing Rider (1928). He also starred in several western films. His age caught up with him and he finished his career appearing in westerns in various character parts. He died November 2, 1949. His western films included: *Deuce Duncan* (1918), *Burning Trail* (1925), *Mystery Rider* (1928), *Sunset Trail*

*William Desmond, center, with Al Taylor, Tom Santschi, and Tom Dugan in the serial,* Phantom of the West *(Mascot, 1931).*

(1932), *Fargo Express, Rustlers Roundup, Straw-berry Roan* (1933), *Way of the West, Powdersmoke Range* (1935), *Song of the Saddle, Nevada,* *Cavalry, Song of the Gringo, Headin' for the Rio Grande* (1936).

### Andy Devine (1905–    )

Andy Devine was born Jeremiah Schwartz in Flagstaff, Arizona, October 7, 1905. He attended Arizona State College and graduated from Santa Clara University. The magnificently gravel-throated comedian started his career as a film extra in 1926. He has appeared in every type of film in addition to his many westerns. In the early 1950s he appeared in the popular *Wild Bill Hickok* series on television as Guy Madison's sidekick, "Jingles." He later had his own show called *Andy's Gang.* He and his family reside in Van Nuys, California. His western films include: *Law and Order* (1932), *Geronimo, Stagecoach* (1939), *When the Daltons Rode* (1940), *Badlands of Dakota* (1941), *Frontier Badmen* (1943), *Frontier Gal* (1945), *Canyon Passage* (1946), *The Michigan Kid* (1947), *Eyes of Texas* (1948), *The Last Bandit* (1949), *New Mexico* (1951), *Montana Belle* (1952), *Two Rode Together* (1961), *The Man Who Shot Liberty Valance* (1962), *The Ballad of Jose* (1968).

*Andy Devine, left, with John Litel and George Brent in* Montana Belle *(RKO, 1952).*

### Joe Dominguez (1894–1970)

Joe Dominguez was born March 19, 1894, in Chihuahua, Mexico. He started his career as an extra at the Lubin Co. in 1913 for a dollar a day plus carfare. This led to acting as an extra at various studios of the time and in 1914 he became a stock player for Vitagraph, appearing in many movies and serials. In 1920 he became a stock player for Universal Studios and in 1921 became a free lance actor and he played in the first sound picture with Al Jolson and the first experimental color film. He appeared in 325 motion pictures and was also a stunt man, technical advisor and assistant director.

His memories of a long film career included the time a platform collapsed at the Santa Monica wharf dumping the entire company, cameras, crew and actors into the ocean. He died April 11, 1970. His western films included: *Riders of the Desert* (1932), *Viva, Villa!* (1934), *Robin Hood of El Dorado* (1936), *Outlaws of the Rio Grande* (1941), *The Kissing Bandit* (1948), *The Streets of Laredo* (1949), *Dallas* (1950), *Ride, Vaquero* (1953), *Gypsy Colt* (1954), *The Broken Star* (1956), *One-Eyed Jacks* (1961).

*Joe Dominguez, center, kneels over the body of Dick Foote as William Bendix and William Holden look on in* The Streets of Laredo *(Paramount, 1949).*

*Dick Elliott spins a disbelieving yarn in* Across the Badlands *(Columbia, 1950). Disinterested listeners are Stanley Andrews, Charles Starrett, and Charles Evans.*

### Dick Elliott (1886–1961)

Dick Elliott excelled in playing a big Texas blowhard. His hearty laughter and mile-a-minute patter were his trademarks. This enabled him to portray politicians at all levels, Texas oilmen, and cattle ranchers. He began his career in stock in 1901 and entered films in the early 1930s. He was also a regular guest on various television programs. He died in Hollywood December 22, 1961. His western films included: *Outcasts of Poker Flat* (1937), *Under Western Stars* (1938), *One Man's Law* (1940), *Sunset in Wyoming* (1941), *Rainbow over Texas* (1946), *The Dude Goes West* (1948), *Across the Badlands* (1950), *Fort Defiance* (1951), *Montana Belle* (1952).

### Douglas Evans (1903–1968)

Douglas Evans journeyed to Los Angeles in 1933 and became a radio announcer. He had just started his film career in 1941 when World War II started. He became an Army Captain and upon his discharge appeared in several Broadway plays before resuming his Hollywood career. The distinguished appearing Evans appeared in over 100 films before his retirement. He died in Hollywood March 25, 1968, at the age of 64. His western films included: *Flashing Guns* (1947), *California Firebrand, Crossed Trails, Cowboy Cavalier* (1948), *The Golden Stallion* (1949), *Rustlers on Horseback, North of the Great Divide* (1950), *South Pacific Trail* (1952).

*Douglas Evans, hatless, with Rex Allen, Estelita and Roy Barcroft in* South Pacific Trail *(Republic, 1952).*

### Frank Faylen (1909–    )

Frank Faylen was born in St. Louis in 1909. His parents were the vaudevillians Ruf and Cusik and he received an early indoctrination to show business. He received his schooling in Chicago and St. Louis. He entered films after a brief fling as an author and backer of a revue in 1936. His film characterizations have been many since this time. He was also seen on television as the frustrated father of Dobie Gillis in *The Many Loves of Dobie Gillis.* His western films include: *California* (1946), *Blood on the Moon* (1948), *Whispering Smith* (1949), *Copper Canyon, The Nevadan, The Eagle and the Hawk* (1950); *Passage West* (1951), *The Lusty Men, Hangman's Knot* (1952), *Seventh Cavalry* (1956).

*Frank Faylen as "Cass Browne" in* Hangman's Knot, *a story of the ambush of a union gold train (Columbia, 1952).*

### William Farnum (1876–1953)

William Farnum's silent screen career is legendary. Starring in his first film, *The Spoilers*, in 1914 he went on to become the highest paid actor in films during his prime. His equally famous brother, Dustin Farnum, starred in *The Squaw Man* the same year. He was born July 4, 1876, in Boston. He began his professional career at the age of 10 in a play with Edwin Booth and at 16 was playing Shakespeare. After touring with *Ben Hur* for five years he tried his hand in motion pictures. He lost his fortune in the 1929 Stock Market Crash, returned to the stage and made his film comeback in 1931. His fine speaking voice enabled him to find work in character parts, mostly westerns. He died of cancer in Hollywood at the age of 76, June 5, 1953. His western films included: *The Spoilers* (1914), *The Plunderer* (1915), *The Lone Star Ranger* (1919), *Drag Harlan* (1920), *Flaming Guns* (1933), *Powdersmoke Range* (1935), *Public Cowboy No. 1* (1937), *Santa Fe Stampede* (1938), *Hi-Yo Silver, Kit Carson* (1940), *Gangs of Sonora,*

*William Farnum, second from left, has just discovered a bonanza mine in Santa Fe Stampede (Republic, 1938). Ready to aid him against claim jumpers are "The Three Mesquiteers", John Wayne, Ray Corrigan and Max Terhune.*

*Last of the Duanes* (1941), *The Lone Star Ranger, The Silver Bullet, Boss of Hangtown Mesa* (1942), *Frontier Badmen* (1943), *Trail of Robin Hood* (1950), *Lone Star* (1952).

### William Fawcett (1894–    )

William Fawcett was born William Fawcett Thompson on September 8, 1894, in High Forest, Minnesota. His father was a minister and he planned to follow in his footsteps and took courses for the ministry at Hamline University. He was going on to divinity school until World War I intervened. He was one of two Americans awarded the *Medaille D'Honneur* for work with the French wounded. Upon his return he switched to acting with stock companies until talking pictures put the stock companies out of business. He then became a teacher of English and dramatic literature at the University of Nebraska where he acquired his M.A. and Ph.D. degrees. He then taught for five years at Michigan State University. Another war, World War II, again changed his career. He worked in shipyards in San Francisco and Oakland during the war and then headed for Hollywood. He started as a writer for commercial films, then made his motion picture debut at the age of 52 in a western titled *The Michigan Kid* released in 1947. This launched the literate Mr. Fawcett on a career of prospectors, saloon loafers, ranch hands and cattle rustlers. In addition to his films he has worked in some 350 television episodes and his favorite role is that of "Pete" the co-star of the *Fury* television series. He again mangled and battered the English language in this series. His western films include: *Ghost Town Renegades, The Michigan Kid* (1947), *The Tioga Kid* (1948), *Ride, Ryder, Ride* (1949), *Hills of Utah* (1951), *Springfield Rifle, Montana Incident* (1952), *The Star of Texas* (1953), *Seminole Uprising* (1955), *Dakota Incident* (1956), *The Quick Gun* (1964).

*William Fawcett.*

### Richard Fiske (1915-1944)

Richard Fiske was born Tom Potts in Shelton, Washington, on November 20, 1915. He started his acting career while attending the University of Washington, participating in school plays. The six-foot one-inch Fiske came to Hollywood by freight train and played leading parts in films and both leads and villains in westerns. Reportedly he died in June of 1944. His western films included: *Man from Sundown, Stranger from Texas* (1939), *Pioneers of the Frontier, Prairie Schooners* (1940), *Outlaws of the Panhandle, North from the Lone Star, Across the Sierras* (1941).

*Richard Fiske, left, with Norman Willis, Eddie Laughton, and Jack Low gang up on Charles Starrett in* Outlaws of the Panhandle *(Columbia, 1941).*

### Paul Fix (1901– )

Paul Fix spent a good deal of the 1930s and 1940s playing gangster and prison roles, but he has also found the time to appear in many westerns. His roles range from the villain to the sheriff and perhaps his greatest recognition came as "Sheriff Mike Torrence" on the *Rifleman* TV series starring Chuck Connors. He was born March 13, 1901, in Dobbs Ferry, New York, where his father was a brewer. His early acting experience was in various stock companies and little theatres and his motion picture career has spanned from early William Farnum films to latter day John Wayne features. His western films include: *South of the Rio Grande* (1932), *Fargo Express* (1933), *Rocky Rhodes* (1934), *Crimson Trail* (1935), *Heritage of the Desert* (1939), *Trail of the Vigilantes* (1940), *A Missouri Outlaw* (1941), *South of Santa Fe* (1942), *In Old Oklahoma* (1943), *Tall in the Saddle* (1944), *Dakota* (1945), *Fighting Man of the Plains* (1949), *The Great Missouri Raid* (1951), *Ride the Man Down* (1952), *The Star of Texas* (1953), *Johnny Guitar* (1954), *Stagecoach to Fury* (1956), *The Sons of Katie Elder* (1965), *Ride Beyond Vengeance* (1966), *El Dorado* (1967), *Young Billy Young* (1969), *Dirty Dingus Magee* (1970), *Shoot Out* (1971).

### Sam Flint (1882– )

Sam Flint was born in Guinette County, Georgia, October 19, 1882. After spending 25 years on the stage he entered films in the early 1930s. He specialized in playing ranchers, but was sometimes found in his early roles as a villain. In addition to western films he made many appearances in other type features in a variety of character parts. His western films include: *New Frontier* (1935), *Winds of the Wasteland* (1936), *Under Fiesta Stars* (1941), *South of Santa Fe* (1942), *The Stranger from Pecos* (1943), *Silver City Kid* (1944), *Along the Navajo Trail* (1945), *My Pal Trigger* (1946), *The Wild Frontier* (1947), *The Strawberry Roan* (1948), *The Gay Amigo* (1949), *The Return of Jesse James* (1950), *The Hawk of Wild River* (1952), *Cow Country* (1953).

*Paul Fix.*

*Sam Flint with a line-up of veteran players from* Cow Country *(Allied Artists, 1953). Reading left to right are: Seated, Robert Lowery, Flint, Barton MacLane. Standing, Edmond O'Brien, Robert Barrat, Jack Ingram, and Raymond Hatton.*

## Francis Ford (1882–1953)

Francis Ford was born Francis O'Ferna in Portland, Maine, August 15, 1882. He graduated from high school, attended Maine University and played stock, road shows, and on the stage before starting his film career as an actor with Edison. He became a director for Universal and doubled as the star opposite Grace Cunard in four exciting silent serials starting in 1914. *The Broken Coin* in 1915 was perhaps the best. He also directed and starred in several other silent serials, his last being in 1921. He was the brother of director John Ford and appeared in character parts in many of his films as well as others. One of his better characterizations was as "The Old Man" in *The Ox-Bow Incident.* Along with Dana Andrews and Anthony

*Francis Ford, right, and Eddy Waller, left, as rival stage line operators square off as Allan (Rocky) Lane tried to restore peace in* Frontier Investigator *(Republic, 1949).*

Quinn he was an innocent victim of mob lynching. He died in Hollywood, September 5, 1953. His western films included: *Trail's End* (1922), *The Devil's Saddle* (1927), *The Indians Are Coming* (1930), *Last Ride* (1932), *Man from Monterey* (1933), *Gun Justice* (1934), *The Arizonian* (1935), *The Texans* (1938), *Stagecoach* (1939), *Lucky Cisco Kid* (1940), *Last of the Duanes* (1941), *The Ox-Bow Incident* (1943), *Dark Canyon* (1947), *Eyes of Texas* (1948), *Frontier Investigator* (1949), *Wagonmaster* (1950), *Toughest Man in Arizona* (1952), *The Sun Shines Bright* (1953).

### Byron Foulger (1899–1970)

Byron Foulger was born in Ogden, Utah, August 27, 1899. He is from a pioneer background as his mother was one of the first babies born crossing the plains in a covered wagon. In his early years he played in tent shows up and down the East Coast as far North as Nova Scotia. Then he spent eight years with the repertory company of the Moroni Olsen Players where he met his wife, screen actress Dorothy Adams. He then directed the Portland Civic Theatre for three years and spent three more at the Pasadena Playhouse as an actor, director and teacher. He made his film debut in 1931. His roles have ranged from a meek bank or hotel clerk to an arch villain in westerns as well as all types of films. He appeared on television as the engineer in *Petticoat Junction* and formerly was the father you never saw behind the newspaper in TV's *Captain Nice*. He was especially fond of the many acquaintances of the talented people he had worked with in the motion picture industry through his long career. He died of a heart attack April 4, 1970. His western films included: *Arizona* (1931), *Heroes of the Saddle* (1940), *Ridin' on a Rainbow* (1941), *Hoppy Serves a Writ*, *Silver*

*Byron Foulger, left, with Don Barry, Tom Neal and Margia Dean in* Red Desert *(Lippert, 1949).*

*Spurs, In Old Oklahoma* (1943), *Swing in the Saddle* (1944), *Plainsman and the Lady* (1946), *Michigan Kid* (1947), *The Dalton Gang, Red Desert* (1949), *Salt Lake Raiders* (1950), *Apache Country, Cripple Creek* (1952), *Bandits of the West* (1953), *Gun Battle at Monterey* (1957), *King of the Wild Stallions* (1959), *The Cockeyed Cowboys of Calico County* (1970).

### Nacho Galindo (1908–    )

Nacho Galindo was born November 7, 1908, in Guadalajara, Jalisco, Mexico, the only son in a family of six. His father was a bullfighter and later promoted bullfights. The veteran western player made his first movie appearance in 1929 in an early Cisco Kid movie starring Warner Baxter. In addition to his western roles he studied singing for over thirty years and had singing roles in opera and operettas with leads in *Cavelleria Rusticana* and *I Pagliacci*. He currently has his own singing and acting academy in Los Angeles. His western films include: *Rose of Santa Rosa, The Gay Cavalier* (1946), *South of St. Louis* (1949), *Montana, The Showdown* (1950), *Lone Star* (1952), *Broken Lance, Border River* (1954), *Thunder over Arizona* (1956).

*Nacho Galindo as he appeared in* Montana *(Warner Bros., 1950).*

### Fred Graham (    -    )

Fred Graham has appeared in many films as an actor, but his most important contribution has been as a stuntsman. His specialty is fighting and he has been at it for over 30 years staging and appearing in many of the famous fight scenes, particularly at Republic Studios in the 1940s and 1950s. This included westerns and many of their famous serials. He has also doubled for many of the top stars during his career. His western films include: *Marshal of Reno, Stagecoach to Monterey* (1944), *Out California Way* (1946), *On the Old Spanish Trail* (1947), *The Bold Frontiersman* (1948), *The Fighting Kentuckian* (1949), *Heart of the Rockies* (1951), *Colorado Sundown, Old Oklahoma Plains* (1952), *The Last Hunt* (1956), *Badman's Country* (1958).

*Fred Graham, center, with June Vincent and Russ Conway* in Colorado Sundown *(Republic, 1951).*

*J. Frank Glendon, black suit and tie, with John Merton, Dick Curtis, Don Barclay, Tim McCoy and Art Felix in* Lion's Den *(Puritan, 1936).*

### J. Frank Glendon (1884–1937)

Jonathan Frank Glendon appeared on Broadway as Clara Kimball Young's leading man in several productions. He entered films in 1918 when he came to Los Angeles from New York. He appeared in many western films and was seen in many Tim McCoy features. In addition to his acting career he was known for his writings on economics and frequently spoke on the radio. He was closely asso-ciated with the Technocracy movement from its inception. He died in Los Angeles March 17, 1937. His western films included: *Border Romance* (1930), *Cheyenne Cyclone* (1932), *Gun Law* (1933), *Texas Tornado* (1934), *Sagebrush Troubador* (1935), *King of the Pecos, Border Caballero, The Lion's Den, Aces and Eights, The Traitor* (1936).

### James Griffith (1916–    )

For a fellow who played Santa Claus in the seventh grade, James Griffith has portrayed many roles since that would be a far cry from that kindly gentleman. This is even true when he does not play the actual heavy of the film. He was born in Los Angeles February 13, 1916, and originally had planned a musical career. He changed his mind and played in many amateur theatricals before turning professional in 1941. He spent two hitches in the Marine Corps and was a Spike Jones musi-cian for half of 1948. He then entered films playing many diversified roles. His favorite is "Doc Holliday" in *Masterson of Kansas*. His western films include: *Daughter of the West* (1949), *The Cariboo Trail, Indian Territory* (1950), *Apache Drums* (1951), *Kansas Pacific* (1953), *Masterson of Kansas, Jesse James vs. The Daltons* (1954), *Apache Ambush* (1955), *The First Texan* (1956), *Return to Warbow* (1958), *Advance to the Rear* (1964).

### Henry Hall (1876–1954)

Henry Hall was born in Missouri, November 5, 1876. He started his film career in 1933, appearing in *Story of Temple Drake*. He appeared in many films thereafter and usually portrayed a rancher in western films. He died December 11, 1954, at the age of 78. His western films included: *Rainbow Ranch* (1933), *Dude Ranger* (1934), *Desert Trail* (1935), *Yodelin' Kid from Pine Ridge* (1937), *Blazing Six-Shooters* (1940), *Pirates on Horseback* (1941), *Stagecoach Buckaroo* (1942), *Sonora Stagecoach* (1944), *Navajo Kid, Lightning Raiders* (1945), *Terrors on Horseback* (1946), *Ghost Town Renegades* (1947), *Crossed Trails* (1948), *Challenge of the Range* (1949).

*James Griffith portraying "Doc Holliday" in* Masterson of
Kansas *(Columbia, 1954).*

*Henry Hall, second from left, with Mady Lawrence, Al St. John and Steve Darrell in* Lightning Raiders *(PRC, 1945).*

### Thurston Hall (1883–1958)

Blustery, pompous Thurston Hall made the ideal businessman or politician in motion pictures. He was born in Boston in 1883. After completing high school he gave up his intended plans to attend Yale for an acting career in 1901. He appeared in tent shows, Broadway plays, and owned his own theatrical company that toured all over the world. He entered silent films in 1915, but did not go to Hollywood until 1935. He died of a heart attack February 20, 1958, in Beverly Hills, California. His western films included: *Call of the Canyon* (1942), *Song of Nevada* (1944), *West of the Pecos, The Gay Senorita* (1945), *Swing the Western Way* (1947), *Rim of the Canyon* (1949), *Belle of Old Mexico* (1950), *Whirlwind* (1951), *Carson City* (1952).

*Thurston Hall as a Chicago tycoon who goes west on doctor's orders with his screen niece, Barbara Hale, in* West of the Pecos *(RKO, 1945).*

### John Hamilton (1887–1958)

John Hamilton spent 25 years on the New York stage before coming to Hollywood in 1937. Very distinguished in appearance, he added dignity to any role he played. He gained his greatest audience on television playing editor Perry White on the *Superman* series. He died of a heart attack in Hollywood, October 15, 1958. His western films included: *Allegheny Uprising* (1939), *Sheriff of Las Vegas* (1944), *Home on the Range, Raiders of the South* (1946), *Bandits of Dark Canyon* (1947), *Desperadoes of Dodge City* (1948), *Canadian Pacific* (1949), *Bells of Coronado* (1950), *Sugarfoot* (1951), *Marshal of Cedar Creek* (1953), *Sitting Bull* (1954).

*John Hamilton, left, with S. Z. Sakall, Randolph Scott, and Robert Warwick as Prescott, Arizona businessmen in* Sugarfoot *(Warner's, 1951).*

### Harry Harvey (1901–    )

Harry Harvey was born in Indian Territory, Oklahoma, January 10, 1901. With a musical background he began his entertainment career in 1918 in Gus Hill's Honey Boy Minstrels. After this he appeared with various minstrel and burlesque shows. This led to many roles in Broadway plays. He came to Hollywood in 1934 and has appeared in many western films. His western films include: *The Oregon Trail* (1936), *Six Shootin' Sheriff* (1938), *In Old Montana* (1939), *Robbers of the Range* (1941), *The Rangers Take Over* (1943), *Return of the Rangers* (1944), *Sunset Pass* (1946), *Code of the West* (1947), *The Arizona Ranger* (1948), *Rio Grande Patrol* (1950), *Silver City*

*Bonanza (1951), Outcasts of Poker Flat (1952), Bandits of the West (1953), Wyoming Renegades (1955), Showdown at Abilene (1956), Shoot-Out at Medicine Bend (1957).*

Harry Harvey, right, with "Big Boy" Williams in Hoedown (Columbia, 1950).

### Paul Harvey (1884–1955)

Paul Harvey was born in Illinois. He started at the bottom in show business, moving scenery and lifting trunks until he worked into small parts in various plays. He joined the old Selig Film Company in Chicago in 1917. He played leads in many plays and in movies had assorted character parts. He died in Hollywood December 14, 1955. His western films included: *Ride on Vaquero* (1941), *Heart of the Golden West* (1942), *The Man from Music Mountain* (1943), *Don't Fence Me In* (1944), *Helldorado* (1946), *Wyoming* (1947), *A Ticket to Tomahawk* (1950), *Thunder in God's Country* (1951), *Calamity Jane* (1953).

Paul Harvey watches as Will Wright swears in Anne Baxter as a deputy marshal in A Ticket to Tomahawk (20th Century-Fox, 1950). Chief Yowlachie and Charles Kemper also look on.

### Earle Hodgins (1899–1964)

Earle Hodgins was a versatile character actor who excelled at playing the medicine show owner, barker, auctioneer, or con man. He also played many other roles during his 35-year career. He was a veteran of many radio programs and appeared on all of the top television series from 1954 through 1964. He died of a heart attack April 14, 1964, in Hollywood. His western films included: *Cyclone Ranger* (1935), *Guns and Guitars* (1936), *Hills of Old Wyoming* (1937), *The Purple Vigilantes* (1938), *Range War* (1939), *The Bad Man from Red Butte* (1940), *Riding the Wind* (1941), *Hoppy Serves a Writ* (1943), *The San Antonio Kid* (1944), *Under Western Skies* (1945), *Gun*

*Town* (1946), *Oregon Trail Scouts* (1947), *Oklahoma Badlands* (1948), *The Savage Horde* (1950), *Thunder over the Plains* (1953), *Bitter Creek* (1954), *The Man Who Shot Liberty Valance* (1961).

*Earle Hodgins, left, with Fred Scott and Al St. John in* Moonlight on the Range *(Spectrum Pictures Corporation, 1937).*

*Jack Holt, second from left, along with Fred Kohler Jr. and Chill Wills, are attentive listeners to Gene Autry's explanation in* Loaded Pistols *(Columbia, 1948).*

### Jack Holt (1881–1951)

Born in Winchester, Virginia, Jack Holt received his education at Virginia Military Institute. He tried many jobs including that of a cowpuncher before settling for an acting career. He became a silent star working with most of the greats of the silent era. He began his career at Paramount in 1916 and played leading roles in a number of Cecil B. DeMille productions. He became Paramount's top rider in a series of westerns based on Zane Grey stories. He later graduated into character parts and played heavies, sheriffs, and ranchers with equal aplomb. His handsome moustache and clear speaking voice were his trademarks for his career in the talkies. He died January 18, 1951, of coronary thrombosis leaving his son, Tim, to carry on the western tradition. His western films included: *The Squaw Man* (1919), *Wanderer of the Wasteland* (1924), *The Enchanted Hill* (1926), *End of the Trail* (1936), *Roaring Timber* (1937), *Northwest Rangers* (1942), *My Pal Trigger* (1946), *The Wild Frontier* (1947), *The Arizona Ranger, Loaded Pistols* (1948), *Return of the Frontiersman, Trail of Robin Hood* (1950), *Across the Wide Missouri* (1951).

*Robert Homans, second from right, with Richard Alexander, Johnny Mack Brown, and Fuzzy Knight in* Son of Roaring Dan *(Universal, 1940).*

### Robert Homans (1877–1947)

Robert Homans was born in Malden, Massachusetts, November 8, 1877. He attended the University of Michigan and his early screen work was with Independent Pictures, Associated Exhibitors, Tiffany, Luma, and Universal. He played in many films throughout a long career and appeared as a policeman in countless non-western films. He died July 28, 1947, of a heart attack at the age of 69. His western films included: *Range Courage, Ride 'Em High* (1927), *Forlorn River* (1937), *Gold Is Where You Find It, Gold Mine in the Sky* (1938), *West of Carson City, Son of Roaring Dan* (1940), *Sierra Sue, Red River Valley* (1941), *The Sombrero Kid* (1942), *Frontier Badmen* (1943).

### Henry Hull (1890–    )

Henry Hull was born October 3, 1890, in Louisville, Kentucky, where his father was a drama critic and city editor of the *Louisville Courier-Journal*. After graduation from college he became a mining engineer, assayer, mineralogist and prospector in Northern Canada. His brother, Shelley,

*Henry Hull as editor Greeley, the local newspaperman who records the ghost killings in his town in* Rimfire *(Screen Guild, 1949).*

was an actor, earning many times Henry's salary so he switched careers. He appeared on the New York stage in 1909 at the age of 18 and went on to become one of the best actors in the theatre. He earned great acclaim for his roles on the stage in *The Man Who Came Back* and *Tobacco Road*. He appeared in his first film in 1924. He has enriched many western films with his expert character portrayals. His western films include: *Jesse James, Return of the Cisco Kid* (1939), *The Return of Frank James* (1940), *The Woman of the Town* (1943), *Belle Starr's Daughter* (1948), *El Paso, Rimfire, Colorado Territory* (1949), *The Return of Jesse James* (1950), *The Treasure of Lost Canyon* (1952), *Thunder over the Plains* (1953), *Man with a Gun* (1955).

### Lloyd Ingraham (1875–1956)

Lloyd Ingraham started his career as a legit actor and director for Oliver Morosco and other stage producers. He began his film career in 1912 and played leading roles. He also directed such stars as Mary Pickford and Douglas Fairbanks. After sound came in he could be found in character roles often playing a rancher, sheriff, or father. He was born in Rochelle, Illinois, and died of pneumonia April 4, 1956, at the Motion Picture Country Hospital. His western films included: *Texas Gun-Fighter* (1932), *Dude Ranger* (1934), *Northern Frontier* (1935), *Rogue of the Range, Empty Saddle* (1936), *Riders of the Dawn* (1937), *Gun Packer* (1938), *Marshal of Mesa City* (1940), *Dude Cowboy* (1941), *Stagecoach Buckaroo* (1942), *Blazing Guns* (1943), *Partners of the Trail* (1944), *Frontier Gal* (1945).

Jack Randall gazes at the murdered Tim Davis held by his sorrowing father, Lloyd Ingraham, in Riders of the Dawn (Monogram, 1937).

### Si Jenks (1876–1970)

Si Jenks was born Howard H. Jenkins in Morristown, Pennsylvania, in 1876. He was active in almost every branch of the entertainment field through a long career. He played in medicine shows, vaudeville, and was with the Miller Brothers 101 Ranch. He also played on Broadway; his most famous stint was with George M. Cohan. He was signed by Fox Studios in 1922 which started his long career in films where he was noted for comedy character parts. He died January 6, 1970, at Woodland Hills, California at the age of 93. His western films included: *Galloping Thru* (1932), *Rider of the Law, Outlaw Deputy* (1935), *Outcasts of Poker Flats* (1937), *Rawhide* (1938),

Si Jenks, right, with Jerry Colonna and James Ellison in Kentucky Jubilee (Lippert, 1951).

*Drums Along the Mohawk* (1939), *Ride, Tenderfoot Ride* (1940), *The Great Train Robbery* (1941), *Wild Horse Stampede* (1943), *The Man* *from Oklahoma* (1945), *The Dude Goes West* (1948), *Kentucky Jubilee* (1951).

*Ben Johnson, left, as a cavalry officer with Peter Mamakos in* Fort Bowie *(United Artists, 1958).*

### Ben Johnson (1918–    )

Ben Johnson was born June 13, 1918, at Foracre, Oklahoma. His father was a cowboy and world's champion steer roper. Ben came to California at the age of 21 and began his film career as a stuntman, doubling for many of the western stars. Director John Ford was impressed and gave him his start as an actor in films. He played many Indian Scout roles in films. Ben was the world's champion steer roper in 1953. His favorite screen role was that of Bob Amory in *One-Eyed Jacks*. One of the soft-spoken actor's most memorable roles was that of "Chris," the fellow who started the famous fight scene in *Shane*. His western films include: *Three Godfathers* (1948), *Rio Grande, Wagonmaster* (1950), *Fort Defiance* (1951), *Wild Stallion* (1952), *Shane* (1953), *Rebel in Town* (1956), *Fort Bowie* (1958), *Ten Who Dared* (1960), *One-Eyed Jacks* (1961), *The Rare Breed* (1966), *Hang 'Em High* (1968), *Chisum* (1970).

### I. Stanford Jolley (1900– )

I. Stanford Jolley was born in Elizabeth, New Jersey, October 24, 1900. His early childhood days were spent on tour with his father's circus and carnival. He later worked in stock, vaudeville, radio, and on Broadway. He came to Hollywood in 1935 and has become a permanent fixture since, never lacking for work in films and television. He appeared in many gangster roles, serials, and then began his western career as one of the bad guys. He found this very rewarding and for the most part has remained in westerns since. He later switched to a variety of western character parts including many sheriff portrayals. His western films include: *Rolling Home to Texas* (1941), *The Sombrero Kid* (1942), *Frontier Fury* (1943), *Oklahoma Raiders* (1944), *Lightning Raiders* (1945), *Ambush Trail* (1946), *Prairie Express* (1947), *The Fighting Ranger* (1948), *Roll Thunder Roll!* (1949), *Colorado Ranger* (1950), *Can-

*I. Stanford Jolley pins a deputy marshal badge on Wayne Morris in* The Marksman *(Allied Artists, 1953).*

yon Raiders* (1951), *Waco* (1952), *The Marksman* (1953), *Two Guns and a Badge* (1954), *The Young Guns* (1956), *13 Fighting Men* (1960).

*Willie Keeler, left, watches Rex Lease about to place a noose around Francis McDonald's neck in* Cheyenne Wildcat *(Republic, 1944). Others in the scene are Tom Smith, Universal Jack, Rudy Bowman, Franklyn Farnum, and Horace B. Carpenter.*

### Willie Keeler (1890–1964)

"Sugar" Willie Keeler was born September 14, 1890, in Colorado. The six-foot three-inch, 230-pound Keeler spent most of his film career as an extra standing around watching the action take place. He appeared in all types of films. He died January 17, 1964, at the age of 73. His western films included: *Cheyenne Wildcat* (1944), *Pursued, Trail Street* (1947), *Black Bart* (1948), *The Fighting Kentuckian* (1949), *Covered Wagon Raid* (1950).

*Frank LaRue, center, with Louise Brooks, Curley Dresden, Henry Otho, Tommy Coats, and Bud McClure in* Overland Stage Raiders *(Republic, 1938).*

### Frank LaRue (1878–1960)

Frank LaRue was born in Ohio, December 5, 1878. He appeared in vaudeville and later on the Broadway stage. He appeared in over 100 films during his long career, including many western features. He died in Hollywood, September 26, 1960, at the age of 81. His western films included: *Sundown Rider* (1933), *Under the Pampas Moon* (1935), *Gun Lords of Stirrup Basin* (1937), *Overland Stage Raiders* (1938), *Song of the Buckaroo* (1939), *Land of Six Guns* (1940), *Gunman from Bodie* (1941), *Lawless Plainsmen* (1942), *Robin Hood of the Range* (1943), *West of the Rio Grande* (1944), *Under Arizona Skies* (1946), *Over the Santa Fe Trail* (1947), *Range Renegades* (1948).

### Harry Lauter (1925– )

Harry Lauter was born June 19, 1925, in White Plains, New York. His father was an artist and musician and his mother was a writer. He always wanted to be an actor, but had to postpone his career until after World War II. He plays good guys and bad guys with equal aplomb, but prefers heavy roles. He has appeared on television in hundreds of series and co-starred as "Clay Morgan" in *Tales of the Texas Rangers*. He also starred in the last serial ever made by Republic Studios, *King of the Carnival* in 1955. In addition to his acting he keeps active today with swimming, golf, and fishing. He also owns outdoor art galleries which feature his own paintings as well as the paintings and sculpture of other artists. His western films include: *Prince of the Plains* (1949), *Silver City Bonanza, Whirlwind* (1951), *Night Stage to Galveston* (1952), *The Marshal's Daughter* (1953), *Apache Ambush* (1955), *Posse from Hell*

*Harry Lauter, center, as the local banker's son is about to be done in by Lane Bradford as Shirley Davis watches in* Prince of the Plains *(Republic, 1949).*

(1961), *Fort Courageous* (1965), *Fort Utah* (1967), *Barquero* (1970).

### Nolan Leary (1891– )

One actor who has been a part of the entire evolution of the motion picture industry is Nolan Leary. Still active, he made his motion picture debut as a pony express rider in a silent western, *Bill Sharkey's Last Game,* in 1911. He was born in Rock Island, Illinois, of railroading heritage. He studied at the Chicago Musical College School of Acting and his first professional role was as a song and dance boy in Victor Herbert's *The Red Mill* in 1909. In addition to his many silent features he also performed on the stage in many plays. One stage commitment kept him from fulfilling a role in The Perils of Pauline, a fact Leary recalls with nostalgic regret. He has authored many one-act plays in addition to appearing in over 150 films and countless TV and stage appearances. In his western films he portrayed a variety of character roles. He particularly cherishes the memory of working with Gary Cooper in *High Noon*. His western films include: *Outlaws of Santa Fe* (1944), *Out California Way, Galloping Thunder, Heading*

*Nolan Leary, second from left, as Doctor Sawyer treats Francis McDonald in* Gene Autry and the Mounties *(Columbia, 1950). With them are Gene Autry and Richard Emory.*

*West* (1946), *West of Dodge City, Over the Santa Fe Trail* (1947), *Outlaw Brand* (1948), *The Cowboy and the Indians* (1949), *Gene Autry and the Mounties* (1950), *High Noon* (1952).

### Edward J. Le Saint (1871–1940)

Edward J. Le Saint was noted for his roles as the heroine's father, rancher or town citizen in scores of westerns. He began his film career as an actor with the old IMP Company in New York in 1909. He later worked as a director for IMP, Selig, Lasky, Universal and Fox before resuming his acting career. His versatility extended to scenario writing. He died in Hollywood September 10, 1940. His western films included: *Fighting Marshal* (1931), *Texas Bad Man* (1932), *Last Trail* (1933), *Frontier Marshal, Dawn Trail* (1934), *Justice of the Range, Thunder Mountain* (1935), *The Oregon Trail, End of the Trail* (1936), *Two Gun Law* (1937), *Cattle Raiders, Colorado Trail* (1938), *Jesse James, Spoilers of the Range, West of Santa Fe* (1939), *Bullets for Rustlers, Texas Stagecoach* (1940).

*Edward Le Saint, center, meets Alma Chester, left, in* The Old Wyoming Trail *(Columbia, 1937). Also shown are Barbara Weeks, Charles Starrett, and Donald Grayson.*

### Theodore Lorch (1880–1947)

Theodore Lorch was born in Springfield, Illinois, September 29, 1880. He started his career in traveling stock companies and was in vaudeville with Frank Tinney. After 20 years with legit road companies he moved to Hollywood where he enacted feature roles for Warners, Universal, Metro and other major studios. He appeared in several westerns as the father of the heroine, a villain or in other supporting roles. He died in Hollywood after a long illness November 11, 1947. His western films included: *The Tenderfoot, Honor of the Mounted, Texas Bad Man* (1932), *Black Beauty, The Whirlwind, The Fugitive, The Gallant Fool* (1933), *Rustler's Paradise, His Fighting Blood* (1935), *Romance Rides the Range* (1936), *Cheyenne Rides Again, Aces Wild* (1937), *Lost Ranch* (1938).

*Theodore Lorch, right, with Tom Tyler, Ed Cassidy, and Lucille Brown in* Cheyenne Rides Again *(1937).*

### J. Farrell MacDonald (1875–1952)

He was born in Waterbury, Connecticut, graduated from Yale and sang in grand opera before embarking on a film career. He started with Biograph and worked as an actor and director for all the film studios in the silent era. He was a member of the original IMP Company in 1911. He appeared in over 300 films and his best remembered western role was that of Corporal Casey in the 1924 production of *Iron Horse* under the direction of John Ford. He died August 2, 1952, in Hollywood. His western films included: *Iron Horse* (1924), *Vanishing Frontier* (1932), *Heritage of the Desert* (1933), *Square Shooter* (1935), *Courage of the West* (1937), *Come on Rangers* (1938), *Knights of the Range, The Dark Command* (1940), *In Old Cheyenne* (1941), *Texas Masquerade* (1944), *My Darling Clementine* (1946), *Fury at Furnace Creek* (1948), *Whispering Smith, The Beautiful Blonde from Bashful Bend* (1949).

*Ranch foreman, J. Farrell MacDonald, is believing Russell Hayden is okay after all after he returns his gun in* Knights of the Range *(Paramount, 1940). Pretty rancher, Jean Parker, looks on.*

### Jock Mahoney (1919–    )

Jock Mahoney has performed on the screen under a variety of names, Jacques O'Mahoney, Jock O'Mahoney and Jack Mahoney. He was born Jacques J. O'Mahoney February 17, 1919, in Chicago, Illinois. He was a star athlete while attending the University of Iowa. He joined the Marines in 1941 and became a fighter pilot and instructor during World War II. He entered films as a stuntman, switched to acting where he normally was a "heavy" in westerns, but also starred as a leading man. On television he starred in two series, *Range Rider* and *Yancy Derringer*. He also became the thirteenth man to portray Tarzan on the screen. His western films include: *South of the Chisholm Trail* (1947), *The Doolins of Oklahoma, Frontier Outpost, The Blazing Trail, Renegades of the Sage* (1949), *Hoedown, The Nevadan, Lightning Guns* (1950), *Santa Fe* (1951), *Smoky Canyon, The Rough, Tough West, The Kid from Broken Gun*

*Jock Mahoney, right, is about to have his tainted career end at the hands of Charles Starrett in* Blazing Trail *(Columbia, 1949).*

(1952), *Overland Pacific* (1954), *Showdown at Abilene* (1956), *Joe Dakota* (1957), *The Last of the Fast Guns* (1958).

### Francis McDonald (1891–1968)

Born in Bowling Green, Kentucky, this veteran performer began his lengthy career in films in 1912 in non-westerns. In 1923 the 5-foot 9-inch McDonald was voted Hollywood's "prettiest" man by a board of magazine editors. To counteract the publicity he had his agent book him as a villain and soon he pillaged, murdered and was strung up in picture after picture. McDonald established himself as a talented character actor specializing in heavy roles, then later in sympathetic parts as a banker, rancher, sheriff, and many Indian roles. McDonald, who held a college degree, was one of the first members of the Hollywood Masquers Club. His first wife was actress Mae Busch. McDonald died September 18, 1968, in the Motion Picture Country Hospital after a lengthy illness. His many western roles included: *The Last Trail* (1921), *The Yankee Senor, Flying Horseman* (1926), *Outlaws of Red River* (1927), *The Lash* (1930), *Hidden Valley, Texas Buddies*

(1932), *Terror Trail* (1933), *Robin Hood of El Dorado* (1936), *Gun Law* (1938), *Range War, Geronimo* (1939), *Northwest Mounted Police, Wyoming* (1940), *Wild Bill Hickok Rides* (1942), *Bar 20, The Kansan, Buckskin Frontier, Texas Masquerade* (1943), *The Great Stage Robbery, Cheyenne Wildcat, Bordertown Trail* (1944), *Corpus Christi Bandits, South of the Rio Grande, Bad Men of the Border, Cisco Kid Returns* (1945), *My Pal Trigger, Roll on Texas Moon* (1946), *Saddle Pals* (1947), *The Bold Frontiersman, Strange Gamble, The Dead Don't Dream* (1948), *Rustlers, Powder River Rustlers, Rim of the Canyon, Apache Chief* (1949), *Gene Autry and the Mounties* (1950), *Fort Osage* (1951), *Rancho Notorious, Desert Passage* (1952), *Ten Wanted Men* (1954), *Canyon River* (1956), *Pawnee, Duel at Apache Wells, Last Stagecoach West* (1957), *Fort Massacre, The Saga of Hemp Brown* (1958).

*Francis McDonald, right, is forced to open the safe fearful of Peggy Stewart's life in* Cheyenne Wildcat *(Republic, 1944). The trio of badmen in foreground are Bud Osborne, Robert Wilke, and Bud Geary.*

### Nelson McDowell (1875–1947)

Nelson McDowell was a leading portrayer of character parts in many non-westerns as well as the sagebrush films. His non-western roles included such classics as *Uncle Tom's Cabin* and *Oliver Twist*. He was born August 8, 1875, in Greenfield, Missouri, and died November 3, 1947, of a self-inflicted wound from a gun that had been used in many cowboy roles. His western films included:

*Border Blackbirds, The Great Mail Robbery* (1927), *Billy the Kid* (1930), *Law and Order* (1932), *Rustler's Roundup* (1933), *Wheels of Destiny, Texas Ranger,* (1934), *Wilderness Trail, Western Frontier* (1935), *The Desert Phantom, Feud of the West* (1936), *Roll Wagons Roll* (1939), *Pioneer Days* (1940).

*Nelson McDowell, left, with Lafe McKee, Robert Brower, Tom Tyler, and Jayne Regan in* Silver Bullet *(Reliable Pictures Corporation, 1934).*

### John P. McGowan (1880–1952)

John P. McGowan gained his greatest fame as a director of silent serials, particularly *Hazards of Helen* with his wife, Helen Holmes, as the star. This was in 1912. He also directed and acted in many westerns of the silent and sound era. He was born in Terowie, Australia, February of 1880. He served in the Boer War with Australian troops. His stage career found him working with the top stars all over the world. He worked as an actor and director with the Kalem Motion Picture Company, then with Famous Players-Lasky as a director. He organized the Signal Film Corporation and produced and directed for Mutual and then to Universal, FBO, RKO, and Monogram. He then became an independent producer. He was

*John P. McGowan and Randolph Scott prepare to fight off the Indians in* Wagon Wheels *(Paramount, 1934).*

the executive secretary of the Screen Director's Guild from 1938 to 1950. He died in Hollywood, March 26, 1952. His western films included: *Somewhere in Sonora* (1933), *Wagon Wheels, Fighting Hero* (1934), *Bar 20 Rides Again* (1935), *The Three Mesquiteers, Ride 'Em Cowboy, Guns and Guitars* (1936), *In Old Montana, Stagecoach* (1939).

### Lafe McKee (1872–1959)

Born Lafayette Stocking McKee in Morrison, Illinois, January 23, 1872, Lafe McKee became one of the most beloved actors in western films. His film career began in 1912. He usually portrayed an honest rancher whose daughter fell in love with the hero. He was menaced at one time or another by nearly every screen villain. His film career continued into the early 1940s when he retired from films. He died August 10, 1959, at the age of 87. His western films included: *Obligin' Buckaroo* (1927), *On the Divide, Trail Riders* (1929), *Under Montana Skies, The Utah Kid* (1930), *Mark of the Spur, Riding Tornado* (1932), *Tombstone Canyon, Fighting for Justice* (1933), *Trail Drive, Riders of Destiny* (1934), *Desert Trail, The Ivory-Handled Gun* (1935), *The Cowboy and the Kid, Idaho Kid* (1936), *Law of the Ranger, Melody of the Plains* (1937), *Rawhide* (1938), *Pioneers of the Frontier, Riders of Pasco Basin* (1940).

*Lafe McKee, second from left, with Dick Curtis, Linda Winters, and Carl Stockdale in* Pioneers of the Frontier *(Columbia, 1940).*

### Kansas Moehring (1897–1968)

Carl (Kansas) Moehring was born July 9, 1897, in Ohio. His appearances in westerns consisted primarily of ranchers, sheriffs, or one of the townspeople. He died October 3, 1968, at the age of 71. His western films included: *Down Texas Way* (1942), *Land of the Outlaws* (1944), *Trailing Danger* (1947), *Frontier Agent* (1948), *The Younger Brothers, Renegades of Sonora* (1949), *The Cariboo Trail* (1950), *The Stranger Wore a Gun* (1953).

*Kansas Moehring, right, as the sheriff with Steve Darrell,*
*Jack Hendricks, and Marshall Reed in* Trailing Danger
*(Monogram, 1947).*

### Walter (Monte) Montague (1892–1959)

Monte Montague started his show business career
with Ringling Brothers Circus as an aerialist. He
later went to Hollywood and played in early westerns with Tom Mix, Buck Jones and Hoot Gibson.
In later-day westerns he portrayed character parts,
particularly sheriff roles. He died in Burbank,
California, April 6, 1959. His western films included: *King of the Rodeo* (1929), *Trigger Tricks*
(1930), *Outlawed Guns* (1935), *Song of the
Saddle* (1936), *Guns of the Pecos* (1937), *Riders
of the Black Hills* (1938), *The Renegade Ranger*
(1939), *Young Buffalo Bill* (1940), *The Apache
Kid* (1941), *The Cyclone Kid* (1942), *Fighting
Frontier* (1943), *The Vigilantes Return* (1947),
*Rustlers* (1949), *The Last Musketeer* (1953).

*Monte Montague, center, has the drop on Richard (Chito)
Martin with Martha Hyer's help in* Rustlers *(RKO, 1949).
The man behind Montague is Stanley Blystone.*

### J. Carrol Naish (1900– )

Versatility is the word for Irishman J. Carrol Naish. As the master of many dialects, he has played almost every conceivable role in almost every type of film. He was born in New York City, January 21, 1900. He appeared on the stage in New York and Paris and left Broadway in November of 1930 and was signed by 20th Century-Fox. He created the role of "Luigi" for radio and later appeared in the television series *Life With Luigi*. He has appeared in over 150 films and his favorite roles were the two times he was nominated for the Academy Award for performances in *Sahara*, 1943, and *A Medal for Benny*, 1945. His western films include: *Last Trail* (1933), *Under the Pampas Moon* (1935), *Robin Hood of El Dorado* (1936), *Thunder Trail* (1937), *Jackass Mail* (1942), *Bad Bascomb* (1946), *Canadian Pacific* (1949), *Rio Grande* (1950), *The Denver and Rio Grande* (1952), *Sitting Bull* (1954), *The Last Command* (1955), *Yaqui Drums* (1956).

*J. Carrol Naish, left, as assistant to Dean Jagger, right, head of the railroad with the love interest, Laura Elliot, and rail boss Edmond O'Brien in Denver and Rio Grande (Paramount, 1952).*

*Parson Frank O'Connor is about to punch Francis Mc-Donald in Gun Law (RKO, 1938). Other interested onlookers are Bob Burns, Rita Oehmen, George O'Brien, and Ethan Laidlaw.*

### Frank O'Connor (1888–1964)

Frank O'Connor probably appeared in as many unbilled parts as any other screen actor. Although he was in many westerns he appeared in untold bit roles as a policeman. He was a former director of stage and screen having co-directed with Marshall Neilan. He was born in New York, April 11, 1888, and died February 24, 1964. His western films included: *His Fighting Blood* (1935), *The Purple Vigilantes, Riders of the Black Hills, Gun Law* (1938), *The Tulsa Kid* (1940), *Saddle Leather Law* (1944), *Days of Buffalo Bill* (1946), *Last Frontier Uprising* (1947), *Fort Dodge Stampede* (1951).

### Bradley Page ( – )

Bradley Page was born in Seattle. He attended the University of Washington where he became interested in an acting career. He moved scenery and became an assistant electrician for a Seattle stock company before getting his first part. From 1917 until 1927 he played in stock and then embarked on his film career. In western films he played a saloon owner or businessman who normally was the leader of the band of outlaws. His western films include: *Sundown Rider* (1933), *Fighting Rangers* (1934), *Law West of Tombstone* (1938), *Beyond the Sacramento, Roaring Frontiers, Badlands of Dakota* (1941), *Sons of the Pioneers* (1942).

*Bradley Page, right, is apprehensive of Bill Elliott's next move in* Beyond the Sacramento *(Columbia, 1941).*

### Vester Pegg (1889–1951)

Vester Pegg was born May 28, 1889, in Appleton City, Missouri. He started his film career at an early age and appeared in character roles in western films for 30 years. He died February 19, 1951, at the age of 61. His western films included: *Cheyenne's Pal* (1917), *The Phantom Riders* (1918), *The Dawn Trail* (1934), *Born to the West* (1938), *Stagecoach* (1939), *West of Abilene, Colorado* (1940).

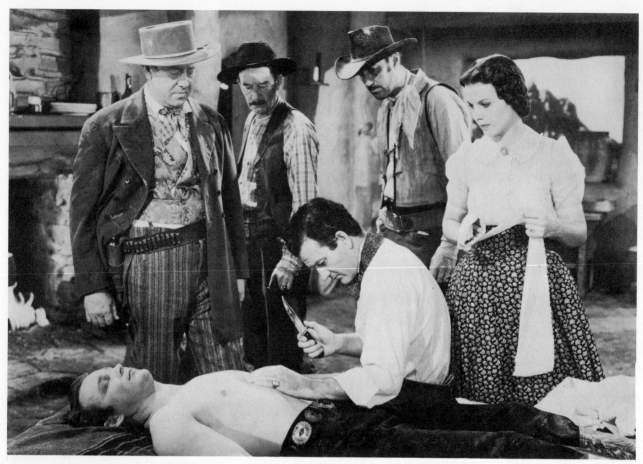

*Vester Pegg, standing, second from left, with Arthur Loft, Charles Baldra, and Pauline Moore watch as Milburn Stone attempts to extract a bullet from Roy Rogers in* Colorado *(Republic, 1940).*

## Edward Peil (1882–1958)

Edward Peil was born in Racine, Wisconsin, in 1882. His screen career began in 1908. He appeared in many films in a variety of parts, but participated in more westerns than any other type. He was normally a rancher or sheriff. He died in Hollywood December 29, 1958, at the age of 76. His western films included: *Gay Buckaroo* (1932), *Tombstone Canyon* (1933), *Blue Steel* (1934), *Come on Cowboys!, Two-Fisted Sheriff* (1937), *Colorado Trail* (1938), *The Man from Sundown* (1939), *One Man's Law* (1940), *The Lone Rider in Ghost Town* (1941), *Robin Hood of the Range* (1943).

*Edward Peil, right, as Sheriff Wiley in* The Man from Sundown *(Columbia, 1939). Others from left to right are Edward Le Saint, Richard Fiske, Oscar Gahan, and Charles Starrett.*

### Jack Pennick (1895-1964)

Jack Pennick played comedy, straight, or heavy parts in films. His classic face was found gracing the screen for over 35 years and he appeared in many of John Ford's westerns. He served in both World Wars and during the second was wounded in action and received the Silver Star. His movie career started when he was employed as a technical advisor on *What Price Glory* in 1926; 26 years later he appeared in the remake of the film. He was born in Portland, Oregon, and died March 16, 1964, in Manhattan Beach, California. His western films included: *Lone Eagle* (1927), *The Virginian* (1929), *Way Out West* (1930), *Phantom Express* (1932), *Renegades of the West* (1933), *Drift Fence* (1936), *Stagecoach* (1939), *The Westerner* (1940), *Fort Apache* (1948), *She Wore a Yellow Ribbon* (1949), *Rio Grande* (1950), *The Horse Soldiers* (1959), *The Alamo* (1960), *The Man Who Shot Liberty Valance* (1962).

*Jack Pennick, left, as Sergeant Shattuck is one of three sergeants feeling the wrath of Master Sergeant Ward Bond in John Ford's brilliant western,* Fort Apache *(RKO, 1948). The other two are Victor McLaglen and Dick Foran.*

### Lee Phelps (1894–1953)

Lee Phelps was one of the many actors that remained unidentified by the vast majority of the audience during his film career. He was a former vaudevillian and appeared in films and serials for almost 35 years. He played on both sides of the law in his western films and his picture has appeared in many film books as the unidentified waiter in Greta Garbo's *Anna Christie* in 1930.

He died in Culver City, California, March 19, 1953. His western films included: *Boss Rider of Gun Creek* (1936), *Boss of Lonely Valley* (1937), *Sudden Bill Dorn* (1938), *Hidden Gold* (1940), *Shadows of the West, Gun Law Justice* (1949), *The Girl from San Lorenzo, Hills of Oklahoma* (1950).

*Lee Phelps, right, has the drop on Leo Carrillo and Duncan Renaldo as Jane Adams looks on in* The Girl from San Lorenzo *(United Artists, 1950).*

### Slim Pickens (1919–    )

Slim Pickens was born Louis Bert Lindley Jr. in Kingsburg, California, June 29, 1919. Able to ride á horse well at an early age he joined his first rodeo at the age of 12. He became the top rodeo clown in the business and the highest paid. In his rodeo career he fought over 3000 Brahma bulls and has broken nearly every bone in his body. He made his motion picture debut in 1950 and played in many Rex Allen features as well as other top feature westerns. His western films include: *Rocky Mountain* (1950), *Border Saddlemates, Colorado Sundown* (1952), *Shadows of Tombstone* (1953), *Red River Shore* (1954), *Santa Fe Passage* (1955), *Gun Brothers* (1956), *Gunsight Ridge* (1957), *The Sheepman* (1958), *Escort West* (1959), *One-Eyed Jacks* (1961), *The Glory Guys* (1965), *Stagecoach* (1966), *Rough Night in Jericho* (1967), *Will Penny* (1968), *The Ballad of Cable Hogue* (1970).

*Slim Pickens, left, and Rex Allen prepare for the worst in* Shadows of Tombstone *(Republic, 1953).*

### Lee Prather (1889–1958)

Oscar Lee Prather began his film career in 1930, after a long career in stock and on Broadway including appearances with Mae West. In western films he usually played the heroine's father. He died in Los Angeles January 3, 1958, after a long illness. His western films included: *Two-Gun Law* (1937), *Born to the West* (1938), *Texas Stampede* (1939), *Bullets for Rustlers* (1940), *Outlaws of the Panhandle* (1941).

*Lee Prather protects his daughter, Iris Meredith, as Charles Starrett draws a bead on Fred Kohler Jr. in* Texas Stampede *(Columbia, 1939).*

### Stanley Price (1892–1955)

Stanley Price was the original Abie in Broadway's *Abie's Irish Rose,* playing the part in 1,100 performances. He later played in many western films and serials both as a heavy and other assorted roles. In addition to his acting career he was also a dialogue director. His last assignment as an actor was in Cecil B. DeMille's *The Ten Commandments.* He was born in Kansas on December

31, 1892, and died in Hollywood of a heart attack July 13, 1955. His western films included: *Range War* (1939), *The Golden Trail* (1940), *Wanderers of the West* (1941), *Range Law* (1944), *Sunset in El Dorado* (1945), *Frontier Gunlaw, Alias Billy the Kid* (1946), *Rimfire* (1949), *Cherokee Uprising* (1950), *Abilene Trail* (1951), *Canyon Ambush* (1952), *The Star of Texas* (1953).

Stanley Price, standing center, with Frank Ellis, Pierce Lyden, Johnny Mack Brown, and Hugh Prosser in Canyon Ambush *(Monogram, 1952).*

### Denver Pyle (1920–   )

A Johnny-Come-Lately as far as most western actors are concerned, Denver Pyle has made up for lost time. His first film was *Man From Colorado* with Glenn Ford and William Holden. Since that time he has appeared with Bill Elliott, Gene Autry, Sunset Carson, Roy Rogers and Johnny Mack Brown. His favorite role was in the non-western hit *Bonnie and Clyde,* but Denver states, "I played the Texas Ranger, Frank Hamer, like a "B" western sheriff." He was born May 11, 1920, in Bethune, Colorado. His western films include: *Man from Colorado* (1948), *Hellfire* (1949), *The Old Frontier, Rough Riders of Durango* (1951), *Canyon Ambush* (1952), *Goldtown Ghost Riders* (1953), *Ride Clear of Diablo* (1954), *Top Gun* (1955), *Seventh Cavalry* (1956), *The Alamo* (1960), *Geronimo* (1962), *The Rounders* (1965), *Gunpoint* (1966), *Welcome to Hard Times* (1967), *Five Card Stud* (1968).

*Denver Pyle.*

### Marshall Reed (1917–    )

From 1945 through 1952 Marshall Reed was as busy as any actor around in western films. The handsome Reed played on both sides of the law in many Monogram, Eagle-Lion, and Republic films. He appeared with Johnny Mack Brown, Tim Holt, and Whip Wilson in scores of features. He was born May 28, 1917, in Englwood, Colorado. After graduation from high school he held a variety of jobs such as a bookkeeper, horse trainer, department store clerk, addressograph operator, and meter reader. He joined the U.S. Navy during World War II and after his discharge started his film career. His western films include: *Tucson Raiders, Mojave Firebrand* (1944), *Law of the Valley* (1945), *Shadows on the Range, Gentleman from Texas* (1946), *The Fighting Vigilantes, Prairie Express* (1947), *The Gallant Legion, Back Trail* (1948), *Law of the West, The Dalton Gang*

*Marshall Reed, left, with Veda Borg and Robert Shayne in* Rider from Tucson *(RKO Radio, 1950).*

(1949), *Over the Border, Silver Raiders* (1950), *Abilene Trail* (1951), *Laramie Mountains* (1952), *Cow Country* (1953).

### Frank Rice (1892–1936)

Frank Thomas Rice was born May 13, 1892, in Muskegon, Michigan. He started his career as an actor in 1918 and appeared in many silents. In the sound era he played in several Buck Jones and Ken Maynard westerns as well as appearing with John Wayne, George O'Brien, and Randolph Scott. He was active until his death January 9, 1936, in Los Angeles of hepatitis. His western films included: *The Slingshot Kid* (1927), *Hound of Silver Creek, Overland Telegraph* (1928), *Shotgun Pass* (1931), *Sunset Trail* (1932), *Somewhere in Sonora, Forbidden Trail, King of the Arena* (1933), *Thundering Herd, Wheels of Destiny* (1934), *Stone of Silver Creek, Powdersmoke Range* (1935), *The Oregon Trail* (1936).

*Frank Rice, left, with Ken Maynard in* King of the Arena *(Universal, 1933).*

### Addison Richards (1902–1964)

Addison Richards played a variety of parts from cavalry officers to ranchers to swindlers, and always gave a good performance. He was born in 1902 in Zanesville, Ohio, and graduated from Washington State University. He began his acting career in 1926 and in 1931 joined the Pasadena Community Playhouse as an actor and associate director. His film career began in 1933 and he also made many

*Addison Richards, right, and Weldon Heyburn are at odds in scene from* Bordertown Trail *(Republic, 1944).*

television appearances. He died March 22, 1964, of a heart attack. His western films included: *Lone Cowboy* (1933), *Eagle's Brood* (1935), *Song of the Saddle* (1936), *Geronimo* (1939), *The Man from Dakota* (1940), *Sheriff of Tombstone* (1941), *Men of Texas* (1942), *Bordertown Trail* (1944), *Bells of Rosarita* (1945), *Renegades* (1946), *Rustlers* (1949), *Fort Yuma* (1955), *Fury at Gunsight Pass* (1956), *Frontier Uprising* (1961).

## Julian Rivero (1890–      )

Julian Rivero has appeared with many of the western greats including Harry Carey, Hoot Gibson and Buck Jones. His early years were spent as a heavy, but he switched to kindlier roles later on. He was born in Galveston, Texas, in 1890 and entered films in 1915. He became a cameraman and also directed comedies. His wife was the former Isabel Thomas, a Mack Sennett bathing beauty. His western films include: *Night Rider* (1932), *Via Pony Express* (1933), *Sagebrush Troubadour* (1935), *Song of the Saddle* (1936), *Heroes of the Alamo* (1937), *Young Buffalo Bill* (1940) *Billy the Kid's Fighting Pals* (1941), *Hands Across the Border* (1943), *Trail to Mexico* (1946), *Robin Hood of Monterey* (1947), *Wild Horse Ambush* (1952), *Broken Lance* (1954), *Thunder Over Arizona* (1956).

*Julian Rivero, right, with Gilbert Roland in* Robin Hood of Monterey *(Monogram, 1947).*

## Willard Robertson (1886–1948)

Willard Robertson could have had a distinguished career in law, but he chose to be an actor. He made his stage debut in 1906 but turned to law shortly thereafter. He became an attorney in the Interstate Commerce Commission and during World War I became supervisor of the Federal Railway Police. He turned down an opportunity to become the United States Chief Attorney and returned to acting. He also became a director and playwright. He was born in Runnels, Texas, Janu-

*Willard Robertson, left, as Nathan Brockway in* Renegades
*(Columbia, 1946), with Eddy Waller and Evelyn Keyes.*

ary 1, 1886, graduated from public and law school in Washington, D.C. He died April 5, 1948, at the age of 62. His western films included: *Gay Caballero, Texas Bad Man* (1932), *The Last of the Mohicans* (1936), *Jesse James, Heritage of the Desert* (1939), *Lucky Cisco Kid* (1940), *Texas* (1941), *The Virginian, Renegades* (1946), *Fury at Furnace Creek* (1948).

### Rad Robinson (1911–    )

Rad Robinson was born November 11, 1911, in Bountiful, Utah. His parents were active in civic and educational programs and his grandparents were pioneers coming across the plains with the early Mormon settlers. After school Rad started singing at an early age. He entered films as a member of a quartet at the age of 18. This quartet eventually became known as "The Kings Men." They were signed by Harry Sherman to star with Bill Boyd in the Hopalong Cassidy series. Rad, in addition to his singing, went on to other types of roles. His favorite role was the smiling, singing, swaggering bandit of *Stagecoach War* in 1940. In looking back on his western roles he stated that he loved the riding, singing and the early morning calls. His western roles include: *Law of the Pampas* (1939), *The Light of the Western Stars, Knights of the Range, The Showdown, Stagecoach War* (1940), *Man from Montana* (1941).

*Rad Robinson as "Brazos" in* Knights of the Range *(Paramount, 1940).*

### Jack Rockwell (    –1947)

One of the regular Charles Starrett stock players at Columbia was Jack Rockwell who more often than not appeared as the honest sheriff. Rockwell was no exception to the sheriff of the era, as he always needed the hero's help to restore law and order to the town. He did occasionally switch roles to a businessman, rancher or villain, but normally was the man behind the badge. He died November 10, 1947. His western films included: *Whistlin' Dan* (1932), *King of the Arena* (1933), *Gun Justice, Smoking Guns* (1934), *Lawless Frontier, Tumbling Tumbleweeds* (1935), *The Singing Cowboy, Roarin' Guns* (1936), *Texas Trail* (1937), *Prairie Moon, Black Bandit* (1938), *Man from Sundown* (1939), *Bullets for Rustlers, Santa*

*Jack Rockwell, left, as the sheriff and U.S. Marshal Charles Starrett in* The Stranger from Texas *(Columbia, 1939).*

*Fe Marshal, Pony Post* (1940), *The Pinto Kid* (1941), *Tombstone* (1942), *The Renegade* (1943), *Trigger Trail* (1944), *Flame of the West* (1945), *Two-Fisted Stranger* (1946), *Code of the Plains* (1947).

### Buddy Roosevelt (1898–    )

Buddy Roosevelt was born Kent Sanderson June 25, 1898, on a ranch near Meeker, Colorado. The one-time law aspirant joined a wild west show in his youth as a stunt rider. This led to attempts to get into films as a stunt man, and in 1915 he appeared briefly in his first film in this capacity. His career was interrupted by World War I and he had a difficult time getting back into films upon his return. He was finally rehired and recognized for his ability. In 1924 he starred in his first of many fast moving westerns. By 1930 his career as a leading man waned but he continued to appear in supporting roles for several years to come and even appeared as one of Tim McCoy's riders in *Around the World in 80 Days* in 1956. His western films include: *Hell's Hinges* (1916), *Rough Ridin'* (1924), *The Ramblin' Galoot, Easy Going* (1926), *The Bandit Buster, The Phantom Buster* (1927), *Mystery Valley* (1928), *The Trail Riders* (1929), *Westward Bound* (1931), *Fourth Horseman, Wild Horse Mesa* (1933), *Powdersmoke Range* (1935), *The Old Corral* (1937).

*Buddy Roosevelt as he appeared in* Westward Bound *in 1931 by Syndicate.*

### Francis Sayles (1891–1944)

Born in Buffalo, New York, in 1891 Francis Sayles started his career on the stage and switched to the screen in 1930. Most of his films were of the western variety where he played many character parts. He died March 19, 1944 in Hollywood. His western films included: *The Texas Bad Man* (1932), *Home on the Range* (1935), *The Purple Vigilantes* (1938), *Riders of Black River, Union Pacific* (1939).

*Francis Sayles, center, with Charles Starrett and Iris Meredith in* Riders of Black River *(Columbia, 1939).*

### Syd Saylor (1895–1962)

Syd Saylor specialized in character or sidekick roles playing with nearly every western star at one time or another. He normally played comedy roles and his trademarks were his bobbing adams apple and slight stutter. He was born Leo Sailor May 24, 1895, in Chicago. He attended the Chicago Art Institute and specialized in art and athletics. After 14 years of stage experience he made 54 two-reel Syd Saylor comedies for Universal. In addition to his many films he also appeared in many television shows. He died of a heart attack in Hollywood December 21, 1962. His western films included: *When a Man Sees Red* (1934), *Wilderness Mail* (1935), *Headin' for Rio Grande* (1936), *Forlorn River, Arizona Days* (1937), *Born to the West* (1938), *Union Pacific* (1939), *Arizona* (1940), *Wyoming Wildcat* (1941), *Navajo Kid* (1945), *Thunder town* (1946), *Big Jack* (1949), *Mule Train* (1950), *The Hawk of Wild River* (1952).

*Syd Saylor, right, with Buster Crabbe in a scene from Zane Grey's* Forlorn River *(Paramount, 1937).*

### Fred F. Sears (1913–1957)

Fred F. Sears was born in Boston, July 7, 1913. He attended Boston College and in little theatre groups was an actor, stage manager, and director. He was an instructor at Southwestern University in Memphis, Tennessee. Primarily a director at Columbia he nevertheless took time out to appear in character roles in many western films. He died November 30, 1957. His western films included:

*Law of the Canyon, West of Dodge City* (1947), *Phantom Valley, Adventures in Silverado* (1948), *Laramie, South of Death Valley, Frontier Out-* *post* (1949), *Hoedown, Texas Dynamo* (1950), *Bonanza Town, Fort Savage Raiders* (1951), *Laramie Mountains, The Rough Tough West* (1952).

*Fred Sears, second from right, with Smiley Burnette and Charles Starrett, in Fort Savage Raiders (Columbia, 1951).*

### Harry Shannon (1890–1964)

Harry Shannon began his film career in 1939 at the age of 49 after a long, successful career in musical comedy, in vaudeville, and on Broadway. The kindly Irish actor was born in Saginaw, Michigan, June 13, 1890, and revealed an aptitude for singing and dancing at an early age. He retired in 1962 and died July 27, 1964, in Hollywood. His western films included: *In Old California* (1942), *Idaho* (1943), *The Yellow Rose of Texas* (1944), *Rustlers* (1949), *Curtain Call at Cactus Creek, The Gunfighters* (1950), *Al Jennings of Oklahoma* (1951), *High Noon* (1952), *Kansas Pacific* (1953), *The Tall Men* (1955), *Hell's Crossroads* (1957).

*Harry Shannon.*

### Dave Sharpe (1911–    )

Dave Sharpe was born in St. Louis in 1911. The handsome Sharpe has long been recognized as one of the finest stuntmen ever to perform in films. His flying leaps and bar room brawls are unparalleled in motion pictures. The athletic Sharpe was a former U.S. tumbling champion and his talents are endless. He excels in boxing, judo, wrestling, jiu jitsu, swimming, diving, fencing, juggling, gymnastics and dancing. He is an expert horseman and can perform numerous two-gun feats including an exceptional "fast-draw." He has played many roles and starred in several "Range Buster" films for Monogram in the early 1940s. He also became a fixture in Republic serials and starred in *Daredevils of the Red Circle*. His western films include: *Roaring Roads* (1935), *Idaho Kid* (1936), *Melody of the Plains* (1937), *Three Texas Steers, Wyoming Outlaw* (1939), *Covered Wagon Trails* (1940), *Silver Stallion* (1941), *Trail Riders* (1942), *Two-Fisted Justice* (1943), *Colorado Serenade* (1946), *Bells of San Angelo* (1947).

*Dave Sharpe, center, with his two fellow range busters, Max Terhune and John King, in* Two Fisted Justice *(Monogram, 1943).*

### Russell Simpson (1880–1959)

Russell Simpson was one of the finest character actors on the screen. The grizzled veteran's career spanned 60 years in a variety of roles, but he was at his best in western films. He was born June 17, 1880, in San Francisco and participated in the Alaskan Goldrush in 1898. He played a number of dramatic leads on the New York stage and began making movies in 1910. He started as a romantic lead playing opposite such stars as Gloria Swanson. One of his most famous silent roles was as gambler Jack Rance in *Girl of the Golden West* in 1923. His "Pa Joad" interpretation in *The Grapes of Wrath* in 1940 was also outstanding. He died December 12, 1959. His western films included: *Girl of the Golden West* (1923), *Rustlin' for Cupid* (1926), *The Bushranger* (1928), *The Lone Star Ranger* (1930), *Law and Order, Ridin' for Justice* (1932), *Frontier Marshal* (1934), *Yodelin' Kid from Pine Ridge* (1937), *Dodge City, Western Caravans* (1939), *Santa Fe Trail* (1940), *Wild Bill Hickok Rides* (1941), *The Lone Star Ranger* (1942), *Border Patrol* (1943), *Texas Masquerade* (1944), *Along Came Jones* (1945), *California Gold Rush* (1946), *The Fabulous Texan* (1947), *Coroner Creek* (1948), *The Gal Who Took the West* (1949), *Wagonmaster* (1950), *Lone Star* (1952), *The Sun Shines Bright* (1953), *Broken Lance* (1954), *The Tall Men* (1955), *The Brass Legend* (1956).

*Russell Simpson, right, with Ward Bond and Jane Darwell as Mormon pioneers heading for fertile land in Wagonmaster (Argosy-RKO, 1950).*

### Carl Stockdale (1874–1953)

Carl Stockdale was a veteran western player normally chosen to play the heroine's rancher-father. He was born in Worthington, Minnesota, February 19, 1874, and graduated from the University of North Dakota. After playing in stock and roadshows he entered films in 1912 with the old Essanay Film Company and then with D. W. Griffith for three years. He died March 15, 1953. His western films included: *Rocky Rhodes* (1934), *The Crimson Trail, The Ivory-Handled Gun* (1935), *Courage of the West* (1937), *Hawaiian Buckaroo* (1938), *Pioneers of the Frontier, Stage to Chino, Wagon Train, Konga the Wild Stallion, Thundering Frontier* (1940), *The Return of Daniel Boone, Along the Rio Grande* (1941).

*Carl Stockdale, as contractor Andrew Belknap, right, shows concern over injured Fred Burns in* Thundering Frontier *(Columbia, 1940). Also shown are his screen daughter, Iris Meredith, and Charles Starrett.*

*Lyle Talbot.*

### Lyle Talbot (1904–    )

Lyle Talbot was born Lysle Hollywood in Pittsburgh February 8, 1904. His last name sounded too fantastic for a screen career and he changed it to Talbot. Both of his parents were in show business in traveling tent shows and he followed in their footsteps. He played in stock companies, was a juvenile magician, a singer and on Broadway prior to being signed in Warner Brothers in 1931 for *Love is a Racket*. He played many leading roles in "B" features and in the 1950s supported Whip Wilson, Johnny Mack Brown, Gene Autry, Roy Rogers, and other stars in westerns. His western films include: *Trail to Gunsight* (1945), *Song of Arizona, Gun Town* (1946), *Border Rangers* (1950), *Colorado Ambush, Stage to Blue River, Abilene Trail, Man from Sonora* (1951), *Desperadoes Outpost, Montana Incident, The Old West* (1952), *Trail Blazers* (1953).

### Forrest Taylor (1883–1965)

Forrest Taylor played every conceivable part in western films. He switched from one side of the law to the other with regular frequency. He was equally at home portraying the gangleader as he was the banker, rancher, father, or judge. He made over 200 appearances in films. He was born in Bloomington, Illinois, December 29, 1883, and died in Garden Grove, California, February 19, 1965. His western films included: *Riders of Destiny* (1933), *Rider of the Law* (1935), *Rio Grande Romance* (1936), *Arizona Days, Riders of the Dawn* (1937), *Gun Packer, Black Bandit* (1938), *Riders of Black River* (1939), *West of Abilene* (1940), *The Lone Star Vigilantes* (1941), *Bullets for Bandits* (1942), *Silver Spurs* (1943), *Sonora Stagecoach* (1944), *The Caravan Trail* (1946), *Rustlers of Devil's Canyon* (1947), *Coroner Creek* (1948), *The Fighting Redhead* (1949), *Cowboy and the Prizefighter* (1950), *Blazing Bullets* (1951), *Border Saddlemates* (1952), *The Marshal's Daughter* (1953), *Bitter Creek* (1954).

*Forrest Taylor, left, and Tex Ritter enjoy a hearty meal in* Bullets for Bandits *(Columbia, 1942).*

### Harry Tyler (1888–1961)

Harry Tyler began his theatrical career at the age of eight, appearing with Anna Held as a boy soprano. This gave him a 65-year career, one of the longest in show business. He played vaudeville with his wife for a number of seasons and returned to the legitimate theatre in 1925. In 1929 he went to Hollywood to appear in *The Shannons of Broadway,* a role he created for the New York stage. He stayed in Hollywood and played many character parts in all types of films including many westerns. He died in Hollywood of cancer September 15, 1961. His western films included: *Jesse James* (1939), *The Untamed Breed* (1948), *The Beautiful Blonde from Bashful Bend* (1949), *Rider from Tucson* (1950), *Al Jennings of Oklahoma* (1951), *Junction City* (1952), *A Lawless Street* (1955), *Day of Fury* (1956), *Alias Jesse James* (1959).

*Harry Tyler, left, is held up by the Jennings Brothers, Dick Foran, and Dan Duryea in* Al Jennings of Oklahoma *(Columbia, 1951).*

### Rick Vallin (1920– )

Rick Vallin was born in Russia in 1920. His mother was the famous Russian ballerina, Nedia Yatsenko. He was brought to New York while a teenager as his mother continued her career in America. He became interested in acting while in school and later played with several stock companies. He was also on radio and appeared at the Pasadena Playhouse. He attracted the attention of film scouts while there and appeared in his first film in 1942. His western films include: *King of the Stallions* (1942), *Wagon Tracks West* (1943), *Northwest Outpost, Last of the Redmen* (1947), *Rio Grande Patrol, Comanche Territory* (1950), *The Star of Texas, Topeka* (1953), *Treasure of Ruby Hills* (1955).

*Rick Vallin, right, as "Little Coyote" and Chief Thundercloud as "Hahawi" in* King of the Stallions *(Monogram, 1942).*

### Robert Warwick (1878–1964)

Former matinee idol Robert Warwick who played opposite many of the leading ladies of the silent screen in the teens found many character roles when sound came in. He was born Robert Taylor Bien in Sacramento, California in 1878. He started his stage career in 1903. A few years later he began his film career. He became a Colonel during World War I and upon his return was signed by Famous Players-Lasky for a long film career. He died at the age of 85 in Hollywood, June 6, 1964. His western films included: *Code of the Mounted, Hopalong Cassidy* (1935), *The Bold Caballero* (1936), *Trigger Trio* (1937), *Law of the Plains* (1938), *In Old Monterey* (1939), *Konga—The Wild Stallion* (1940), *Fury at Furnace Creek* (1948), *Gun Smugglers* (1949), *Sugarfoot* (1951), *Silver Lode* (1954), *Chief Crazy Horse* (1955).

*Robert Warwick discusses ranch expenses with Rochelle Hudson in* Konga—The Wild Stallion *(Columbia, 1940).*

### Pierre Watkin (1889–1960)

Banker, rancher, businessman or respected citizen —Pierre Watkin was at home in any role. He even showed up now and then as the secret leader of the gang of outlaws. He appeared in over 100 films after 1935. Very distinguished in both appearance and dress, he also appeared in many non-westerns. He was born December 29, 1889, in Sioux City, Iowa and had planned to be a lawyer but followed his brother's footsteps to a stage career and then the movies. He died February 3, 1960, after a lengthy illness. His western films included: *Geronimo* (1939), *Nevada City, Jesse James at Bay* (1941), *Heart of the Rio Grande* (1942), *Song of the Range* (1944), *Dakota* (1945), *Sioux City Sue* (1946), *The Wild Frontier* (1947), *Frontier Outpost* (1949), *Over the Border* (1950), *In Old Amarillo* (1951), *Thundering Caravans* (1952), *The Stranger Wore a Gun* (1953), *The Maverick Queen* (1956).

*Pierre Watkin, left, with Johnny Mack Brown in* Over the Border *(1950).*

### Minor Watson (1890–1965)

One of the more familiar faces in films was that of Minor Watson. When the role required dignity and prestige he was a logical choice. He normally played sheriffs, the father of the beautiful girl, landowner, or judge. His acting career spanned 45 years starting in 1911 until his retirement in 1956. After a long stage career he entered films in 1933. Although he preferred the stage the depression caused him to look for a more lucrative position in his chosen field. He was born in Alton, Illinois, and died there July 28, 1965. His western films included: *The Llano Kid* (1939), *Viva Cisco Kid* (1940), *Western Union, They Died With Their Boots On* (1941), *Untamed Frontier* (1952), *Ten Wanted Men* (1955), *The Rawhide Years* (1956).

*Minor Watson, seated, as the crippled cattle baron who refuses to let the settlers cross his land in* Untamed Frontier *(Universal, 1952). Pictured also are John Alexander and Katherine Emery.*

*Sheriff Chill Wills congratulates Gene Autry in tracking down a killer as Barbara Britton looks on in* Loaded Pistols *(Columbia, 1949).*

### Chill Wills (1903–

Chill Wills has a habit of calling everyone "cousin." This is undoubtedly due to this great storyteller's fondness for people; the feeling must be mutual as the people in his home state of Texas have dubbed him "Mr. Texas." Chill was born July 18, 1903, on the hottest day in Texas and as he is fond of telling folks this is how he got his name. He entered motion pictures after being spotted by an RKO executive while singing at a Hollywood restaurant. He is a fine actor and his film credits are many, both westerns and otherwise. In addition to his many roles where he appeared on the screen he was also the voice of "Francis" in the talking mule series. His western films include: *Allegheny Uprising* (1939), *The Westerner* (1940), *Belle Starr, Billy the Kid, Western Union* (1941), *The Omaha Trail* (1942), *Northwest Stampede, Loaded Pistols* (1948), *Red Canyon* (1949), *The Sundowners, Rio Grande* (1950), *Cattle Drive* (1951), *Bronco Buster* (1952), *The Man from the Alamo* (1953), *Santiago* (1956), *The Alamo* (1960), *Gold of the Seven Saints* (1961), *McLintock!* (1963).

### Guinn "Big Boy" Williams (1900–1962)

Guinn Williams was born April 26, 1900, in Decatur, Texas. Prior to entering films he toured the rodeo circuit. He was nicknamed "Big Boy" by humorist Will Rogers when Williams was making his first film as an extra in 1919. "Big Boy" went on to star in many westerns of the 1930s. In addition to his appearances with Tom Mix, Harry Carey, and Buck Jones, he also played straight dramatic roles as well as comedy in non-westerns. He graduated to character parts, playing every conceivable role in many oaters. He and Will Rogers became good friends through their common interest in polo. Williams captained one of the film colony's teams in the late 30s and at one time owned more than 200 polo ponies His last film was with John Wayne in *The Comancheros*, 1961. Williams, who speciailzed in the role of the happy-go-lucky, perplexed muscular types, died June 6, 1962, of uremic poisoning. His western films included: *Rounding Up the Law* (1922), *Black Cyclone* (1925), *Heritage of the Desert* (1933), *Thunder Over Texas, Cowboy Holiday* (1934), *Powdersmoke Range* (1935), *End of the Trail* (1936), *The Bad Man of Brimstone* (1938), *Dodge City* (1939), *Virginia City* (1940), *Billy*

*Deputy Sheriff, Guinn "Big Boy" Williams, right, doesn't see eye to eye with Sheriff Ken Curtis in* That Texas Jamboree *(Columbia, 1946).*

*the Kid* (1941), *The Desperadoes* (1943), *The Cowboy and the Senorita* (1944), *Nevada* (1945), *Cowboy Blues* (1946), *Over the Santa Fe Trail* (1947), *Bad Men of Tombstone* (1948), *Rocky Mountain* (1950), *Springfield Rifle* (1952), *Southwest Passage* (1954), *Hidden Guns* (1956), *The Alamo* (1960), *The Comancheros* (1961).

### Jay Wilsey (1896–1961)

Jay Wilsey was born in 1896 in Hillsdale, Wyoming. He followed the same route to stardom in early westerns that many others had also taken, that of being a member of wild west shows and rodeos and of appearing as a stunt man and bit parts. In 1924 he was given the name of "Buffalo Bill Jr." and his career blossomed. His easy-going manner and ability to ride allowed him a few

years of stardom before he started appearing in supporting roles. He died October 25, 1961, at the age of 65. His western films included: *Rarin' to Go* (1924), *Rawhide* (1926), *The Interferin' Gent, The Ballyhoo Buster, Roarin' Broncs* (1927), *Pals in Peril* (1928), *Westward Bound* (1931), *Dynamite Denny, Terror Trail, Deadwood Pass* (1953), *Rainbow Valley, Powdersmoke Range* (1935).

*Jay Wilsey, second from right, with Ben Corbett and Tom London (on the horse) in* Westward Bound *(Syndicate, 1931).*

### Clarence H. Wilson (1876–1941)

Clarence Hummel Wilson was born November 17, 1876, in Cincinnati. The skilled character actor appeared in many films during the early sound era, making his presence felt in every role. He died October 5, 1941, at the age of 64. His western films included: *The Mysterious Rider, Smoke Lightning, Flaming Guns* (1933), *The Texans* (1938), *Drums Along the Mohawk* (1939), *Melody Ranch* (1940).

*Clarence H. Wilson, center, with E. H. Calvert and Irving Pichel in* The Mysterious Rider *(Paramount, 1933).*

### Britt Wood (1895–1965)

As a boy he began his career in vaudeville. He became an accomplished harmonica player and often played the New York Palace. As vaudeville was fading he headed for Hollywood where he appeared in many westerns. He was used as one of the comedy reliefs in Hopalong Cassidy films, playing the role of "Speedy." He died in Hollywood, April 13, 1965. His western roles included:

*Trail Dust* (1936), *Range War* (1939), *Santa Fe Marshal, Knights of the Range, The Showdown, Stagecoach War, Hidden Gold* (1940), *Pirates on Horseback, Border Vigilantes* (1941), *Down Rio Grande Way* (1942), *Cheyenne* (1947), *Riders of the Whistling Pines* (1949), *Return of the Frontiersman* (1950).

*Britt Wood as he appeared in one of his rustic roles as "Laigs," in* Knights of the Range *(Paramount, 1940).*

### Will Wright (1891–1962)

Will Wright normally portrayed an apparently hard-hearted man who proved more often than not that this was a surface characterization. He was born in San Francisco, March 26, 1891, and was a newspaper reporter, then made the rounds in vaudeville and stock. He became a producer for the New York stage and radio. He died of cancer in Hollywood, June 19, 1962. His western films included: *In Old Oklahoma* (1943), *Relentless, Whispering Smith, Black Eagle* (1948), *A Ticket to Tomahawk, Dallas* (1950), *Vengeance Valley* (1951), *The Last Posse* (1953), *The Raid* (1954), *The Tall Men* (1955), *The Iron Sheriff* (1957), *Quantrill's Raiders* (1958), *Alias Jesse James* (1959), *The Deadly Companions* (1961).

*Will Wright, center, with Marguerite Chapman and Joseph Crehan in* Relentless *(Columbia, 1948).*

## Non-Biographical Section

*Frank Ball: Ball, second from left, steps between Charles King and Bob Steele in* Ridin' the Lone Trail *(Republic, 1937). Also pictured are Ernie Adams and Claire Rochelle. His western films include:* Mark of the Spur, Man from New Mexico *(1932),* When a Man Rides Alone, Galloping Romeo *(1933),* Courageous Avenger, Between Men *(1935),* Rogue of the Range, The Fugitive Sheriff *(1936),* The Gun Ranger, The Trusted Outlaw *(1937),* Paroled—To Die *(1938).*

*Buzz Barton (1914–    ): Barton, right, with Jack Luden's assistance tries to contain Harry Woods in* Rolling Caravans *(Columbia, 1938). His western films include:* Slingshot Kid *(1927),* Pioneer Scout *(1928),* Human Targets *(1932),* Lucky Larrigan *(1933),* Fighting Pioneers, Powdersmoke Range, *(1935),* Feud of the West, The Riding Avenger *(1936),* Phantom Gold, Rolling Caravans *(1938).*

*Stanley Blystone (1894–1956): Blystone, right, restrains Holly Bane from fighting with Riley Hill in* Six Gun Mesa *(Monogram, 1950). The girl is Gail Davis. His western films included:* Galloping Thru *(1932),* Lucky Larrigan, Man of Action *(1933),* Trail's End, Saddle Aces *(1935),* The Riding Avenger *(1936),* Boots and Saddles *(1937),* Stranger from Arizona *(1938),* Three Texas Steers *(1939),* The Tulsa Kid *(1940),* Sunset in Wyoming *(1941),* Jesse James Jr. *(1942),* Navajo Kid *(1945),* Six Gun Man *(1946),* Eyes of Texas *(1948),* Ride, Ryder Ride *(1949),* Six Gun Mesa *(1950),* Road Agent *(1952),* Jack McCall, Desperado *(1953).*

*Rocky Camron (1903–1967): Camron, right, with Bob Steele, Hoot Gibson, and Chief Thundercloud in* Outlaw Trail *(Monogram, 1944). His western films included:* Sonora Stagecoach, Outlaw Trail *(1944),* Song of Old Wyoming *(1945),* The Enchanted Valley *(1948),* Treachery Rides the Range *(1936),* The Golden Trail *(1940),* The Pioneers, Dynamite Canyon, Arizona Bound *(1941).*

*Ed Brady (1889–1942): Brady, second from left, with Gabby Hayes, Roy Rogers, Frank Thomas, and Jack Ingram in Saga of Death Valley (Republic, 1939). His western films included:* The Squaw Man *(1931)*, Forbidden Trail, Galloping Romeo, Lone Avenger *(1933)*, Texas Ranger *(1934)*, Riders of the Dawn *(1937)*, Thunder in the Desert *(1938)*, Saga of Death Valley *(1939)*, Shooting High *(1940)*, Wyoming Wildcat, Fugitive Valley *(1941)*.

*Harry Cheshire (1891—1968): Cheshire, as Doctor Chadwick with Patricia White in* Riders of the Whistling Pines, *starring Gene Autry. (Columbia, 1949). His western films included:* My Darling Clementine *(1943),* Springtime in the Sierras *(1947),* Black Eagle *(1948),* Riders of the Whistling Pines, Fighting Man of the Plains, Sand *(1949),* Thunder in God's Country *(1951).*

*Buck Connors: Connors, center, with Tom London and Harry Carey in* Thundering Herd *(Paramount, 1934). His western films include:* The Phantom Riders *(1918),* The Mojave Kid *(1927),* Fearless Rider *(1928),* The Last Round Up, Thundering Herd *(1934),* West of Santa Fe *(1939).*

*Jim Davis: Davis, second from left, with Bill Elliott, Paul Fix and Lane Chandler in* Hellfire *(Republic, 1949). His western films include:* Frontier Fury *(1943),* Cyclone Prairie Rangers *(1944),* The Fabulous Texan *(1947),* Hellfire *(1949),* The Showdown *(1950),* Cavalry Scout *(1951),* Rose of Cimarron, Ride the Man Down *(1952),* Woman They Almost Lynched *(1953),* The Outlaw's Daughter *(1954),* The Last Command *(1955),* The Maverick Queen *(1956),* Noose for a Gunman *(1960),* Frontier Uprising *(1961),* Fort Utah *(1967).*

*William Duncan (1879–1961): Duncan, second from left, with Buster Crabbe, June Martel and John Patterson in* Forlorn River *(Paramount, 1937). His western films included:* Nevada, Three on the Trail *(1936),* Hopalong Rides Again, Forlorn River, Thunder Trail *(1937),* Bar 20 Justice, The Frontiersman *(1938),* Law of the Pampas *(1939).*

*John Elliott (1876–1956): Elliott, right, holds back the crowd in* Ridin On, *starring Tom Tyler (Reliable Pictures, 1934). His western films included:* Galloping Thru, Riders of the Desert, Texas Pioneers *(1932)*, The Gallant Fool *(1933)*, Cowboy Holiday, Ridin' On *(1934)*, Fighting Pioneers, Sunset Range, Saddle Aces, *(1935)*, Roamin' Wild, The Fugitive Sheriff *(1936)*, Headin' East *(1937)*, Cassidy of Bar 20 *(1938)*, Jesse James *(1939)*, The Apache Kid *(1940)*, Pirates of the Prairie *(1941)*, Two-Fisted Justice *(1942)*, Oklahoma Raiders *(1944)*, Frontier Gunlaw *(1946)*, Law of the Lash *(1947)*.

*Frank Ferguson: Ferguson, left, with Roy Barcroft, Rex Allen, and Walter Coy in* Under Mexicali Stars *(Republic, 1950). His western films include:* Under Mexicali Stars *(1950)*, Warpath, Thunder in God's Country, Santa Fe *(1951)*, Rancho Notorious, Rodeo *(1952)*, The Star of Texas *(1953)*, Johnny Guitar, Drum Beat *(1954)*, A Lawless Street, At Gunpoint *(1955)*.

*Martin Garralaga: Garralaga, left, with Howard Duff in* Blackjack Ketchum, Desperado *(Columbia, 1956). His western films include:* Gay Caballero *(1932)*, Lawless Border *(1935)*, Rose of the Rio Grande *(1938)*, The Fighting Gringo *(1939)*, Rhythm of the Rio Grande *(1940)*, The Laramie Trail *(1944)*, West of the Pecos *(1945)*, South of Monterey *(1946)*, Twilight on the Rio Grande *(1947)*, Four Faces West, *(1948)*, The Big Sombrero *(1949)*, The Outriders *(1950)*, Branded *(1951)*, The Fabulous Senorita *(1952)*, San Antone *(1953)*, Jubilee Trail *(1954)*, Blackjack Ketchum, Desperado *(1956)*.

*Roy Gordon: Gordon, left, with Dennis Morgan in* The Gun That Won the West *(Columbia, 1955). His western films include:* The Last Round Up *(1947)*, Riders of the Whistling Pines, Apache Chief *(1949)*, Beyond the Purple Hills, Sons of New Mexico, Indian Territory *(1950)*, Silver Lode *(1954)*, The Gun That Won the West *(1955)*.

*Don Haggerty: Haggerty, left, with Barry Sullivan in* Texas Lady *(RKO Radio, 1955). His western films include:* Gun Smugglers *(1948)*, Storm Over Wyoming, The Sundowners, Dynamite Pass *(1950)*, Bronco Buster, Wild Stallion *(1952)*, Texas Lady *(1955)*.

*Riley Hill: Hill, center, with Max Terhune and Fred Kohler Jr. in* Range Justice *(Monogram, 1949). His western films include:* Flame of the West, Sheriff of Cimarron *(1945),* The Haunted Mine, Under Arizona Skies *(1946),* Range Renegades, Frontier Agent *(1948),* Shadows of the West, Range Justice *(1949),* Six Gun Mesa, Gunslingers *(1950),* Nevada Badmen, Canyon Raiders *(1951),* Target, The Raiders *(1952),* White Lightning *(1953).*

*Chubby Johnson: Johnson, left, with Allan (Rocky) Lane in* Fort Dodge Stampede *(Republic, 1951). His western films include:* Rocky Mountain *(1950),* Fort Worth, Fort Dodge Stampede, Night Riders of Montana, Wells Fargo Gunmaster *(1951),* The Treasure of Lost Canyon, Last of the Comanches *(1952),* Gunsmoke *(1953),* Overland Pacific, Queen of Montana *(1954),* The Far Country *(1955),* The First Texan, Fastest Gun Alive, The Rawhide Years *(1956).*

*Jack Kirk (1895–1948): Kirk, left, with Kermit Maynard in Silver Spurs (Republic, 1943). His western films included:* The Singing Cowboy, Guns and Guitars *(1936),* Pals of the Saddle *(1938),* Rough Riders' Roundup *(1939),* The Tulsa Kid *(1940),* Kansas Cyclone *(1941),* South of Santa Fe, Sunset Serenade *(1942),* Silver Spurs, Death Valley Manhunt *(1943),* Beneath Western Skies, The Vigilantes Ride *(1944),* Lone Texas Ranger, The Topeka Terror *(1945),* California Gold Rush, Texas Panhandle *(1946),* Oregon Trail Scouts *(1947),* Oklamhoma Badlands *(1948).*

*Pierce Lyden: Lyden, left, with Johnny Mack Brown in* Texas City *(Monogram, 1952). His western films include:* Dead Man's Gulch, The Black Hills Express *(1943),* Riders of the Deadline, Texas Masquerade *(1944),* Alias Billy the Kid, Roll on Texas Moon *(1946),* Valley of Fear, Adventures of Don Coyote *(1947),* Back Trails, Silver Trails *(1948),* Shadows of the West *(1949),* Sons of New Mexico *(1950),* Nevada Badmen *(1951),* Wagon Team *(1952).*

*Rory Mallinson: Mallinson, right, deputy sheriff, listens to Gene Autry discuss wanted poster in* Rim of the Canyon *(Columbia, 1949). The faces on the poster are those of Jock Mahoney, Francis McDonald, and Walter Sande. His western films include:* King of the Bandits *(1947),* Last of the Wild Horses, Bad Men of Tombstone, Panhandle *(1948),* Rim of the Canyon, Prince of the Plains *(1949),* Short Grass *(1950),* Rodeo King and the Senorita *(1951),* Laramie Mountains *(1952),* Cow Country *(1953),* Jesse James vs. The Daltons *(1954),* Seminole Uprising *(1955).*

*Frank Marvin: Marvin, center, with Bob Burns, Gene Autry, and Sterling Holloway in* Twilight on the Rio Grande *(Republic, 1947). His western films include:* Tumbling Tumbleweeds *(1935)* The Singing Cowboy, Guns and Guitars *(1936),* Round'Up Time in Texas, Springtime in the Rockies *(1937),* Gold Mine in the Sky, Man from Music Mountain *(1938),* Mountain Rhythm, Colorado Sunset *(1939).*

*Montie Montana: Montana, right, with Roy Rogers and Dale Evans in* Down Dakota Way *(Republic, 1949). His western films include:* Circle of Death *(1935),* Riders of the Deadline *(1944),* Down Dakota Way *(1949).*

*George Morrell (1872–1955): Morrell, third from left, with Art Mix, Charles Starrett, Ed Peil, Ed Cobb, Alan Sears, and Tex Cooper in* Two Fisted Sheriff *(Columbia, 1937). His western films included:* Wild Mustang *(1935),* Two-Fisted Sheriff *(1937),* Buzzy and the Phantom Pinto *(1941),* Buckskin Frontier *(1943),* Marked Trails, Law of the Valley, The Whispering Skull *(1944),* Law of the Valley *(1945),* Ghost of Hidden Valley *(1946).*

*Steve Pendleton: Pendleton, with Steve Darrell, Charles Starrett, and Marjorie Stapp in* The Blazing Trail *(Columbia, 1949). His western films include:* Unknown Valley *(1933),* Trail's End *(1935),* Young Buffalo Bill *(1940),* Ride, Ryder, Ride!, The Blazing Trail *(1949),* Gunfire *(1950),* The Great Missouri Raid, Buckaroo Sheriff of Texas *(1951).*

*Hal Price (1886–1964): Price, right, with Tex Ritter and Bill Elliott in* Prairie Gunsmoke *(Columbia, 1942). His western films include:* Ranger's Code *(1933),* The Fugitive Sheriff, The Desert Phantom *(1936),* Melody of the Plains, The Trusted Outlaw *(1937),* Call the Mesquiteers *(1938),* Overland Mail *(1939),* Arizona Frontier *(1940),* Gangs of Sonora *(1941),* Prairie Gunsmoke *(1942),* Fugitive of the Plains *(1943),* Outlaw Trail *(1944),* Law of the Valley *(1945),* Raiders of Red Rock *(1947)* Frisco Tornado *(1950),* Rough Riders of Durango *(1951),* Junction City *(1952).*

*Lee Roberts: Roberts, left, with Phyllis Coates in* Canyon Ambush *(Monogram, 1952). His western films include:* Wild West *(1946)*, Law of the Lash, Ghost Town Renegades *(1947)*, Prairie Outlaws, Fighting Mustang *(1948)*, The Cowboy and the Indians, Haunted Trails *(1949)*, Law of the Panhandle, Cherokee Uprising *(1950)*, Colorado Ambush, Abilene Trail *(1951)*, Canyon Ambush, Kansas Territory *(1952)*, Battle of Rogue River *(1954)*, Fort Yuma *(1955)*.

*Joe Sawyer: Sawyer, right, as Sergeant Keough with George Montgomery in* Indian Uprising *(Columbia, 1952). His western films include:* The Westerner, The Arizonian *(1935)*, Frontier Marshal *(1939)*, The Dark Command, Melody Ranch, Santa Fe Trail *(1940)*, Belle Starr, Last of the Duanes *(1941)*, Buckskin Frontier *(1943)*, The Singing Sheriff *(1944)*, Coroner Creek *(1948)*, Deputy Marshal, Tucson *(1949)*, Red Skies of Montana, Indian Uprising *(1952)*, Taza, Son of Cochise, Riding Shotgun *(1954)*.

*Emmett Vogan (1893–1969): Vogan, right, with Allan (Rocky) Lane in* The Denver Kid *(Republic, 1948). His western films included:* Badlands of Dakota *(1941)*, Stardust on the Sage *(1942)*, Song of Nevada *(1944)*, Utah, Along the Navajo Trail *(1945)*, Smoky River Serenade *(1947)*, The Denver Kid *(1948)*, Brothers in the Saddle *(1949)*, Red River Shore *(1954)*.

*Hank Worden: Worden, left, with Jane Darwell, George Brent, Ann Blyth, and James Seay in* Red Canyon *(Universal-International, 1949). His western films include:* Stranger from Arizona *(1938)*, Black Market Rustlers *(1943)*, Prairie Express *(1947)*, Three Godfathers *(1948)*, Red Canyon *(1949)*, Wagonmaster *(1950)*, Sugarfoot *(1951)* Apache War Smoke *(1952)*, The Indian Fighter *(1955)*, The Searchers *(1956)*, The Alamo *(1960)*, One-Eyed Jacks *(1961)*, Mclintock! *(1963)*, True Grit *(1969)*.

*Lee "Lasses" White (1888–1949): White, hatless, struts his stuff in the musical short "Corralling a School Marm" (RKO, 1940). Music is provided by Ray Whitley and his Six Bar Cowboys. His western films included: Rovin' Tumbleweeds (1939), Oklahoma Renegades (1940), The Bandit Trail, Cyclone on Horseback (1941), Song of the Range (1944), Moon over Montana, Trail to Mexico (1946), Song of the Sierras, Six Gun Serenade (1947), Indian Agent, The Valiant Hombre (1948).*